THE SOCIAL WORK SKILLS WORKBOOK

Barry Cournoyer

Indiana University

Wadsworth Publishing Company
Belmont, California
A Division of Wadsworth, Inc.

Social Work Editor: Peggy Adams
Editorial Assistant: Tammy Goldfeld
Production Editor: Carol Dondrea, Bookman Productions
Print Buyer: Martha Branch
Designer: Judith Levinson
Copy Editor: Candace Demeduc
Compositor: Patricia Douglass
Cover: Harry Voigt

Printed in the United States of America

1 2 3 4 5 6 7 8 9 10 — 95 94 93 92 91

ISBN 0-534-14730-5

CONTENTS

CHAPTER ONE   INTRODUCTION   1

CHAPTER TWO   SELF-AWARENESS AND SELF-UNDERSTANDING   10

CHAPTER SIX   BEGINNING   114

CHAPTER SEVEN   EXPLORING   143

CHAPTER ELEVEN ENDING   335

APPENDIX ONE

APPENDIX TWO

PREFACE

The impetus for developing this workbook originated with the observations and, yes, the complaints from students that social work professors and their textbooks tend to "talk *about* practice" rather than helping students learn to do what actually needs to be done. Comments such as "They communicate at such abstract levels that it's impossible to translate what they say into what to do" led me to prepare a workbook in which students could actually practice some of the fundamental social work skills through the use of exercises and simulated case situations.

This workbook is designed for use in the following contexts: (1) as the primary text or source book for social work skills laboratory courses (which might be entitled "interviewing skills," "interpersonal skills," "interactional skills," or "helping skills" labs); (2) as a secondary text and workbook for social work practice courses; (3) as a workbook for use by social work students and field instructors during practicum experiences; and (4) by professional social workers interested in refreshing their proficiency with basic social work skills. Social workers and social work students who are currently providing service to actual clients may be able to alter some of the workbook exercises, particularly the summary exercises, for use in their agency setting. However, in so doing, they should carefully consider the implications for social work values and ethics in order to ensure that clients' rights are securely protected.

The workbook provides beginning social workers and social work students with a means to understand and practice the essential skills of direct social work practice. The skills presented in this workbook do not represent an exhaustive collection of all those that have relevance for social workers. Indeed, there are other skills of great significance. However, I have limited the workbook to those skills that are most applicable to and congruent with (1) the phases or processes of social work practice (Perlman, 1957; Compton & Galaway, 1989) and (2) seven essential qualities that effective social workers must reflect.

The social work skills are presented so as to coincide with the phases or processes of social work practice. The adoption of such a phase-to-phase approach involves the risk of concluding that work with every client always follows a similar pattern and that the characteristics of one phase as well as the skills relevant to it are distinctly different from those of another. This is not the case. Many of the dynamics, tasks, functions, and skills applicable to one phase may, in work with a particular client, be evident in other phases. Some skills may be used over and over again throughout the course of the social worker's efforts with and for a client.

The workbook is organized in the following manner: An introductory chapter provides overall perspective. The second chapter engages the student in a series of self-awareness and self-understanding exercises in preparation for social work practice. The third chapter introduces the student to the process of ethical decision making in social work practice. The fourth chapter addresses the fundamental interpersonal skills of talking and listening. Chapters Five through Eleven address the skills associated with the preparing, beginning, exploring, assessing, contracting, working, and ending phases or processes of social work practice. Each of these chapters includes a general introduction to the overall purpose, dynamics, and tasks associated with the work of that particular phase. After the introduction, the social work skills commonly used during the phase are identified and illustrated. Exercises intended to help students learn to apply each skill are provided within and at the end of each chapter.

Cases and situations selected as illustrative examples and for use in the exercise sections have been drawn from a variety of agency settings and circumstances. Most of the case vignettes involve interaction with individual persons. However, an attempt has been made to include some examples of other types of clients (e.g., dyads, families, groups) and extra-client systems (e.g., referral sources, community resources, or related social systems) with whom social workers interact. The cases have been selected in order to include persons of differing age, socioeconomic, racial, and ethnic status as well as those of each gender and sexual preference. (To avoid gender stereotyping, use of the pronouns *he* and *she* for social worker and client alternate from chapter to chapter, except where the context of the material makes such use clearly inappropriate.)

Instructors who employ the workbook in their social work courses may use the exercises in a variety of ways. As part of a homework assignment, students may be asked to respond to selected exercises. During the classroom session, the instructor may then call on students to share their responses and discuss the characteristics that account for superior and inferior applications of the skills. Alternately, an instructor may assign certain exercises as written homework to be submitted for evaluation. During classroom meetings, students may be asked to form pairs, triads, or small groups in order to engage "live" in selected exercises. Role-plays in which students alternately assume the part of client and social worker are often powerful learning experiences, particularly when constructive feedback is provided by other students and the instructor. In general, instructors should recognize that the social work skills are ultimately used in the context of helping clients. As such, teaching-learning processes that approximate the actual *doing* are preferred.

ACKNOWLEDGMENTS

The preparation of this workbook is the culmination of more than fifteen years of social work practice and a decade of teaching courses to beginning social work students. Over the years, clients have been my most important teachers. Time and time again, they forgave my mistakes and guided me toward more fruitful paths. I have learned more from them than from any other source. I am forever indebted to those clients who allowed me a glimpse into their worlds, and I feel privileged to have participated with them on their heroic journeys. In a similar fashion, students in the skills laboratory course and in various social work practice courses have been my educators. They have taught me a great deal. If they have learned half of what I have learned from them, I will feel satisfied. Without their teachings, this workbook would not have been possible.

I would also like to recognize those social workers whose teachings and writings have affected me professionally and contributed to the approach taken in this workbook. Dr. Eldon Marshall, my former professor and now colleague, was the first to introduce me to the "helping skills." I shall never forget his class nor the impact of my first videotaped interview. During my doctoral program, Dr. Dean Hepworth, through both his teaching and his writing, furthered the skills emphasis begun during my master's education. Even now, I recall the competence with which he prepared course syllabi. And my former colleague, Dr. Beulah Compton, deserves much credit. Her clear conception of fundamental social work processes has served me well. I shall long remember our sometimes heated but always stimulating conversations about social work practice.

I also want to credit the extraordinary staff at Wadsworth. Peggy Adams, Carol Dondrea, and Candace Demeduc somehow managed to transform my manuscript into readable prose—a remarkable accomplishment.

Finally, I wish to thank my partner, Catherine Hughes Cournoyer, and our children, John Paul and Michael, for their love and patience. Catherine is the most generous person I have ever met and, without question, the best social worker. She and the boys continue to make me more and better than I could possibly be without them.

LIST OF SOCIAL WORK SKILLS

Self-Awareness and Self-Understanding
Understanding the Influence of One's Family of Origin
Understanding the Influence of Current Situational Factors
Assessing One's Self-Esteem
Assessing One's Acceptance of Others
Assessing One's Assertiveness
Assessing One's Readiness for Social Work Practice

Ethical Decision Making
Understanding the Legal Duties of Professional Helpers
Understanding the Fundamental Values and the Ethics of Social Work
Identifying Ethical and Legal Implications
Ethical Decision Making

Talking and Listening—The Basic Interpersonal Skills
Using Voice and Speech
Using Body Language
Listening: Hearing, Observing, Encouraging, and Remembering
Active Listening

Preparing
Preparatory Reviewing
Preparatory Exploring
Preparatory Consulting
Preparatory Arranging
Preparatory Empathy
Preliminary Planning
Preparatory Self-Exploration
Centering
Recording During the Preparing Phase

Beginning
Introducing Oneself
Seeking Introductions
Describing Initial Purpose
Outlining the Client's Role
Discussing Policy and Ethical Considerations
Seeking Feedback

Exploring

Probing
Seeking Clarification
Reflecting Content
Reflecting Feeling
Reflecting Complex Communications
Partializing
Going Beyond What Is Said

Assessing

Organizing Descriptive Information
Formulating a Tentative Assessment

Contracting

Reflecting the Problem
Sharing Worker's View of the Problem
Specifying Problems for Work
Establishing Goals
Developing a Program for Change
Identifying Action Steps
Planning for Evaluation
Summarizing the Contract

Working

Rehearsing Action Steps
Reviewing Action Steps
Evaluating
Focusing
Educating
Advising
Representing
Responding with Immediacy
Reframing
Confronting
Pointing Out Endings
Recording During the Work Phase

Ending

Reviewing the Process
Final Evaluating
Sharing Ending Feelings and Saying Goodbye
Recording the Closing Summary

LIST OF FIGURES

INTRODUCTION

Social work is an exciting and challenging profession that provides helping services to people in all walks of life and in all kinds of situations. Social workers serve in child protection capacities, responding to indications that a minor child may be at risk of abuse or neglect and helping families to improve their child caring capacities. Some social workers serve in the emergency rooms of hospitals, intervening with persons and families in crisis situations. Others lead groups for children who have been sexually victimized and provide education and counseling to perpetrators of incest. Many social workers serve couples whose relationships are faltering or single parents who seek guidance and support in rearing their children. Others serve persons who are addicted to or abuse alcohol and drugs as well as family members who have been affected by the substance abuse of a parent, child, spouse, or sibling. Many social workers serve in prisons and institutions; others serve in school systems. Still others advocate for persons who have been subjected to discrimination or exploitation, often due to racism, sexism, or ageism. Many social workers serve persons stricken with physical illnesses such as cancer or AIDS and help the families of patients cope during and after hospitalization. Some help persons locate needed services or resources by providing information and making referrals. Other social workers help individuals who experience mental illness, such as schizophrenia, and provide support and education to their families. Social workers serve in nursing homes for aged persons, often leading groups or counseling family members. And, increasingly, social workers serve in industry, providing consultation to employers and employees concerning problems that affect their health and productivity.

The range of settings in which social workers practice their profession and the variety of functions that they serve are enormous indeed. Sometimes the diversity seems so great that beginning social work students feel overwhelmed. Many ask themselves, Can I possibly learn what I need to in order to be a competent social worker in all those places, serving such different people with such diverse problems? Well, the answer to that question is certainly *no!* An individual social worker could never become truly competent in all the arenas in which social workers practice, since it would require a greater breadth of knowledge and expertise than any one person could ever acquire. There is a specialized body of knowledge and expertise needed for each practice setting, each special population group, and each psychosocial problem. Nonetheless, there are also certain skills common to social work practice in all settings, with all population groups, and with all psychosocial problems. These skills exist because social workers, as professionals, adhere to several common guideposts, regardless of setting, function, population, or problem. In large part, these fundamental commonalities serve to make social work a coherent profession despite its incredible diversity.

Although professional social workers practice in widely differing contexts, they all have earned a baccalaureate, master's, or doctoral degree in social work. They have adopted certain common professional values that pervade all aspects of their social work practice and have pledged adherence to a social work code of ethics. In addition, social workers in all settings view the *person-and-situation* as the basic unit of attention and the *enhancement of social functioning* as the overriding purpose of their practice. Social workers tend to conceive of people and situations both as having a potential for change and as continuously changing. They view professional practice as predominantly *for* the client and the community; its primary purpose is not for the social worker's personal benefit. Social workers tend to reflect a special sensitivity for at-risk individuals and oppressed groups. In their practice, social workers assume multiple professional roles and functions. They recognize that social work practice involves powerful interpersonal processes that have potential for harm as well as for helpfulness. Social workers recognize that professional practice requires a highly developed and developing self-awareness and self-understanding. They realize that social work practice demands extraordinary personal discipline and self-control. It requires a great deal more than admirable personal qualities and compassionate feelings. Rather, social workers understand that their practice must be based upon professional knowledge and guided by social work values, ethics, and obligations. Finally, social workers tend to conceive of practice as a helping process that follows fairly predictable phases during the course of work with and on behalf of persons called clients. Each of these phases requires competence in certain essential skills. These social work skills constitute the primary focus of this workbook.

SOCIAL WORK SKILLS

The term *skill* has become extremely popular in social work and the other helping professions during the past two decades. Currently, several widely adopted social work textbooks incorporate *skill* or *skills* in their titles (Henry,

1981; Hepworth & Larsen, 1986; Shulman, 1982; 1984). However, the term *skill* is not always used in the same way. It means different things to different authors. For example, Sue Henry (1981, p. vii) suggests that skills are "finite and discrete sets of behaviors or tasks employed by a worker at a given time, for a given purpose, in a given manner." Henry (1981, p. vii) also cites Phillips, who characterizes skill as "knowledge in action." L. C. Johnson (1986, p. 62) defines skill as "the practice component that brings knowledge and values together and converts them to action as a response to concern and need." Smalley (1967, p. 17) states that "*Skill* . . . refers to the social worker's capacity to *use* a method in order to *further* a process directed toward the accomplishment of a social work purpose as that purpose finds expression in a specific program or service."

For the purposes of this workbook, a social work skill may be defined as *a set of discrete cognitive and behavioral actions that derive from social work knowledge and from social work values, ethics, and obligations; are consistent with the essential facilitative qualities; and comport with a social work purpose within the context of a phase of practice.* Although they are associated with different phases or processes, social work skills, as viewed here, are not technical tasks that the social worker enacts, robotlike, at the same relative time and in the same way with all clients, all problems, and all situations. Rather, the social worker selects and adapts the skills in order to suit the particular needs and characteristics of the person-problem-situation.

The skills chosen for incorporation into this workbook are primarily derived from the tasks associated with commonly identified phases of social work practice and the essential qualities exhibited by effective professional helping persons. As viewed here, the phases of practice (see Perlman, 1957; Compton & Galaway, 1989) are: (1) preparing, (2) beginning, (3) exploring, (4) assessing, (5) contracting, (6) working, and (7) ending. The essential facilitative qualities that effective social workers tend to exhibit throughout the course of their work with clients include: (1) empathy, (2) respect, (3) authenticity, (4) self-awareness and self-understanding, (5) understanding of social work values and ethics, (6) professional social work knowledge, and (7) assertiveness. The tasks associated with each phase are organized into small, manageable units of thought and action—into social work skills—compatible with the seven essential qualities.

ESSENTIAL QUALITIES

The results of research attempting to identify the characteristics of effective professional helpers remain somewhat confusing. During the 1960s and 1970s, research studies (Lambert, 1982, pp. 31–33) tended generally to suggest that qualities such as accurate empathy, nonpossessive warmth, and genuineness reflected by counselors are modestly related to positive client changes. However, identifying and measuring all the potential factors that affect the outcome of helping processes is an enormously complex undertaking. Definite conclusions may never be reached. For social workers, who fulfill disparate professional functions in extremely varied settings with an incredibly wide range of different populations and psychosocial problems, the picture is even more cloudy. As Alfred Kadushin (1983, p. 84) suggests, the roles that social workers assume in their professional practice are diverse indeed:

> The warm, accepting qualities necessary for interviews whose primary purpose is therapeutic are not those required for the interview whose primary purpose is assessment. The "therapeutic" interviewer in an assessment interview may fail to probe inconsistencies or may make compassionate allowance for interviewee reluctance to discuss essential but difficult areas. The interview whose primary purpose is reliable judgment, diagnostic assessment, may require a reserved, extraceptively oriented person; the therapeutic interview may require a warmer, more spontaneous, intraceptively oriented person. The interviewer engaged in advocacy may need a more aggressive, directive, dominant approach to the interview.

In spite of the diversity inherent in social work and the inconclusive nature of the research findings, it is possible to identify certain aspects of the worker-client experience that are likely to enhance the probability of an effective outcome. Donald F. Krill (1986, p. xi) suggests that for the experience between a worker or therapist and a client to be effective:[1]

1. Client and counselor need to like one another. The matching of client and therapist is therefore important.
2. The use of positive, clear-cut suggestion in the structuring of the client's expectations of the counseling process is valuable.
3. The counselor's natural expression of the "core conditions" (warmth, empathy, genuineness) is of key importance.
4. Core conditions need to be connected with problem-solving actions. These rest, first, upon attitude change in relation to problem understanding. Attitude change needs to occur at such time the client is experiencing a strong emotion in relation to the problem.
5. Behavior change, as homework or "in interview" task, is the second component to problem-solving action.
6. The involvement of a client's significant other in both problem understanding and solving is especially useful.

As mentioned by Krill, among the characteristics of effective helpers are those that have been called the "core conditions" or the "facilitative qualities" (Rogers, 1957; 1961; Carkhuff & Truax, 1965; Truax & Carkhuff, 1967; Carkhuff, 1969; Ivey, 1971; Ivey & Authier, 1978; and Marshall, Charping, & Bell, 1979).

---

[1] From *The beat worker: Humanizing social work and psychotherapy practice* by Donald F. Krill. Copyright 1986. Used by permission of the publisher, University Press of America, Lanham, MD.

These qualities, when consistently demonstrated by the helping person, often aid in the development and maintenance of a special kind of relationship between worker and client. It is sometimes called "the helping relationship," "the working relationship," or "the therapeutic alliance." According to Helen Harris Perlman (1979, pp. 48–77) the professional working relationship is distinguished from other relationships by the following characteristics:

- It is formed for a recognized and agreed-upon purpose.
- It is time-bound.
- It is *for* the client.
- It carries authority.
- It is a controlled relationship.

It is within the context of this special relationship between worker and client that the "facilitative qualities" become so essential. When consistently reflected by the worker, the risk of doing harm to the person-and-situation is usually decreased and the probability of being helpful is usually increased. However, the manifestation of these qualities alone is rarely enough to enable clients to reach their goals. The social worker must nearly always add expert knowledge in helping the client toward goal attainment. Nonetheless, it is clear that *both* aspects—the facilitative qualities *and* professional expertise—are necessary to the process of helping most clients address most problems in most situations. One element without the other is usually incomplete and ineffective.

The facilitative qualities that are most commonly identified by helping professionals and that should nearly always be consistently reflected by the social worker in the helping relationship are empathy, respect, and authenticity.

Empathy

Empathy (Rogers, 1975) is a term that, although widely used, is often not accurately understood. Derived from the Greek work *empatheia*, it may be defined as a process of "joining in the feelings of another"; of "feeling with" another person—feeling how and what the other is feeling. It is not an expression of "feeling for" or "feeling toward," as in pity or romantic love. Rather it is a conscious and intentional joining with others in their subjective experience.

Hammond, Hepworth, and Smith (1977, p. 3) suggest that "empathy is an understanding *with* the client, rather than a diagnostic or evaluative understanding *of* the client." Of course, there are limits to any helper's ability and willingness to "feel with" and "feel as" the other does. In fact, the professional helper must always retain a portion of herself for herself and her professional responsibilities. She cannot adopt the client's feelings as her own; she must be able both to "feel with" the client and then leave those feelings with the client. They are his, not hers to be assumed.

As a result of empathy, the worker gains an understanding of, appreciation for, and sensitivity to the person who is the primary focus of attention.

Respect

The facilitative quality of respect (Hammond, Hepworth, & Smith, 1977, p. 5; 170–203) refers to the helper's attitude of noncontrolling, warm, caring acceptance of the other. It reflects unconditional positive regard (Rogers, 1957; 1961). There are very few relationships in which people are truly cared about and accepted as unique human beings with full rights and privileges *without regard* to their views and actions. In social circumstances, people generally tend to spend time with people who have views similar to their own; tend to be friendly with persons who are affectionate toward them; and tend to be less friendly toward persons who hold views that differ from their own, or who are insulting or demeaning to them.

In the professional helping relationship, the worker maintains respect for and caring acceptance of the client and his rights and preferences regardless of the client's views and actions. The helper may personally disagree with and perhaps disapprove of a particular attitude or action of a client but nonetheless continues to care about the client as a unique person and continues to respect the client's right to make his own decisions. This ability on the part of the professional helper to see and value the client neither because of nor in spite of the client's attributes or behavior is a critical facilitative condition in the helping relationship.

Respect for the client as a person and respect for his rights does not imply that the client has license to behave in any way he wishes. Nor does it suggest that the helper must never make professional judgments about the client. It also does not mean that the worker neglects to consider other persons or groups as she focuses upon the client. For example, in working with an adult male client who, during the course of an interview, indicates that frequently he severely beats his nine-year-old daughter, the social worker would attempt to ensure the safety of the child. However, in doing so, she would demonstrate respect for the client by (1) informing him as completely and as accurately as possible what steps she intends to take, (2) requesting input from him concerning his views of the possible consequences of those steps, (3) asking him whether he might like to join her in taking those steps, (4) informing him of his rights in the situation, and (5) exploring ways in which she or other potential resources might be helpful to him during this difficult time.

Authenticity

Hammond, Hepworth, and Smith (1977, p. 7) suggest that "authenticity refers to a sharing of self by behaving in a natural, sincere, spontaneous, real, open, and nondefensive manner. An authentic person relates to others personally, so that expressions do not seem rehearsed or contrived." Genuineness, congruence, transparency, or authenticity (Rogers, 1961) may sometimes seem contrary to the notion of the *professional* as always and completely cool, calm, and collected. However, professionalism in social work does not mean adopting such an overcontrolled attitude. The worker need not and should not present herself as an unfeeling, detached, computerlike technician. People seeking social work services almost always prefer to talk with a professional who, yes, presents herself as knowledgeable and competent, but also comes across as a living, breathing, feeling human being; not as someone playing a canned role, spouting cliches, or repeating the same phrases again and again.

However, being authentic in the working relationship does not mean that the professional social worker may say whatever she thinks or feels. She must always remember that the helping relationship is *for* the client—not for the worker. Expression of her own thoughts and feelings for any other purpose than that of serving the client and working toward the mutually agreed-upon goals is, at best, inefficient and, at worst, harmful.

ADDITIONAL ESSENTIAL QUALITIES

In addition to empathy, respect, and authenticity, there are four additional qualities necessary for effective social work practice. These are self-awareness and self-understanding, understanding of social work values and ethics, professional social work knowledge, and assertiveness.

Self-Awareness and Self-Understanding

In order to use themselves effectively in attempting to help others, it is vital that social workers have a well-developed understanding of self (Compton & Galaway, 1989, pp. 302–306). Although striving for self-understanding is, of course, a lifelong process—one that is never really finished—social workers must know themselves as well as possible, in order to minimize the chance of doing damage to clients. Otherwise, even with the best motivation and intention, they may inadvertently express themselves in an unhelpful or perhaps even harmful way (Keith-Lucas, 1972).

As is the case with most worthwhile endeavors, engaging in self-awareness activities involves certain risks. A worker may discover aspects of herself that have long been denied or minimized and that she would prefer to keep hidden. For example, she may learn that she has an alcohol or drug problem; or that she suffers from occasional periods of depression; or even that she is unsuited for a career in social work. Such self-discovery may evoke disturbing thoughts and feelings that cause her to reconsider significant life choices. The process of self-examination itself involves certain dangers. For example, it is possible to become self-absorbed almost to the point of narcissism. A worker may become so dedicated to the pursuit of self-understanding that she becomes introspective and self-analytical during interviews with clients. This may interfere with her capacity to serve the client and detract from the attention to which the client is entitled.

Understanding of Social Work Values, Ethics, and Obligations

In addition to self-knowledge, social workers must also have a thorough understanding of social work values and ethics (Compton & Galaway, 1989, pp. 175–201) as well as the legal obligations of professional helpers as they affect and inform their work with and on behalf of others. Understanding, in this case, refers to a great deal more than familiarity with the ethical code. It means that the worker knows the code and can identify the ethical principles that apply in specific practice situations. Furthermore, it means that the worker has developed the capacity to address in logical fashion those dilemmas that inevitably occur in social work practice when principles conflict. Understanding involves the ability to determine which ethical principle or legal obligation takes precedence over others in which situations.

Needless to say, the arena of values and ethics in social work practice is a complex one indeed. However, all social workers must pay consistent attention to professional ethics and obligations because they apply to virtually every aspect of professional life.

Professional Knowledge

Professional knowledge is a third additional characteristic of the effective social worker (Compton & Galaway, 1989, pp. 89–113). The knowledge required for competent social work practice varies according to the unique characteristics of the setting, the problems for work, the populations served, and the roles assumed. However, there is a common base of knowledge required of all social workers. Among other subjects, this base includes an understanding of (1) the nature of systems and their interactions; (2) individual, family, and group development; and (3) the processes associated with problem-solving activities. The substantive material in these areas are, of course, beyond the scope of a skills workbook.

Assertiveness

Assertiveness is the final additional characteristic of effective social workers (Cournoyer, 1983). This dimension is reflected within many of the skills presented in the workbook. It reflects the worker's personal and professional power and authority. Assertiveness is necessary in order to fulfill most social work roles and functions. For our purposes, let's consider the concept of responsible assertiveness to incorporate both the ability to and the manner in which the social worker expresses her knowledge, opinions, and values with and on behalf of others.

Empathy, respect, and authenticity are essential characteristics of professional social workers. To these, we have added self-understanding, understanding of professional values and ethics, professional knowledge, and assertiveness. Typically, these qualities are reflected by the professional helper throughout the entire social work process—from preparing for and beginning with the client on through the conclusion of work. However, their manifestation varies according to the phase of social work practice, the agency mission, and the unique characteristics of the person, problem, and situation.

SELF-AWARENESS AND SELF-UNDERSTANDING

Social work is a professional practice involving the conscious and deliberate use of self. The social worker's self is the medium through which knowledge, attitudes, and skill are conveyed. Professional social workers must have a well-developed and developing self-awareness and self-understanding. Rather than a product or an outcome that can be completed and then set aside, self-awareness and self-understanding are neverending (but not all-consuming) processes that enable social workers to grow and expand developmentally while diminishing the risk of harm to others that occurs all too often when social workers do not "know" themselves.

To be effective professionally, a social worker must have a substantial and sophisticated understanding of who he is, how he appears to others, what mannerisms he commonly exhibits, what issues stimulate closed thinking, what topics trigger maladaptive emotional reactions, and what kinds of people or behavior elicit unhelpful responses from him. Of course, such a level of self-understanding does not occur as a result of one set of exercises, one course, or even a complete program of university study. Self-understanding is a lifelong process. It is frequently aided through personal counseling or psychotherapy, consultation with and supervision by experienced social workers, and is often enhanced through participation in professional workshops and training institutes. Also, it occurs, if people are open to it, as a natural outgrowth of interaction with peers, clients, friends, and families.

This chapter contains a series of exercises that you may find useful in gaining a greater awareness and understanding of yourself—the self that you use to help others.

THE FAMILY: CONTEXT FOR DEVELOPMENT OF SELF

Social workers (Hartman & Laird, 1983) have long recognized that a person's family of origin powerfully influences his social, psychological, and even biological development.[1] His family significantly affects the nature of the attitudes, beliefs, values, personality characteristics, and behavioral patterns he reflects. Unless the social worker is keenly aware of the way in which his family of origin has influenced him, he may inadvertently "play out" a family role or pattern in his work with clients. Some of the common family roles (see Satir, 1972; Wegscheider-Cruse, 1985, p. 41) that occur in the backgrounds of social workers include those of "rescuer," "peacemaker," "hero," "enabler," or "parental child." Of course, sometimes it is entirely proper for a social worker to use a part of his family-based self in social work practice. However, the professional social worker should be aware that he is doing so.

One means by which people may become more aware of the ways in which their family of origin has influenced them is through the use of the family genogram. A family genogram is a graphic representation of one's "family tree." It provides a picture of the parties involved and a chronology of significant events or themes. Additionally, a genogram may be used as "a subjective interpretive tool" (McGoldrick and Gerson, 1985, p. 2) for the purpose of developing hypotheses concerning a person's psychosocial characteristics or a family's interactional patterns.

Certain symbols are commonly used in the preparation of a family genogram (McGoldrick and Gerson, 1985). Males are usually characterized by squares and females by circles. Spousal relationships are represented by bracket lines. A solid bracket line (|_____|) reflects a married couple; a dashed bracket line (|-----|) reflects an unmarried couple. A line extended downward from a relationship line indicates a pregnancy or offspring from that relationship. Separations and divorces are indicated by one and two slash marks (/ and //) respectively, cutting across the relationship line. Pregnancies and births from each relationship are placed in order from earliest to latest proceeding from left to right. Deaths are indicated by an X symbol placed within the circle or square. Names of persons and dates, if known, of birth, marriage, separation, divorce, and death are written alongside the symbols. For example, just above or beneath a bracket line indicating a marriage relationship may be placed "m. 3/18/67." This reflects the date of marriage as March 18, 1967. If this same relationship later results in separation, that event may be indicated by "sep. 4/23/74." A subsequent divorce may be reflected by "div. 5/7/75."

In addition, it is frequently useful to characterize persons and relationships with brief notations. For example, a family member may have served in the military during a war or have suffered from diabetes. Significant events, such as major accidents, injuries, crimes, changes in residence or occupation, may also be recorded. Additional symbols or notations may be used to characterize the nature of selected relationships (McGoldrick & Gerson, 1985, p. 21). Very

---

[1] Not all people have "families of origin." For those reared in foster care, children's institutions, or other nonbiological-family contexts, consider "family of origin" to be the "people who raised you." In some circumstances, an eco-map (see next section) may be more applicable than a genogram.

close relationships, those that are emotionally cool, those that are strained, and those that involve conflict may be identified. Toward the bottom of the genogram are placed the date and the person or persons who provided the information upon which it was based, as well as the name and title of the social worker who prepared the genogram.

A family genogram can be as brief or as extensive as the person collecting the information desires. Some individuals pursue its creation with great zeal, spending hours interviewing parents, aunts and uncles, and grandparents. They may even contact distant relatives. Many others, however, base their genogram solely upon information they personally recall. Usually, the amount of energy expended in collecting data and preparing genograms varies according to the purposes for which they are created. In addition, genograms can be prepared in the present tense—the family as it is now—or on the basis of how it existed at some point in the past. Many people find it useful to take genogrammatic snapshots of the family as they remember it at significant points in their development (e.g., at the time they started school, graduated from school, left home, or had children).

As an illustrative example, let's consider the case of Mrs. Lynn Chase. Later, we will learn more about her and her family, but at this point we are primarily concerned with presenting a typical genogram.

As you can observe from the genogram in Figure 2-1, the social worker put together a considerable amount of information in readily accessible form. She has also concisely noted a few of the major intergenerational family themes and patterns. This genogram will be an important reference in the social worker's service to Mrs. Chase.

■ Exercise 2-1: Family Genogram

As part of an effort to enhance your understanding of self, prepare a genogram of three generations of your family. Use a large piece of paper. If possible, include your grandparents and parents, as well as yourself and your siblings. If you have children, you may include them as the fourth generation. Use your own memory primarily, rather than a lot of investigation. Try to include the approximate dates and categories of significant family events such as births, deaths, marriages, divorces, separations, graduations, military service, hospitalizations, changes in place of residence, injuries, and victimizations. If you do not remember details, enter question marks instead of facts. For each of the most significant family members in your experience, develop a succinct synopsis of their personal characteristics. In addition, briefly characterize the nature of the relationships within your family.

When you have completed the genogram, reflect upon your experience with your family and address the following questions. Record your responses in the spaces provided.

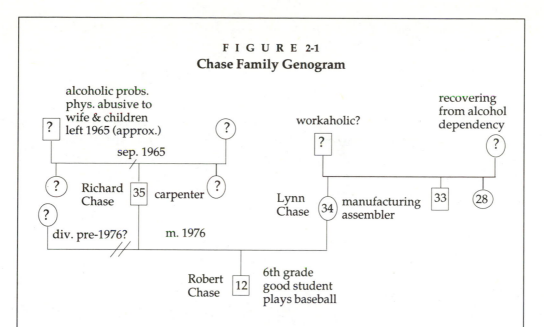

F I G U R E 2-1
Chase Family Genogram

Notes: Richard's father appears to have left the family when Richard was nine years old (1965). Richard, his siblings, and his mother were probably physically and emotionally abused by his father and subject to the insults and inconsistencies associated with a chemically dependent person.

As eldest child in a family where father was rarely at home or involved in family affairs and mother was often intoxicated, Lynn may have assumed parental responsibilities at a very young age. She may have some of the characteristics of an "adult child of an alcoholic system."

There are noticeable family themes of substance abuse and perhaps workaholism. Both Richard and Lynn may have been parental children and may assume more than their fair share of responsibility.

Prepared by: _____
Social Worker
From Perspective of: Lynn Chase
Date: June 20, 1989

---

1. Which roles did each family member assume in your family (e.g., family hero, scapegoat, peacemaker, rescuer, parental child)? Which roles did you tend to play?

2. How were affection and nurturance expressed in your family? By whom? How do you currently express affection and nurturance?

3. How did family members seek help and support in your family? From whom? Currently, when you need help and support, how do you seek it?

4. How was anger expressed in your family? Sadness? Fear? Joy? Currently, how do you express these feelings?

5. How were children corrected and disciplined in your family? Who did so? Currently, how do you correct and/or discipline others?

6. What are the five most important (positive or negative) things you learned from your family experience?

7. What is your fantasy of the "ideal" family? How does it compare with your own?

SITUATIONAL ASSESSMENT

In addition to their families, social workers are also affected by the broader social context in which they live. An eco-map (Hartman, 1978) is an extremely useful tool for reflecting this social context, because it provides a diagrammatic representation of a person's social world—the situation that significantly affects his beliefs, feelings, and actions, which in turn influence his experience and performance as a social worker and a social work student. In addition to presenting an overview of a person, family, or household in the context of the ecological situation, it readily identifies the energy-enhancing and energy-draining relationships between members of a primary social system (e.g., family or household) and the outside world. The graphic nature of the eco-map tends to highlight social deficiencies and excesses as well as areas of conflict. It often points out areas where change may be needed. It is a natural adjunct to the genogram.

As in genograms, squares or circles are used to represent members of the primary social system (e.g., household). These are drawn in the middle of a sheet of paper and placed in a large circle. Other significant social systems with which the person, family, or household members interact are also identified and encircled. The nature of the relationships between the identified social systems are characterized by lines. A solid line (————) reflects a strong (generally positive) relationship; a dashed line (- - - - - -) reflects a tenuous relationship; and a hatched line (++++++) reflects a stressful or conflicted relationship. Arrows (→) are used to indicate the direction of the flow of energy or resources between systems. These relationship lines may also be used to characterize the exchange of energy among family members.

For an illustrative example of an eco-map, let's return to the case of Lynn Chase.

As you can determine from the eco-map in Figure 2-2 (page 18), the social worker has identified important social systems with which the Chase family members interact. She has also indicated the general nature of the relationships among the systems. The eco-map provides the worker and client with much information in graphic form. As is readily observed, Mrs. Chase appears to expend a great deal more energy than she receives from her interactions with others.

■ Exercise 2-2: The Eco-Map

On a large piece of paper, prepare an eco-map of your current social situation. Using the guidelines described above, identify and characterize the significant social systems, including the school or department of social work with which you interact. Identify sources of stress or conflict and sources of support and nurturance. Indicate the direction of energy or resource flow between yourself and other people and systems.

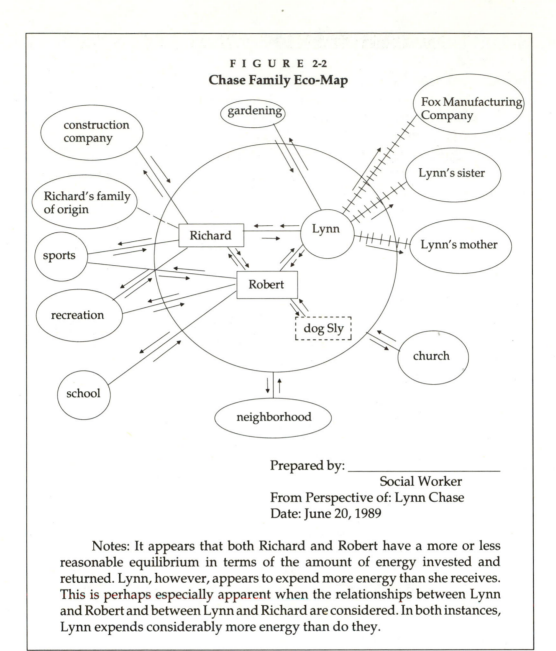

FIGURE 2-2
Chase Family Eco-Map

Prepared by: _____
Social Worker
From Perspective of: Lynn Chase
Date: June 20, 1989

Notes: It appears that both Richard and Robert have a more or less reasonable equilibrium in terms of the amount of energy invested and returned. Lynn, however, appears to expend more energy than she receives. This is perhaps especially apparent when the relationships between Lynn and Robert and between Lynn and Richard are considered. In both instances, Lynn expends considerably more energy than do they.

When you have completed the eco-map, reflect upon your current social situation and address the following questions. Record your responses in the spaces provided.

1. Which elements in your current situation are energizing? Which tend to deplete energy?

2. How does your situation affect the amount of physical, intellectual, and emotional energy you have available for use in your work with clients and for investment in other aspects of your student and professional social work roles?

3. What is your fantasy of the "ideal" social situation? How does it compare with your current situation?

4. Given the nature of your present situation, what kinds of clients and client situations would be likely to generate within you strong emotional reactions?

5. What might you do to enhance your current situation so that you have sufficient psychological, emotional, physical, spiritual, and social resources to succeed in school and to provide professionally competent social work services to clients?

SELF-ESTEEM

Self-esteem, an important concept in social work practice, is recognized by virtually all social workers. It is frequently applied in a social worker's efforts to understand something of the inner world of another person.

Self-esteem is defined in various ways but usually refers to the nature of one's view of and feelings toward oneself. A positive, strong, or high self-esteem is generally regarded as desirable; a negative, weak, or low self-esteem as undesirable.

Often, social work practice is directed toward the development and enhancement of clients' self-esteem, a process in which the social worker's level of self-esteem is also relevant. Since professional practice involves considerable emotional stress and strain, social workers with strong self-esteem are better able to cope with the stress and function in an effective manner than are those whose self-esteem is less well developed.

■ Exercise 2-3: Self-Esteem Index[2]

Complete the following measure of self-esteem. (Place 0 by an item if it is not true; 1 if it is somewhat true; 2 if it is largely true; 3 if true.)

Score	Statement of Present Condition or Action
_____	1. I usually feel inferior to others.
_____	2. I normally feel warm and happy toward myself.
_____	3. I often feel inadequate to handle new situations.
_____	4. I usually feel warm and friendly toward all I contact.
_____	5. I habitually condemn myself for my mistakes and shortcomings.
_____	6. I am free of shame, blame, guilt and remorse.
_____	7. I have a driving need to prove my worth and excellence.
_____	8. I have great enjoyment and zest for living.
_____	9. I am much concerned about what others think and say of me.
_____	10. I can let others be "wrong" without attempting to correct them.
_____	11. I have an intense need for recognition and approval.
_____	12. I am usually free of emotional turmoil, conflict and frustration.
_____	13. Losing normally causes me to feel resentful and "less than."
_____	14. I usually anticipate new endeavors with quiet confidence.
_____	15. I am prone to condemn others and often wish them punished.
_____	16. I normally do my own thinking and make my own decisions.
_____	17. I often defer to others on account of their ability, wealth or prestige.
_____	18. I willingly take responsibility for the consequences of my actions.

---

[2] Published by The Barksdale Foundation, P. O. Box 187, Idyllwild, CA 92349 and reprinted with written authorization of the copyright holder, Lilburn S. Barksdale.

_____ 19. I am inclined to exaggerate and lie to maintain a desired image.

_____ 20. I am free to give precedence to my own needs and desires.

_____ 21. I tend to belittle my own talents, possessions and achievements.

_____ 22. I normally speak up for my own opinions and convictions.

_____ 23. I habitually deny, alibi, justify or rationalize my mistakes and defeats.

_____ 24. I am usually poised and comfortable among strangers.

_____ 25. I am very often critical and belittling of others.

_____ 26. I am free to express love, anger, hostility, resentment, joy, etc.

_____ 27. I feel very vulnerable to others' opinions, comments and attitudes.

_____ 28. I rarely experience jealousy, envy or suspicion.

_____ 29. I am a "professional people pleaser."

_____ 30. I am not prejudiced toward racial, ethnic or religious groups.

_____ 31. I am fearful of exposing my "real self."

_____ 32. I am normally friendly, considerate and generous with others.

_____ 33. I often blame others for my handicaps, problems and mistakes.

_____ 34. I rarely feel uncomfortable, lonely and isolated when alone.

_____ 35. I am a compulsive "perfectionist."

_____ 36. I accept compliments and gifts without embarrassment or obligation.

_____ 37. I am often compulsive about eating, smoking, talking or drinking.

_____ 38. I am appreciative of others' achievements and ideas.

_____ 39. I often shun new endeavors because of fear of mistakes or failure.

_____ 40. I make and keep friends without exerting myself.

_____ 41. I am often embarrassed by the actions of my family or friends.

_____ 42. I readily admit my mistakes, shortcomings and defeats.

_____ 43. I experience a strong need to defend my acts, opinions and beliefs.

_____ 44. I take disagreement and refusal without feeling "put down" or rejected.

_____ 45. I have an intense need for confirmation and agreement.

_____ 46. I am eagerly open to new ideas and proposals.

_____ 47. I customarily judge my self-worth by personal comparison with others.

_____ 48. I am free to think any thoughts that come into my mind.

_____ 49. I frequently boast about myself, my possessions and achievements.

_____ 50. I accept my own authority and do as I, myself, see fit.

_____ Self-Esteem Index Score

To determine your Self-Esteem Index (SEI), add the scores associated with all the _even numbered items_. From that sum, subtract the total of the scores associated with all the *odd numbered items*. The answer represents your Self-Esteem Index. Please note that the potential range of scores is -75 to +75.

Self-esteem is an abstract concept. It is hard to define and difficult to measure accurately. However, whatever it is, it does change! It changes both as a consequence of changing circumstances and as a result of a person's consciously planned efforts. In assessing the results of the self-esteem scale, be aware that the score you reflect may be affected by various temporary factors. Your mood and physical health, along with your current social situation, may influence your score. In addition, as is the case in most scales, there is an error factor. Your actual score may be a certain number of points (plus or minus) from the score reflected here. Therefore, be somewhat cautious in reaching final conclusions based upon the results. Rather, consider the results as hypotheses that should be examined further in light of other forms of evidence.

In evaluating your own results please consider that the average score for a typical college graduate is about +22 and the average score for a typical MBA executive is approximately +28 (Dauw, 1980, pp. 13–16). Compare your scores to these and recognize that most of us could improve our self-esteem.

Dauw suggests that if your SEI is +65 or above you probably have a well-developed (high) sense of self-esteem across a range of areas. If your SEI is between +35 and +64, you probably have a generally favorable self-esteem but may be somewhat handicapped within certain areas of your life. You might benefit from efforts designed to improve your self-esteem in these areas. If your SEI is between +1 and +35, you score in the general range of typical college students (+22) and MBA executives (+28). But if your score is toward the lower end of this range, you may be significantly handicapped in several areas of your life and a systematic program of self-esteem enhancement may be warranted. If your SEI is zero or a minus score you are probably severely handicapped by a lack of self-esteem. For persons reflecting such a score, it may be advisable to seek professional help.

When you have completed and scored the self-esteem scale, reflect upon its implications by addressing the following questions. Record your responses in the spaces provided.

1. How might you define the concept of self-esteem?

2. What characteristics indicate to you that a person has high self-esteem?

3. How do you think people develop high or low self-esteem?

4. How do you respond to people who reflect high self-esteem? How about those who reflect low self-esteem?

5. In what professional areas and situations is your current level of self-esteem likely to be an asset? In what contexts might it be a liability?

6. In what ways would you like to change your self-esteem? How might you do so?

ACCEPTANCE OF OTHERS

It is exceedingly difficult in this highly competitive and evaluative society to develop and maintain genuine tolerance for and acceptance of others. However, in the practice of social work, acceptance of others is crucial. The social worker must have the capacity to accept others who are different in appearance, attitudes, and behavior. He must be able to tolerate and value diversity and to accept others on their own terms.

Social workers who possess or can develop the capacity to accept others are more likely to conform to the values and ethics of the profession and to be effective in their practice. Persons who do not have or cannot develop sincere tolerance for and acceptance of others are incapable of fulfilling the tasks, functions, and obligations of professional social work practice.

■ Exercise 2-4: Acceptance of Others Scale[3]

Please respond to items on this scale by marking 1 if the item is almost always true; 2 if it is usually true; 3 if it is true half of the time; 4 if it is only occasionally true; 5 if it is very rarely true.

Score	Statement of Present Condition or Action
_____	1. People are too easily led.
_____	2. I like people I get to know.
_____	3. People these days have pretty low moral standards.
_____	4. Most people are pretty smug about themselves, never really facing their bad points.
_____	5. I can be comfortable with nearly all kinds of people.
_____	6. All people can talk about these days, it seems, is movies, TV, and foolishness like that.
_____	7. People get ahead by using "pull," and not because of what they know.
_____	8. Once you start doing favors for people, they'll just walk all over you.
_____	9. People are too self-centered.
_____	10. People are always dissatisfied and hunting for something new.
_____	11. With many people you don't know how you stand.
_____	12. You've probably got to hurt someone if you're going to make something out of yourself.
_____	13. People really need a strong, smart leader.
_____	14. I enjoy myself most when I am alone, away from people.

---

[3] William F. Fey, "Acceptance by others and its relation to acceptance of self and others: a revaluation," *Journal of Abnormal and Social Psychology*, 1955, 30, pp. 274–276. Copyright 1955 by the American Psychological Association. Permission to reprint this instrument has been granted.

_____ 15. I wish people would be more honest with me.
_____ 16. I enjoy going with a crowd.
_____ 17. In my experience, people are pretty stubborn and unreasonable.
_____ 18. I can enjoy being with people whose values are very different from mine.
_____ 19. Everybody tries to be nice.
_____ 20. The average person is not very well satisfied with himself.

_____ Acceptance of Others Score

The Acceptance of Others Scale is scored as follows: first, reverse score items 2, 5, 16, 18, and 19. (_Reverse score_ means to change an answer of 1 to 5; 2 to 4; 3 remains 3; 4 to 2; and 5 to 1.) Then, add the answers for all twenty items to find your total score.

As with the self-esteem evaluation, please interpret the results of this scale cautiously. Use the results to formulate hypotheses to test by examining evidence from other sources. The guidelines that follow will help you evaluate your results (Fey, 1955).

Persons who score in the 85–100 range generally tend to accept other people, to experience others as accepting of them, and to be accepted by others. Persons scoring in the 66–84 range reflect the average range of scores of the majority of people. Approximately two-thirds of all people taking the scale score in this medium range. Such midrange scores tend to reflect a mixture of caution toward and acceptance of people. Although less accepting of certain persons, they clearly have the capacity to fully accept others. Persons scoring in the 0–65 range may be very cautious about and intolerant of others. This hesitancy about other people may be a consequence of significant social, emotional, or perhaps even physical pain caused by another person or persons at some point in the past.

When you have completed and scored the scale, reflect upon its implications by addressing the following questions. Record your responses in the spaces provided.

1. How might you define the concept of "acceptance of others"?

2. Have you ever been truly and completely accepted by someone else? If so, what did it feel like? If not, what do you think it might feel like?

3. Have you ever truly and completely accepted someone else? If so, what do you think enabled you to do so? If not, what do you think prevented you?

4. What characteristics indicate to you that a person is accepting of others?

5. How do you think people develop the capacity to accept others?

6. How do you react to people that you consider intolerant of others?

7. In what ways is your current level of acceptance of others likely to represent a positive influence upon your performance as a social worker? In what ways is it a negative?

8. In what ways would you like to change your capacity for accepting others? How might you do so?

ASSERTIVENESS

Like self-esteem and acceptance of others, social workers must be able to express themselves in an assertive fashion. In social work practice, assertiveness involves the capacity of a worker to express his knowledge, opinions, and, where appropriate, feelings in a manner that respects both his own as well as others' rights and preferences as persons. Responsible assertive expression is not indirect or passive, thereby violating one's own rights and preferences, nor is it aggressive, thereby violating the rights and preferences of others.

■ **Exercise 2-5: Assertiveness**

To assess your current level of assertiveness, complete the following Assertion Questionnaire.[4] As you begin to take this instrument, please realize that there are no right or wrong, good or bad, answers. The intent of the questionnaire is to provide you with an estimate of your current level of assertiveness. To complete the questionnaire, you must go through the list of questions twice. First, use the guidelines provided in the Frequency Scale below to rate each situation on how often it has occurred during the past month. Record your responses in the Frequency column.

Frequency Scale

> 1 = This has not happened in the past thirty days.
> 2 = This has happened a few times (one to six times) in the past thirty days.
> 3 = This has happened often (seven times or more) in the past thirty days.

When you have finished recording your frequency responses, go through the list of items again. This time, use the guidelines provided in the Comfort Scale below to rate your comfort level during each situation. If a situation has not occurred during the month, rate it on the basis of how you would probably feel if it had happened. If a situation has come up several times during the month, estimate your "average" rating. Record your responses in the Comfort column.

Comfort Scale

> 1 = I felt very uncomfortable or upset when this happened.
> 2 = I felt somewhat uncomfortable or upset when this happened.
> 3 = I felt neutral when this happened (neither comfortable nor uncomfortable; neither good nor upset).
> 4 = I felt fairly comfortable or good when this happened.
> 5 = I felt very comfortable or good when this happened.

---

[4] From the book, *Control Your Depression* by Peter M. Lewinsohn, Ricardo F. Munoz, Mary Ann Youngren, and Antonette M. Zeiss. © 1978. Used by permission of the publisher, Prentice-Hall, Inc., Englewood Cliffs, N.J.

Assertion Questionnaire

		Frequency	Comfort
1.	Turning down a person's request to borrow my car	_____	_____
2.	Asking a favor of someone	_____	_____
3.	Resisting sales pressure	_____	_____
4.	Admitting fear and requesting consideration	_____	_____
5.	Telling a person I am intimately involved with that he/she has said or done something that bothers me	_____	_____
6.	Admitting ignorance in an area being discussed	_____	_____
7.	Turning down a friend's request to borrow money	_____	_____
8.	Turning off a talkative friend	_____	_____
9.	Asking for constructive criticism	_____	_____
10.	Asking for clarification when I am confused about what someone has said	_____	_____
11.	Asking whether I have offended someone	_____	_____
12.	Telling a person of the opposite sex that I like him/her	_____	_____
13.	Telling a person of the same sex that I like him/her	_____	_____
14.	Requesting expected service when it hasn't been offered (e.g., in a restaurant)	_____	_____
15.	Discussing openly with a person his/her criticism of my behavior	_____	_____
16.	Returning defective items (e.g., at a store or restaurant)	_____	_____
17.	Expressing an opinion that differs from that of a person I am talking with	_____	_____
18.	Resisting sexual overtures when I am not interested	_____	_____
19.	Telling someone how I feel if he/she has done something that is unfair to me	_____	_____
20.	Turning down a social invitation from someone I don't particularly like	_____	_____
21.	Resisting pressure to drink	_____	_____
22.	Resisting an unfair demand from a person who is important to me	_____	_____
23.	Requesting the return of borrowed items	_____	_____
24.	Telling a friend or co-worker when he/she says or does something that bothers me	_____	_____
25.	Asking a person who is annoying me in a public situation to stop (e.g., smoking on a bus)	_____	_____
26.	Criticizing a friend	_____	_____
27.	Criticizing my spouse	_____	_____
28.	Asking someone for help or advice	_____	_____
29.	Expressing my love to someone	_____	_____
30.	Asking to borrow something	_____	_____
31.	Giving my opinion when a group is discussing an important matter	_____	_____

Assertion Questionnaire	Frequency	Comfort
32. Taking a definite stand on a controversial issue	_____	_____
33. When two friends are arguing, supporting the one I agree with	_____	_____
34. Expressing my opinion to someone I don't know very well	_____	_____
35. Interrupting someone to ask him/her to repeat something I didn't hear clearly	_____	_____
36. Contradicting someone when I think I might hurt him/her by doing so	_____	_____
37. Telling someone that he/she has disappointed me or let me down	_____	_____
38. Asking someone to leave me alone	_____	_____
39. Telling a friend or co-worker that he/she has done a good job	_____	_____
40. Telling someone he/she has made a good point in a discussion	_____	_____
41. Telling someone I have enjoyed talking with him/her	_____	_____
42. Complimenting someone on his/her skill or creativity	_____	_____
Total Assertiveness Scores	_____	_____

Two scores are calculated from this questionnaire (Lewinsohn, Munoz, Youngren, & Zeiss, 1978). To determine your assertion frequency score, add the numbers you have placed in the Frequency column. To find your assertion comfort score, add the numbers you have placed in the Comfort column. The majority of people score between 61 and 81 in frequency and between 102 and 137 in comfort. If your score is toward or above the high end of these ranges, you probably have a well-developed ability to express yourself in appropriately assertive ways. If your scores are toward the lower end of the ranges, you may wish to identify specific areas where you are less likely to express yourself directly and then work on them in a systematic fashion. If you score well below the ranges indicated, being comfortably assertive may be of general concern to you. You may be wise to enroll in an assertiveness training course or program.

When you have completed the Assertion Questionnaire, address the following items. Record your responses in the spaces provided.

1. How might you define the concept "assertiveness"?

2. What do you feel like when you are responsibly assertive in a situation where assertiveness is appropriate? When you are aggressive (rather than assertive) in a situation where assertiveness is appropriate? When you are nonassertive (passive) in a situation where assertiveness is appropriate?

3. What characteristics indicate to you that a person is capable of assertive behavior with others?

4. How do you think people develop the capacity to be assertive?

5. How do you react to people that are assertive with you?

6. In what ways is your current level of assertiveness likely to represent a positive influence upon your performance as a social worker? In what ways is it a negative?

7. In what ways would you like to change your capacity for assertiveness? How might you do so?

SOCIAL WORK READINESS

Social workers come from all sorts of backgrounds and reflect diverse personality profiles. They are attracted to the profession and motivated to serve as social workers for many different reasons. Many social workers have a strong sense of altruism and desire to give of themselves to others. Others have a philosophical commitment to a better world. Some are proponents of a particular cause that they can appropriately pursue through their professional practice. Others follow in the footsteps of a relative or other significant person who is a social worker. Some see social work as a way to continue in a family role, such as caretaker, with which they are personally familiar, while others see social work as an efficient route to becoming a psychotherapist. Some select social work as a "second choice," having been denied admission to a clinical psychology program or a law school. Others choose it because they believe that the course work is less difficult and the grading less rigorous than in other schools or departments. Still others have personal or social problems that they believe might be resolved through schooling in social work and through service to others, or have been clients themselves and have identified with the social workers who served them.

Of all the various and complex forms of self-understanding that social workers must pursue, none is more important than that of a person's "goodness of fit" with the profession. At some point, every social worker must honestly and fully address the question, Am I personally ready and suited for this profession and for the nature of the work it entails? As a way to move toward an answer, the social work readiness assessment is provided. It builds upon earlier exercises and is intended to help you explore your motives for selecting social work and evaluate your overall readiness to pursue it as a profession.

■ **Exercise 2-6: Social Work Readiness Assessment**

Now that you have completed several exercises intended to increase your self-awareness and self-understanding, it is time to integrate the results in terms of an assessment of your overall readiness for the roles of social work student and professional social worker. Toward this end, address each of the following questions. Record your responses in the spaces provided.

1. Look ahead to the professional social work career to which you aspire after graduation. Describe the setting, the nature of the problems, and the kinds of people with whom you would prefer to work. Identify and describe the personal qualities and attributes that you think will be required of you as you practice social work in such a context.

2. Identify those settings, problems, and people with whom you would prefer *not* to work. Discuss the reasons for these preferences. What are the implications of those reasons for your personal and professional development?

3. What are the three major factors or incidents in your personal, familial, or situational experience that have contributed to your choice of social work as a career?

4. What do you anticipate will be the single most rewarding or satisfying part of being a professional social worker? What will be the single most difficult?

5. Reflect upon your family genogram, the eco-map, and the results of the questionnaires on self-esteem, acceptance of others, and assertion. In your judgment, do you have or can you develop the personal capacities necessary to function effectively as a professional social worker? If the answer is no, briefly outline a plan by which you can confirm your current assessment (e.g., through a meeting with an advisor, a social work professor, or a guidance counselor) and, if applicable, identify other careers for which you may be better suited. If the answer is yes, identify the personal areas that require further exploration and indicate those capacities that need strengthening. Briefly outline the major elements of a plan by which you can begin to address those objectives.

6. Finally, based upon your current level of self-awareness and self-understanding, what are the three issues most significant to you that you would want to explore with an outstanding, experienced social worker? Identify three specific questions that you would ask.

_____

ETHICAL DECISION MAKING

To make decisions concerning the actions they will take, social workers use information from a variety of invaluable sources: theoretical knowledge; knowledge from research studies; wisdom gained from experiences with their clients; practice experiences of colleagues and supervisors; agency policies and practices; and their own intuitions, hunches, and "gut feelings." However, one source of information also serves as a screen for all the others—the values, ethics, and obligations of the profession itself. Every aspect of practice, every decision, every assessment, every intervention, and virtually every action social workers take should be considered from the perspective of their professional ethics and obligations. This dimension supersedes all others. Ethical decision making constitutes the sine qua non of professional social work practice. Ethical responsibilities take precedence over theoretical knowledge, research findings, practice wisdom, agency policies, and, of course, the social worker's own personal values, preferences, and beliefs.

Assumption of the role of professional social worker entails considerable personal sacrifice, enormous intellectual effort, and extraordinary self-discipline. Because they affect, for better or worse, the lives of the clients they serve and because they pledge adherence to the ethical code of the social work profession, social workers carry weighty responsibilities and obligations. All social workers *must* consistently use ethical decision-making skills throughout their practice.

The skill of ethical decision making involves several dimensions. First, social workers must understand the central legal duties that apply to all professional helpers and understand the core social work values and the social work Code of Ethics to which they pledge allegiance. Second, they must be able to identify which ethical principles and legal duties pertain to specific social work practice situations. Finally, when several competing obligations apply, social workers must be able to determine which take precedence. When there is no conflict among the ethical and legal responsibilities relevant to a case situation, making a decision and taking appropriate action is straightforward. The social worker need simply conform to the obligations. However, much of the time the applicable principles and duties do conflict. Deciding which obligation takes precedence is the most complex and challenging element in the skill of ethical decision making.

UNDERSTANDING THE LEGAL DUTIES OF PROFESSIONAL HELPERS

Along with counselors, psychiatrists, psychologists, and nurses, social workers are societally sanctioned members of the professional helping community. As such, they are subject to certain legally determined responsibilities or *duties*. These derive from common law, legislation, and court decisions. Some legal obligations coincide with the responsibilities suggested by social work values and the Code of Ethics. Some do not. Nonetheless, it is each social worker's responsibility to understand both the legal duties applicable to all professional helpers as well as those ethical obligations that apply specifically to social workers.

Unfortunately, the legal duties of professional helpers are not always clear. They are certainly not permanent. New laws and regulations are continually enacted by local, state, and federal governmental bodies. Thousands of court cases are processed every year. As these laws and regulatory policies emerge, the nature and extent of the legal duties of professional helpers change. Nonetheless, they are subject to these evolving responsibilities.

In 1985 more than two thousand lawsuits were filed against social workers (Besharov & Besharov, 1987). We may expect that figure to increase substantially as the years pass. Of course, the filing of a lawsuit against a social worker does not mean that she is, in fact, guilty of malpractice. Unwarranted lawsuits do take place. Although ethical and competent social work practice is undoubtedly the best defense should litigation take place, it does not guarantee one freedom from legal action. Competent and ethical or incompetent and unethical, the worker may still be required to defend herself against even unjustified charges.

Although the increasing frequency of legal action taken against social workers and other professional helpers is certainly cause for concern, it need not immobilize them. Serving others remains a satisfying and rewarding endeavor. However, the possibility of legal action against social workers does serve to underscore the importance of understanding the legal duties that apply to them and other helpers in professional practice.

Besharov and Besharov (1987, pp. 519–520) identify several common categories of lawsuits that can be filed against social workers. These include: (1) Treatment Without Consent, (2) Inappropriate Treatment, (3) Failure to Consult with or Refer to a Specialist, (4) Failure to Prevent a Client's Suicide,

(5) Causing a Client's Suicide, (6) Failure to Protect Third Parties, (7) Inappropriate Release of a Client, (8) False Imprisonment, (9) Failure to Provide Adequate Care for a Client in Residential Settings, (10) Assault and Battery, (11) Sexual Involvement with a Client, (12) Breach of Confidentiality, (13) Defamation, (14) Violation of a Client's Civil Rights, (15) Failure to Be Available When Needed, (16) Termination of Treatment, and (17) Inappropriate Bill Collection Methods.

Certain kinds of social work practice and certain settings constitute a somewhat greater risk for litigation against social workers. For example, because child welfare work often involves the provision of *involuntary* services, there is a greater likelihood of both civil and criminal legal action against social workers who work in such settings. Besharov and Besharov (1987, p. 520) specifically identify some of the issues in child welfare practice that can lead to legal action: (1) Reporting Suspected Child Abuse and Neglect, (2) Inadequately Protecting a Child, (3) Violating Parental Rights, and (4) Inadequate Foster Care Services.

Although over time there probably will be changes in the nature and extent of the legal duties applying to social workers and other professional helpers, it is possible to outline a list of general *legal duties* (see Figure 3-1) likely to remain in effect for several years (see Everstine and Everstine, 1983, pp. 227–251).

Duty of Care

Professional social workers must provide reasonable care in delivering social work services. Services provided must meet at least an adequate standard of care as determined in part by the social work profession and in part by common expectations of helping professionals. Assessments, diagnoses, treatments, and interventions must therefore have theoretical or empirical support. Atypical interventions and those activities without a sound professional rationale may not meet the duty of care obligation. These also may constitute an increased risk of liability.

F I G U R E 3-1
Legal Duties of Helping Professionals

1. Duty of Care
2. Duty to Respect Privacy
3. Duty to Maintain Confidentiality
4. Duty to Inform
5. Duty to Report
6. Duty to Warn

There are several additional responsibilities that can be included within the general duty of care category. For example, professional social workers must be available to the clients they serve. Arrangements concerning emergency situations should be discussed with clients. Similarly, before going on vacation, workers must inform clients and arrange for substitute coverage. Social workers must also take action to ensure the physical protection of clients determined to be (1) dangerous to other persons, (2) dangerous to self, or (3) so gravely disabled as to be unable to provide minimal self-care (Everstine & Everstine, 1983, p. 232). Often in these cases, the worker would seek to arrange for the hospitalization of such clients.

Duty to Respect Privacy

Professional social workers have a duty to respect the privacy of people with whom they interact during the course of their practice. Under most circumstances, social workers are not entitled to invade or infringe upon the privacy of prospective or actual clients. Privacy includes an individual's physical space (e.g., home) as well as those aspects of his personal life that constitute a "symbolic region" (Everstine et al., 1980), which is his alone to share or reveal as seen fit. The worker should have a sound professional reason for exploration within these regions.

Duty to Maintain Confidentiality

Professional social workers have a duty to maintain the confidentiality of what is said to them during the course of their professional practice. Because much of what is communicated during the helping process falls within the area of personal privacy, the worker is obligated to maintain confidentiality. Generally, the information shared remains the property of the client and, ultimately, remains within his control. Essentially, the worker is merely using the information in order to help the client; it is not the worker's. Usually, clients must give *informed consent* before such confidential information may be shared with another person or organization.

Duty to Inform

Professional social workers have a duty to inform and educate clients and prospective clients concerning the nature and extent of the services—cost, length, probability of success, risks, and alternate services that may be appropriate. Clients should also be informed concerning relevant policies and laws that could affect them at some point during the provision of social services. For example, most clients should be told about the social worker's obligations to report child abuse and child neglect. Typically, clients should be informed about the worker's qualifications, fields of expertise, and, when relevant, areas about which the worker has limited knowledge or experience. Under most circumstances, clients must provide informed consent before professional treatment may begin. Similarly, clients must be informed well before the worker concludes the working relationship or transfers them to another helping professional.

Duty to Report

Professional social workers have a duty to report to designated governmental authorities indications of certain "outrages against humanity" (Everstine & Everstine, 1983, p. 240). Although the specific process of reporting is defined by each state, social workers must report knowledge of certain criminal behavior, including "child abuse, child neglect, child molestation, and incest" (Everstine & Everstine, 1983, p. 240). Increasingly, states are expanding the kinds of behaviors that must be reported. These include abuse and neglect of the elderly and exploitation of the mentally retarded and disabled.

Duty to Warn

If, during an interview with a worker, a client reveals an intention to harm another person and the worker determines that the client might act on his impulse in such a way as to endanger another, then the worker must (1) try to arrange for the client's hospitalization or an equivalent form of protection from his own harmful impulses and (2) warn the intended victim or victims of the threat.

UNDERSTANDING THE FUNDAMENTAL VALUES AND THE ETHICS OF SOCIAL WORK

In addition to the legal duties to which all helping professionals are subject, social workers must also conform to the fundamental values and the Code of Ethics of the social work profession. Social workers and social work educators have energetically discussed the topic of social work values since the emergence of the profession around the beginning of the twentieth century. The discussion continues today and will undoubtedly continue as long as there is a social work profession. While there is some divergence of opinion regarding the application of fundamental values, there is considerable consensus concerning the values themselves. For example, in 1982 the board of directors of the Council on Social Work Education (CSWE), the accrediting body for schools of social work in the United States, adopted as part of the revised curriculum policy statement the social work values outlined in Figure 3-2.

The National Association of Social Workers (NASW), in its *Standards for the Classification of Social Work Practice* (NASW, 1981, p. 18) identified the values for social work practice outlined in Figure 3-3.

The fundamental social work values provide social workers with an extremely useful point of departure for ethical decision making. They are invaluable in helping workers define a professional identity and establish a social work frame of reference. However, since values are abstract concepts, they provide

---

FIGURE 3-2
Social Work Values
Council on Social Work Education
Curriculum Policy Statement*

A. Social workers hold that people should have equal access to resources, services, and opportunities for the accomplishment of life tasks, the alleviation of distress, and the realization of their aspirations and values in relation to themselves, the rights of others, the general welfare, and social justice.

B. Among the values and principles that guide professional social workers in their practice and that should be manifest throughout every social work curriculum are the following:

1. Social workers' professional relationships are built on their regard for individual worth and human dignity and are furthered by mutual participation, acceptance, confidentiality, honesty, and responsible handling of conflict.
2. Social workers respect people's rights to choose, to contract for services, and to participate in the helping process.
3. Social workers contribute to making social institutions more humane and responsive to human needs.
4. Social workers demonstrate respect for and acceptance of the unique characteristics of diverse populations.
5. Social workers are responsible for their own ethical conduct, for the quality of their practice, and for maintaining continuous growth in the knowledge and skills of their profession.

_____

*This excerpt was first published by the Council on Social Work Education, and is reprinted here with permission.

limited guidance for making specific practice decisions. That function is served by the social work Code of Ethics, derived from the fundamental social work values but presented in more concrete terms. It aids social workers in making practice decisions that are both ethical and congruent with the fundamental social work values. One without the other is insufficient. In order to practice ethically, social workers must have a thorough understanding of both the fundamental social work values *and* the ethical principles that guide them in making ethical decisions. In the United States, the National Association of Social Workers' *Code of Ethics* serves as the primary guide to which social workers must adhere. The Code reflects the relationship between values and ethics. The preamble (NASW, 1980, p. iii) states: "This code is based on fundamental values of the social work profession that include the worth, dignity, and uniqueness of all persons as well as their rights and opportunities. It is also based on the nature of social work, which fosters conditions that promote these values."

In order to practice ethically, social workers must be thoroughly familiar with the Code of Ethics. If a social worker does not have it subject to memory, she should carry a copy of the Code with her; during her professional activities, she will frequently need to refer to it. The Code of Ethics is reproduced in Figure 3-4.

FIGURE 3-4

National Association of Social Workers
Code of Ethics*

I. The Social Worker's Conduct and Comportment as a Social Worker
   A. Propriety—The social worker should maintain high standards of personal conduct in the capacity or identity as social worker.
      1. The private conduct of the social worker is a personal matter to the same degree as is any other person's, except when such conduct compromises the fulfillment of professional responsibilities.
      2. The social worker should not participate in, condone, or be associated with dishonesty, fraud, deceit, or misrepresentation.
      3. The social worker should distinguish clearly between statements and actions made as a private individual and as a representative of the social work profession or an organization or group.
   B. Competence and Professional Development—The social worker should strive to become and remain proficient in professional practice and the performance of professional functions.
      1. The social worker should accept responsibility or employment only on the basis of existing competence or the intention to acquire the necessary competence.
      2. The social worker should not misrepresent professional qualifications, education, experience, or affiliations.
   C. Service—The social worker should regard as primary the service obligation of the social work profession.
      1. The social worker should retain ultimate responsibility for the quality and extent of the service that individual assumes, assigns, or performs.
      2. The social worker should act to prevent practices that are inhumane or discriminatory against any person or group of persons.
   D. Integrity—The social worker should act in accordance with the highest standards of professional integrity and impartiality.
      1. The social worker should be alert to and resist the influences and pressures that interfere with the exercise of professional discretion and impartial judgment required for the performance of professional functions.
      2. The social worker should not exploit professional relationships for personal gain.
   E. Scholarship and Research—The social worker engaged in study and research should be guided by the conventions of scholarly inquiry.
      1. The social worker engaged in research should consider carefully its possible consequences for human beings.
      2. The social worker engaged in research should ascertain that the consent of participants in the research is voluntary and informed, without any implied deprivation or penalty for refusal to participate, and with due regard for participants' privacy and dignity.

_____

*Code of Ethics of the National Association of Social Workers. As adopted by the 1979 Delegate Assembly, effective July 1, 1980. National Association of Social Workers, Silver Spring, Maryland. Reproduced with permission.

3. The social worker engaged in research should protect participants from unwarranted physical or mental discomfort, distress, harm, danger, or deprivation.
4. The social worker who engages in the evaluation of services or cases should discuss them only for the professional purposes and only with persons directly and professionally concerned with them.
5. Information obtained about participants in research should be treated as confidential.
6. The social worker should take credit only for work actually done in connection with scholarly and research endeavors and credit contributions made by others.

II. The Social Worker's Ethical Responsibility to Clients
   F. Primacy of Clients' Interests—The social worker's primary responsibility is to clients.
      1. The social worker should serve clients with devotion, loyalty, determination, and the maximum application of professional skill and competence.
      2. The social worker should not exploit relationships with clients for personal advantage, or solicit the clients of one's agency for private practice.
      3. The social worker should not practice, condone, facilitate or collaborate with any form of discrimination on the basis of race, color, sex, sexual orientation, age, religion, national origin, marital status, political belief, mental or physical handicap, or any other preference or personal characteristic, condition or status.
      4. The social worker should avoid relationships or commitments that conflict with the interests of clients.
      5. The social worker should under no circumstances engage in sexual activities with clients.
      6. The social worker should provide clients with accurate and complete information regarding the extent and nature of the services available to them.
      7. The social worker should apprise clients of their risks, rights, opportunities, and obligations associated with social service to them.
      8. The social worker should seek advice and counsel of colleagues and supervisors whenever such consultation is in the best interest of clients.
      9. The social worker should terminate service to clients, and professional relationships with them, when such service and relationships are no longer required or no longer serve the clients' needs or interests.
     10. The social worker should withdraw services precipitously only under unusual circumstances, giving careful consideration to all factors in the situation and taking care to minimize possible adverse effects.
     11. The social worker who anticipates the termination or interruption of service to clients should notify clients promptly and seek the transfer, referral, or continuation of service in relation to the clients' needs and preferences.
   G. Rights and Prerogatives of Clients—The social worker should make every effort to foster maximum self-determination on the part of clients.

1. When the social worker must act on behalf of a client who has been adjudged legally incompetent, the social worker should safeguard the interests and rights of that client.
2. When another individual has been legally authorized to act on behalf of a client, the social worker should deal with that person always with the client's best interest in mind.
3. The social worker should not engage in any action that violates or diminishes the civil or legal rights of clients.

H. Confidentiality and Privacy—The social worker should respect the privacy of clients and hold in confidence all information obtained in the course of professional service.
1. The social worker should share with others confidences revealed by clients, without their consent, only for compelling professional reasons.
2. The social worker should inform clients fully about the limits of confidentiality in a given situation, the purposes for which information is obtained, and how it may be used.
3. The social worker should afford clients reasonable access to any official social work records concerning them.
4. When providing clients with access to records, the social worker should take due care to protect the confidences of others contained in those records.
5. The social worker should obtain informed consent of clients before taping, recording, or permitting third party observation of their activities.

I. Fees—When setting fees, the social worker should ensure that they are fair, reasonable, considerate, and commensurate with the service performed and with due regard for the clients' ability to pay.
1. The social worker should not divide a fee or accept or give anything of value for receiving or making a referral.

III. The Social Worker's Ethical Responsibility to Colleagues
J. Respect, Fairness, and Courtesy—The social worker should treat colleagues with respect, courtesy, fairness, and good faith.
1. The social worker should cooperate with colleagues to promote professional interest and concerns.
2. The social worker should respect confidences shared by colleagues in the course of their professional relationships and transactions.
3. The social worker should create and maintain conditions of practice that facilitate ethical and competent professional performance by colleagues.
4. The social worker should treat with respect, and represent accurately and fairly, the qualifications, views, and findings of colleagues and use appropriate channels to express judgments on these matters.
5. The social worker who replaces or is replaced by a colleague in professional practice should act with consideration for the interest, character, and reputation of that colleague.
6. The social worker should not exploit a dispute between a colleague and employers to obtain a position or otherwise advance the social worker's interest.

7. The social worker should seek arbitration or mediation when conflicts with colleagues require resolution for compelling professional reasons.
8. The social worker should extend to colleagues of other professions the same respect and cooperation that is extended to social work colleagues.
9. The social worker who serves as an employer, supervisor, or mentor to colleagues should make orderly and explicit arrangements regarding the conditions of their continuing professional relationship.
10. The social worker who has the responsibility for employing and evaluating the performance of other staff members should fulfill such responsibility in a fair, considerate, and equitable manner, on the basis of clearly enunciated criteria.
11. The social worker who has the responsibility for evaluating the performance of employees, supervisees, or students should share evaluations with them.

K. Dealing with Colleagues' Clients—The social worker has the responsibility to relate to the clients of colleagues with full professional consideration.
1. The social worker should not solicit the clients of colleagues.
2. The social worker should not assume professional responsibility for the clients of another agency or a colleague without appropriate communication with that agency or colleague.
3. The social worker who serves the clients of colleagues, during a temporary absence or emergency, should serve those clients with the same consideration as that afforded any client.

IV. The Social Worker's Ethical Responsibility to Employers and Employing Organizations
L. Commitments to Employing Organization—The social worker should adhere to commitments made to the employing organization.
1. The social worker should work to improve the employing agency's policies and procedures, and the efficiency and effectiveness of its services.
2. The social worker should not accept employment or arrange student field placements in an organization which is currently under public sanction by NASW for violating personnel standards, or imposing limitations on or penalties for professional actions on behalf of clients.
3. The social worker should act to prevent and eliminate discrimination in the employing organization's work assignments and in its employment policies and practices.
4. The social worker should use with scrupulous regard, and only for the purpose for which they are intended, the resources of the employing organization.

V. The Social Worker's Ethical Responsibility to the Social Work Profession
M. Maintaining the Integrity of the Profession—The social worker should uphold and advance the values, ethics, knowledge, and mission of the profession.

1. The social worker should protect and enhance the dignity and integrity of the profession and should be responsible and vigorous in discussion and criticism of the profession.
2. The social worker should take action through appropriate channels against unethical conduct by any other member of the profession.
3. The social worker should act to prevent the unauthorized and unqualified practice of social work.
4. The social worker should make no misrepresentation in advertising as to qualifications, competence, service, or results to be achieved.

N. Community Service—The social worker should assist the profession in making social services available to the general public.
1. The social worker should contribute time and professional expertise to activities that promote respect for the utility, the integrity, and the competence of the social work profession.
2. The social worker should support the formulation, development, enactment and implementation of social policies of concern to the profession.

O. Development of Knowledge—The social worker should take responsibility for identifying, developing, and fully utilizing knowledge for professional practice.
1. The social worker should base practice upon recognized knowledge relevant to social work.
2. The social worker should critically examine, and keep current with, emerging knowledge relevant to social work.
3. The social worker should contribute to the knowledge base of social work and share research knowledge and practice wisdom with colleagues.

VI. The Social Worker's Ethical Responsibility to Society

P. Promoting the General Welfare—The social worker should promote the general welfare of society.
1. The social worker should act to prevent and eliminate discrimination against any person or group on the basis of race, color, sex, sexual orientation, age, religion, national origin, marital status, political belief, mental or physical handicap, or any other preference or personal characteristic, condition, or status.
2. The social worker should act to ensure that all persons have access to the resources, services, and opportunities which they require.
3. The social worker should act to expand choice and opportunity for all persons, with special regard for disadvantaged or oppressed groups and persons.
4. The social worker should promote conditions that encourage respect for the diversity of cultures which constitute American society.
5. The social worker should provide appropriate professional services in public emergencies.
6. The social worker should advocate changes in policy and legislation to improve social conditions and to promote social justice.
7. The social worker should encourage informed participation by the public in shaping social policies and institutions.

IDENTIFYING ETHICAL AND LEGAL IMPLICATIONS

In addition to understanding the legal duties of all professional helpers and knowing the Code of Ethics, social workers must be able to identify those principles and duties that might apply in a given practice situation. This requires inductive thinking skills as the social worker considers a specific situation and determines which ethical principles and duties are relevant.

Consider the following example. A social worker in an agency that provides crisis intervention services receives a phone call from a former client who says, "I have locked myself in my basement. I have a gun and I am going to shoot myself today. I wanted to let you know that you did not help me at all! Goodbye."

There are several ethical and legal obligations that the worker would consider in responding to this situation. The following elements from the Code probably apply:

> II.F.1. The social worker should serve clients with devotion, loyalty, determination, and the maximum application of professional skill and competence.
>
> II.F.8. The social worker should seek advice and counsel of colleagues and supervisors whenever it is in the best interest of clients.
>
> II.G.3. The social worker should not engage in any action that violates or diminishes the civil or legal rights of clients.
>
> II.H. Confidentiality and Privacy—The social worker should respect the privacy of clients and hold in confidence all information obtained in the course of professional service.
>
> II.H.1. The social worker should share with others confidences revealed by clients, without their consent, only for compelling reasons.

The legal duties that deserve consideration in this particular situation are the duty of care, including the responsibility to try to prevent suicidal action; the duty to inform; the duty of confidentiality; and the duty to respect clients' privacy.

In spite of the fact that this is a "former client" who is angry at the social worker, the Code suggests that the worker should maintain her professional role and continue to serve him enthusiastically (II.F.1.). Because the client reflects disappointment in the worker and may not respond to her attempt to telephone him, it is probably in the client's best interest that the worker seek advice from her supervisor or colleagues (II.F.8.). According to the Code, the worker should also respect the client's civil and legal rights (II.G.3.). Additionally, the worker should maintain the confidentiality of information that the client reveals (II.H.) or share such information with others only for compelling reasons (II.H.1.). These latter three principles apply if or when the worker considers contacting the caller's family members, a medical physician, an ambulance service, or the police in her efforts to help him.

As a professional helper, the social worker should attempt to prevent the client from taking his own life. This is consistent with legal duty of care through which the worker is obligated to be available, to try to prevent suicidal action, to avoid causing suicidal action, and to ensure the physical protection of clients who are dangerous to themselves. The worker also has a duty to inform the client concerning the actions that she might take and to respect the client's privacy. Finally, she has a legal, as well as ethical, duty to maintain confidentiality.

When we consider the relevance of these various ethical and legal obligations, it becomes clear that it is impossible for the worker in this case to meet *all* of them. If she attempts to serve the client with devotion, determination, and meet the legal duty to try to prevent his suicide by telephoning family members, a medical doctor, or the police, she violates his right to confidentiality and, potentially, his privacy. (Imagine the police and emergency medical personnel entering his home!) If she maintains his right to confidentiality and privacy, she neglects her legal duty to attempt to prevent his suicide. How is she to decide what to do?

ETHICAL DECISION MAKING

Identifying the various ethical principles and legal duties pertaining to a case situation is the first step in the process of ethical decision making. However, it is often not enough, since numerous principles and legal duties may apply and sometimes conflict. When they do, social workers are caught between them.

To help social workers decide which principle or legal duty takes precedence over another in situations where ethical obligations conflict, Loewenberg and Dolgoff (1988) have developed a decision-making hierarchy.

Loewenberg and Dolgoff's Hierarchy of Ethical Obligations

Loewenberg and Dolgoff (1988, pp. 120–123) identify and rank-order professional social work's ethical obligations. The obligations are reproduced in Figure 3-5. (*Rank-order* means that in ethically conflicting situations, Obligation 1 takes precedence over Obligations 2 through 7; Obligation 2 takes precedence over Obligations 3 through 7, and so on.) In any given practice situation, the social worker must first identify the relevant principles and legal duties that apply. If conflicts emerge, she then classifies them into the categories suggested by Loewenberg and Dolgoff's Hierarchy. Finally, she gives priority to the stronger (higher) obligation and takes action accordingly.

To resume the discussion of the man who locked himself in his basement and threatened suicide, the ethical principles and legal duties that may apply to the situation have been identified. Loewenberg and Dolgoff's Hierarchy can

F I G U R E 3-5
Loewenberg and Dolgoff's Hierarchy of Obligations*

1. A social worker should make professional decisions that guarantee the basic survival needs of individuals and/or of society. The protection of human life (whether the life of a client or someone else) takes precedence over every other obligation. The means for protecting human life might include emergency or health services, food, shelter, income, and so on as appropriate in a given situation.

2. A social worker should make practice decisions that foster a person's autonomy, independence, and freedom. Freedom, though highly important, does not override the right to life or survival of the person himself or of anyone else. A person does not have the right to harm himself or herself or anyone else on the grounds that the right to make such a decision is her or his autonomous right. When a person is about to make such a decision, the social worker is obligated to intervene, as Obligation 1 takes precedence.

3. A social worker should make practice decisions that foster equality of opportunity and equality of access for all people.

4. A social worker should make practice decisions that promote a better quality of life for all people.

5. A social worker should make practice decisions that strengthen every person's right to privacy. Keeping confidential information inviolate is a direct derivative of this obligation.

6. A social worker should make practice decisions that permit her to speak the truth and to fully disclose all relevant information.

7. A social worker should make practice decisions that are in accord with the rules and regulations which she has voluntarily accepted.

---

* Reproduced by permission of the publisher, F. E. Peacock Publishers, Inc., Itasca, Illinois. From F. Loewenberg & R. Dolgoff, *Ethical Decisions for Social Work Practice* (3rd ed.), 1988, pp. 121–122.

now be used to determine which of these several, conflicting responsibilities take precedence.

As suggested by the hierarchy, the social worker's first obligation is to save or protect human life. This is consonant with the ethical responsibility to "serve clients with devotion, loyalty, determination, and the maximum application of professional skill and competence" and consistent with the duty of care that includes the responsibility to prevent suicidal action. The protection of human life takes precedence over every other obligation. Therefore, assuming that, in the worker's best professional judgment, the man who telephoned indeed intends to attempt suicide, the worker must intervene—even if such intervention violates other ethical principles or legal duties. Of course, the worker would usually first try to intervene in a manner that would not infringe upon other obligations. For example, in this situation, the worker or her supervisor (as the client seems to have targeted the worker as a source of dissatisfaction) might return the person's telephone call in an effort to engage him in conversation in the attempt to defuse the intensity of the situation. The attempt to crisis intervene directly with the client by telephone is congruent with the second ethical obligation, that is, to "make practice decisions that foster a person's autonomy, independence, and freedom." Such intervention would also support the fifth ethical obligation, to "strengthen every person's right to privacy" and to keep information confidential. However, the man may not answer the telephone or it may be apparent that further contact by the worker or other agency personnel would represent provocation. If such is the case, the worker may have to infringe upon the client's right to privacy, his right to confidentiality, and perhaps even his right to freedom—should involuntary hospitalization become necessary. In her attempt to save the man's life, the worker may have to call a family member, inform him about the situation, and ask for his cooperation and help. She may have to telephone the local police and ask them to go to the house. She may also have to contact medical personnel in order to facilitate hospitalization. Taken by themselves, these actions do, in fact, infringe upon certain of the client's rights and do represent violations of some principles and legal duties. However, if the worker determines that the person intends to attempt suicide, the worker is ethically and legally bound to forgo the lower-level obligations in order to adhere to those at the higher level.

SUMMARY

The values, ethics, and duties that guide social workers enter into every aspect of professional practice. Indeed, our ethical obligations must be considered more important than theoretical knowledge, research findings, agency policies, and personal views.

In order to make sound ethical decisions, social workers must know and understand the values of the profession, the Code of Ethics, and the legal duties affecting social work practice. In addition, workers must be able to identify the ethical principles and legal duties that may apply to case situations. Finally, when several obligations apply, social workers must be able to determine which take precedence over others. The skill of ethical decision making is fundamental to professional social work practice. Without such skill, a person cannot legitimately claim to have achieved professional status.

■ **Exercise 3-1: Ethical Decision Making**

In the space provided, identify the ethical principles and legal duties that you believe may apply to each of the case examples presented below. Then classify and rank-order each principle or duty according to Loewenberg and Dolgoff's Hierarchy of Obligations. Finally, based upon your prioritization, describe the actions you might take as a social worker in each situation.

1. As a social worker in the oncology unit of the general hospital, you frequently work with clients who are dying. An intelligent, articulate eighty-eight-year-old woman, Ms. T., who has suffered from enormous pain for several months, informs you that she has hoarded powerful analgesic medicines and intends to take her own life during the night. She says that she wants to say goodbye to you and to thank you for all your help during this time. However, she asks that you please do not interfere with her plans.

2. As a social worker in an elementary school system, you frequently work with young school children in small groups. During a meeting with several girls in the eight- to ten-year-old age range, one girl says that almost every night her father comes into her bedroom, puts his hands under her pajamas, and touches between her legs.

3. A twenty-five-year-old man, father of two children aged one and three, comes to a first interview with you, a social worker in a family counseling agency. During the course of the interview, he says that he and his wife argue a lot. He reports that she won't stop arguing once she starts and that when he tries to walk away, she pursues him, yelling. He says that in those situations he becomes enraged. He reports that on several occasions he has pushed her and once punched her in the face.

4. You have recently been employed in an agency whose clientele is primarily black and Hispanic. All the professional staff are white; several of the secretarial and support staff members are black.

5. You have been working with a married couple who have indicated a desire to improve the quality of their relationship. Direct, open, and honest communication has been agreed upon as a relationship goal. Each has also expressed that sexual fidelity is an important dimension of their marriage. Between the fifth and sixth meetings, you receive a telephone call from one of the partners who says, "I think it would help you to help us in the counseling sessions if you knew that I am involved romantically with another person. My spouse does not know and I know that you will not reveal this information. I want you to know because I respect your expertise. You are doing a wonderful job."

6. Using the rating scales below (where 0 = no proficiency and 10 = complete proficiency), assess your current level of proficiency in the following dimensions of the skill of ethical decision making.

Knowledge and Understanding of Legal Duties

```
|   |   |   |   |   |   |   |   |   |   |
0   1   2   3   4   5   6   7   8   9   10
```

Knowledge and Understanding of Core Social Work Values

```
|   |   |   |   |   |   |   |   |   |   |
0   1   2   3   4   5   6   7   8   9   10
```

Knowledge and Understanding of Social Work Code of Ethics

```
|   |   |   |   |   |   |   |   |   |   |
0   1   2   3   4   5   6   7   8   9   10
```

Ability to Identify Principles and Legal Duties Relevant to Specific Cases

```
|   |   |   |   |   |   |   |   |   |   |
0   1   2   3   4   5   6   7   8   9   10
```

Ability to Prioritize Applicable Principles and Legal Duties

```
|   |   |   |   |   |   |   |   |   |   |
0   1   2   3   4   5   6   7   8   9   10
```

7. Finally, review your ratings to identify those dimensions of ethical decision making in which you remain less proficient (e.g., a score of 7 or less). Then, outline the steps you might take to improve your skill in those areas.

TALKING AND LISTENING—THE BASIC INTERPERSONAL SKILLS

This chapter is intended to aid the student in developing competence in the basic interpersonal skills of talking and listening. These fundamental communication skills (Nelsen, 1980) are so integral and so essential to all phases of social work practice (indeed, to all aspects of human interaction) that even a minimal deficiency in their use is likely to interfere with the development of a positive professional relationship and a successful outcome. The overall purpose of these basic interpersonal skills is to enable workers to engage in effective social interaction with others. Their use enables workers to hear, to understand accurately, and to express themselves clearly and directly.

In order to interact effectively, social workers must be skilled in talking—using voice, speech, and body language—as well as in listening—hearing, observing, encouraging, and remembering. Finally, workers must be able to combine talking and listening in the form of active listening, a form of talking through which the listener demonstrates that he has heard and accurately understood the speaker.

Some common errors made by social workers in talking and listening include: (1) interacting in a patronizing or condescending manner; (2) interrogating rather than interviewing by asking questions in rapid, staccatolike fashion; (3) attending exclusively to either the thinking or the feeling dimensions of a person's experience; (4) frequently interrupting with a comment or question; (5) failing to listen; (6) mispronouncing a person's name or not using it; (7) neglecting to demonstrate understanding through active listening; (8) making suggestions or proposing solutions too early in the process (on the basis of incomplete or inaccurate understanding of the person-problem-situation); (9) prematurely disclosing too much of the worker's own personal feelings or life experiences; (10) confronting or challenging a person before establishing a base of accurate understanding and a solid relationship; (11) interpreting or speculating about causes of problems before adequate exploration has been undertaken; (12) prematurely pushing for action or progress from a person; (13) using cliches and jargon; (14) making critical or judgmental comments, including pejorative remarks about other professionals; and (15) displaying inappropriate or disproportionate emotions (e.g., extraordinarily happy to see a person just met or sobbing uncontrollably when a person expresses painful feelings).

VOICE AND SPEECH

The words the social worker chooses, the quality of pronunciation, the sound and pitch of voice, and the rate and delivery of speech communicate a great deal to clients and others with whom the worker interacts. During a typical first contact, whether that interaction be face-to-face, by telephone, or even by letter, the worker should use words that are understandable to most people. In addition, she should avoid evaluative terms. Even words such as *good* or *right*—intended to convey support and encouragement—may suggest to a client that the worker is making judgments. She may wonder, If he positively evaluates me this soon without knowing much about me, can he really be objective? Or, He approves of me. I guess I'd better not say anything that might disappoint him.

As an interview proceeds, the worker may attempt to match the client's language mode. Some people favor words associated with hearing; others prefer those identified with seeing; still others like words that indicate touching. For example, the worker who uses words such as *hear, sound, noise,* or *loud* with people who respond to words about hearing increases the probability of being understood and valued by them. A similarly favorable reaction is likely when a worker uses *see, view,* and *perceive* with people who tend to experience life visually, or *feel, sense,* and *touch* with those who respond to words about touching (Bandler and Grinder, 1979, pp. 5–78).

Tone of voice often has an impact on others. A worker who communicates in a voice that is monotonous, dramatic, high pitched, loud, or soft may distract the other from the substance of the message and thereby interfere with the communication process. Speech that is fast or slow, delivered in a halting fashion, or punctuated by the frequent use of *uhhs* and *you knows* may also impede understanding. Similarly, the worker whose verbal responses are not consistent with the topic under consideration or incongruent with his own nonverbal presentation sends a confusing set of messages.

In general, social workers should adopt speaking styles moderate in vocal tone, volume, and speed of delivery. Through their voice and speech, they should communicate that they are truly interested in what the client has to say (Ivey, 1988, p. 22). Sometimes, however, the worker deliberately increases or decreases the rate of speech in order to match the pace of the client. On other occasions, the worker may purposely slow his pace in order to "lead" a fast-speaking client into a somewhat more moderate rate. In some circumstances, for example when working with a moderately hearing-impaired client, a worker may significantly change the pitch of his voice in order to be more easily heard. Active voice is usually preferred over passive and each unit of speech should not be so long or complex as to impede understanding.

■ **Exercise 4-1: Voice and Speech**

The following exercises are intended to help you become more aware of the sound of your voice and the nature of your speech patterns.

1. Tape record your voice for five minutes at four periods during the day. First, record your voice upon awakening, again at a point around midday, once more late in the afternoon, and finally just prior to bedtime. Make these recordings when you are alone. Speak approximately the same statement on each occasion (but do not read from a script). You might, for example, imagine that you are introducing yourself to a new client.

   How does your voice sound at the different times? Are the samples similar or different? In general, how would you characterize the sound of your voice? Do you like it? How clear is your pronunciation? Is your speech modulated or does it tend to be monotonous? How would you characterize the pitch or tone of your speech (high or low)? How about the rate of speech (fast or slow)? When you listen to the sound of your voice, what do you feel? Does it remind you of anything or anyone? If so, what or whom?

   In the space below, indicate what you have learned about your voice and speech through this exercise, and what you want to change.

2. Tape record your voice as you express, with emotion, the following statements:

Anger   I am angry. I deserved an *A* but I got a *B*.
          I hate your guts!

Fear   I am scared when I go alone into the public housing project.
          I'm frightened that you are going to leave me.

Caring   I truly care a great deal about you.
          You are very important to me.

Sadness I am so sad and depressed that I cannot even get out of bed.
          I just can't go on anymore.

Request I need some help. My car has broken down and I need a
          ride to get to work in the morning. Would you be willing
          to drive me in?
          Would you please give me an extension for this paper?

Demand   You must pick up your room before you may go out to play.
          Get that report in to me by the end of the workday today.

Replay the tape. As you listen to these different expressions of your voice, what do you notice? Do you seem equally capable of expressing each of these emotions? Which, if any, appear to reflect discomfort? With which do you seem to be at ease? In your everyday life, which emotions do you tend to reflect in your interactions with others? Are there any that you only rarely express?

In the space below, indicate what you have learned through this exercise that may relate to your roles as a professional social worker.

BODY LANGUAGE

Because a great deal of communication is nonverbal, social workers must appreciate the potency of body language. Factors such as posture, facial expression, eye contact, gait, proxemics, and body positioning represent powerful forms of communication (Ivey, 1988, pp. 26–27). Generally, social workers want their body language to be congruent with their verbal language. All people, including children, notice discrepancies and incongruities between what people say verbally and what they express nonverbally. Also, social workers usually want their body language to communicate attention and interest in the other, as well as caring, concern, respect, and authenticity. Frequently, social workers want their message to carry power or authority and to reflect assertion. In order to emphasize one element or another, changes in body language are necessary.

As a general guide for beginning interviews with prospective clients, the social worker should typically adopt an open or accessible body position (Egan, 1982a, pp. 60–62) in which, if standing, arms and hands are held loosely along the sides or, if seated, in the lap. Arms held across the chest, behind the head, or draped over an adjoining chair are likely to express inattention or nonreceptiveness. Tightly clasped hands, swinging legs, pacing, looking at a clock, or drumming fingers may communicate nervousness or impatience. Slouching in a chair may reflect fatigue or disinterest. Sometimes, however, a deliberately informal body position may be necessary to increase the comfort and decrease the threat experienced by another. For example, in work with children, social workers often sit on a floor and talk while playing a game. With teenage clients, significant encounters may occur while eating ice cream cones, shooting pool, or leaning against a fence.

The frequency and intensity of eye contact varies depending upon the people involved, the purpose for the meeting, the topic under discussion, and a host of other factors. As a general guide, however, the social worker should adopt seating or standing arrangements that allow for but do not force eye contact between the persons. Although it is common for workers to attempt rather frequent eye contact, especially when clients are talking, the degree and intensity should vary according to the individual and cultural characteristics of the person, the problems of concern, and the context of the meeting. In many cultures, regular eye contact is experienced as positive. In several, however, it is not. "Some cultural groups (for instance, certain Native American, Eskimo, or aboriginal Australian groups) generally avoid eye contact, especially when talking about serious subjects" (Ivey, 1988, p. 27). In all cases, eye contact should never involve staring. It should not represent a violation of the other's territory or be so intense as to constitute an invasion or challenge.

Attending (Carkhuff & Anthony, 1979, pp. 31–60) is a term frequently used to describe the process of nonverbally communicating to another that the social worker is open, nonjudgmental, accepting of the other as a person, and interested in what she has to say. A general purpose of attending is, in fact, to encourage the other to express herself as fully and as freely as possible. During the beginning phase, the worker's nonverbal presentation is at least as important as any other factor in influencing the client's response to him.

There is a substantial literature that addresses the skill of attending. For example, Carkhuff and Anthony (1979, pp. 39–42) suggest that counselors face their clients squarely, at a distance of three to four feet, without tables or other potential obstacles between the participants. They further recommend regular eye contact, facial expressions of interest and concern, and a slight lean or incline toward the other.

Many of these guidelines are useful. However, they may tend to reflect nonverbal characteristics common among adult, majority-member, middle- and upper-class North Americans. Many persons of ethnic minority status commonly demonstrate quite different nonverbal characteristics in their interactions with others. Facing some people too directly, too squarely, and too closely may, on occasion, represent a violation of personal territory and privacy. For others, a distance of four feet would be much too far for an intimate conversation. Therefore, the social worker must be flexible in his attending and physical positioning. He must closely observe the nonverbal expressions of the other and respect them. Also, within the general guidelines suggested above, he should assume a body position comfortable for him: trying to understand another person requires energy and concentration, and if the worker is distracted by an uncomfortable position, he is likely to be less attentive to the other.

However, the worker must avoid becoming so comfortable that he becomes less alert (falling asleep during an interview does not indicate interest and concern!).

When seated positions are desirable and available (e.g., when interviewing an adult in an office setting), it is often advantageous to place the chairs so that they create an angle of between 90 and 135 degrees. Such an angle allows the other to more easily direct her eyes and body toward or away from the worker as desired. It affords the social worker the same opportunity. Matching, moveable chairs are preferred for their flexibility and in order to avoid symbolic distinction between the worker's chair and the client's. Physically leaning toward the client at points when she is sharing emotionally charged material usually demonstrates concern and compassion. However, carefully observe her reaction. Some clients may find the added closeness invasive or too intimate, especially during the early stages of the relationship.

Of course, many times the social worker has limited control over the placement of chairs or even the interview setting. Often an exchange will occur during a walk or an automobile drive, in a kitchen during mealtime, while someone cares for children, and sometimes even while a person watches television. As a relationship develops and the worker begins to gain a sense of the meaning of different gestures to the client, it may become appropriate to ask to move a chair closer or lower the volume on the television. These are frequently messages of great significance to clients ("My, he actually does want to hear what I have to say!").

■ **Exercise 4-2: Body Language**

Recruit a friend or colleague to join you in a few nonverbal experiments.

1. Maintaining eye contact, slowly walk toward your partner (who remains standing in position) until it becomes uncomfortable for either one of you. Then stop. Observe the approximate distance between you. Ask your partner to describe his thoughts and feelings as you came closer. Make mental note of his comments as well as your own thoughts and feelings.

2. Stand face-to-face with your partner at a distance of approximately four feet. Look directly into one another's eyes until either of you becomes uncomfortable. When that occurs, simply avert your eyes. Now, move to three feet, then to two feet, each time looking directly into one another's eyes until one of you experiences discomfort and turns away. Share your reactions with each other. Now, experiment with different kinds and degrees of eye contact within a two-to-four-foot range. For example, try looking at your partner's cheekbone instead of directly into his eyes. Look at his mouth. Share your reactions. Experiment further by looking into your partner's eyes for several seconds and then slightly change your focus so that you look at his cheekbone for a few seconds and then return your gaze into his eyes. Follow that by looking at his

mouth for a few seconds and then return to the eyes. Share your responses to this form of eye contact. Make mental note of the form of eye contact you and your partner seem to prefer as well as those that you dislike.

3. Place two chairs squarely facing one another (front-to-front) approximately two feet apart in which each of you take a seat. Share your thoughts and feelings as you sit face-to-face and knee-to-knee. Is it comfortable for both of you, for only one, for neither? If it is uncomfortable, ask your partner to gradually alter the distance until he becomes comfortable. Then move your chair until you become comfortable. Finally, compromising if necessary, move the chairs until they are placed at a mutually comfortable distance. Make mental note of your partner's remarks as well as your own experiences in this exercise.

4. Change the placement of the chairs so that instead of facing one another, they now are side by side in parallel position approximately six inches apart. As you and your partner take your seats, share your respective thoughts and feelings. Now increase the angle so that the chairs form a ninety-degree right angle. Share with one another your reactions to this arrangement. Now increase the angle an additional forty-five degrees. Describe your reactions to this position. Which arrangement does your partner prefer? Which do you?

5. Based upon the results of your experimentation, place the chairs in the position and at the angle that is reasonably comfortable for both you and your partner. Some compromise may be necessary. Now, maintaining a more or less neutral facial expression and without saying a word, try to show through your body language, but without moving your face or head, that you care about your partner and are interested in his thoughts and feelings. Continue with this experiment with three or four different body positions, attempting to demonstrate concern and interest, for approximately one minute each. Following each position, seek verbal feedback from your partner concerning his reactions to the position. Make mental note of his comments as well as your own reactions.

6. Based upon what you have learned through your experimentation with various body positions, assume a position that your partner indicates reflects caring and interest. Now begin to experiment with different facial expressions. First, let your face become relaxed in its more or less usual state. Retain this facial expression for about one minute while your partner experiences the effect. After a minute, seek feedback from him concerning his observations and reactions. Then experiment with other facial expressions through which you hope to express silently, in turn, affection, compassion, joy, sadness, disappointment, disapproval, fear, and anger. Hold each facial expression for a minute or so while your partner tries to determine the feeling you are trying to express. Share your respective thoughts and feelings about this exercise.

7. In the space below, summarize those things you discovered from these nonverbal experiments that may help you to become a more effective social worker.

LISTENING

Listening (Kadushin, 1983, pp. 276–286) refers to the processes of attentively *hearing* another's words and speech, *observing* (Carkhuff & Anthony, 1979, pp. 42–47) her nonverbal gestures and positions, *encouraging* (Ivey, 1988, pp. 93–95) her to express herself fully, and *remembering* what she communicates. Most people are rather poor listeners; tending to pay more attention to their own thoughts and feelings than to the messages that others are trying to convey. Competent listening rarely comes naturally. Yet listening, perhaps more than any other skill, is essential for effective social work practice. It is a skill requiring two actions of the worker. First, the worker must minimize attention to his own experiences (e.g., thoughts, feelings, and sensations). Then he must energetically concentrate upon the client with a determination to understand—not to evaluate—what the client is experiencing and expressing.

For most people, being truly heard and understood by another person is one of the genuinely humanizing events in life. It conveys respect. It demonstrates that the listener values them and is interested in what they have to say. In a real sense, careful listening is a gesture of love. Because of this, listening is a dynamic factor in social work practice. It has several purposes. First, effective listening enables the worker to gather information essential for assessment and planning. Second, effective listening leads the client to *feel* better—often in the form of reduced tension or anxiety, heightened feelings of personal safety and well-being, and greater hope and optimism. Third, it tends to encourage the client to express herself more freely and fully. Fourth, effective listening usually enhances the image of the worker in the eyes of the client. Finally, listening, by itself, is a powerful intervention tool often contributing significantly to positive change in a client's self-understanding, self-esteem, and problem-solving capacities.

In order to listen effectively, the social worker must be able to manage his own impulses. Containing self (Shulman, 1984, p. 61) is essentially a matter of restraint, self-control, and self-discipline on the part of the worker. It suggests a holding back from fully experiencing and freely expressing one's reactions, ideas, or opinions. Containing self involves temporarily suspending judgment and action in order to better hear and understand the client. Social workers tend to be highly motivated to help people who are troubled. In their desire to serve, they may sometimes rush to conclusions and solutions. Although immediate intervention is certainly warranted in life-threatening situations, engaging in premature assessment, solution making, or action taking interferes with effective listening and frequently has deliterious consequences. In most circumstances, workers would be wise to listen carefully and fully before assessing or intervening. As Shulman (1984, p. 61) says, "Workers who attempt to find simple solutions often discover that if the solutions were indeed that simple, then the client could have found them alone without the help of the worker."

Containing self is integrally related to the use of silence (Kadushin, 1983, pp. 286–294). Social workers "frequently perceive silence as a hindrance and a hazard to the progress of the interview. . . . The professional assumption is that talking is better" (Kadushin, 1983, p. 286). This is certainly not always the case. Periods of silence, pauses in the exchange, are vital elements in effective communication. As Shulman (1984, p. 63) suggests, the worker should not let silence continue so long that it becomes a test to see "who will speak first." However, he should also recognize that with some clients, at certain moments, silence can be a powerfully helpful experience. "Instead of a threat, silence should be seen and utilized as an opportunity" (Kadushin, 1983, p. 294).

Hearing refers to the process of listening that involves attending to the voice and speech of another person. Hearing can be prevented or impeded by numerous factors. A room might be noisy, or another person might speak in a soft or mumbled fashion, a foreign language, or an unfamiliar dialect. She might use words the worker does not understand or that connote meanings to her that differ from the worker's. Effective hearing involves diminishing the obstacles and focusing the aural capacities entirely upon the words and sounds of the other. It also involves reducing tendencies to hear selectively as a result of judging, comparing, criticizing, or evaluating the words and sounds of the other. In attempting to hear, social workers are usually interested primarily in taking in and remembering the messages sent by the speaker. Because social workers recognize that process is as important as content, they try to hear more than simply the words themselves. They are also keenly interested in the person's voice and manner of speaking. Does she speak rapidly or slowly? Is there hesitancy in the speech? Does she "block" at points? Is there a stammer? Is the voice loud or soft; well modulated or monotonous? Does she seem to speak in words that reflect greater emphasis upon intellect and thinking or upon feelings and emotions? Does the speech reflect specificity and concreteness or is it more abstract and sometimes vague? Is a characteristic language mode reflected in the speech? If so, does the speaker reflect a visual, auditory, or kinesthetic mode of experience?

Another vital element in the listening process is the skill of observation. Through observing (Carkhuff & Anthony, 1979, pp. 42–47), which may be thought of as "listening with one's eyes," the worker notices the client's physical characteristics and nonverbal behaviors. Frequently, the worker pays attention to indications of energy level, emotions, and degree of congruence between verbal and nonverbal expression.

The purpose of observing is to enable the worker to gain a better and more complete understanding of the ways in which the client experiences the world. During interviews, social workers watch for subtle communications related to themes of power or authority, ambivalence about seeking or receiving help, difficulties in discussing topics associated with a societal stigma or taboo, and inhibitions concerning the direct and full expression of powerful feelings (Shulman, 1984, pp. 20–22, 85–91). Generally, since workers are more likely to pick up indirect communications from nonverbal rather than verbal communications, they must observe closely.

Among the specific aspects to observe are included (1) facial expression, (2) eye contact, and (3) body language, position, and movement. When observing, the social worker should ask himself the following questions: Are the client's face and head active or inactive during communication exchanges? Are there spontaneous facial movements? If so, what do they seem to communicate? What moods or feelings are reflected? Does she appear to be happy, sad, angry, tense, or fearful? Does she look at the worker? If so, does the client avert her gaze when the worker focuses upon the client's eyes or face? Does she look at the worker when he is talking? When she is talking? How would the worker characterize the client's physical build, dress, and grooming? What is her general posture when standing or walking and what is her body position when seated? Is her body turned toward or away from the worker? Is the client more physically open or closed? Are there characteristic gestures? Is her body flexible or rigid, erect or slouched, relaxed or tight? Does she appear to prefer physical distance or closeness? Does she move her body, including hands and arms, to aid in communication? Does she walk quickly or slowly? Does she reflect high or low energy and alertness?

What might these expressions, gestures, and behaviors suggest about how this person thinks and feels about herself, the problem, and this meeting with the worker? Are the various aspects of the client's presentation and communication congruent or incongruent? Do nonverbal expressions match the verbal? What might the degree of congruence indicate about the person, problem, and situation?

Encouraging (Ivey, 1988, pp. 93–94) is an element of listening that very closely approaches talking. Encouraging involves making very brief responses in the form of single words, brief phrases, or sounds and gestures that stimulate others to continue their expression. Some examples of brief verbal encouragers include: *Please go on; And?; Uh uh; Mmmm; Yes; Please continue.* Head nods, eye contact, some hand motions, and leaning toward the client are illustrative of nonverbal encouraging.

Repeating a portion of a phrase or a key word that the client uses may also constitute encouragement. Such brief responses enable the worker to demonstrate that he wants to hear more. And the worker does so without interrupting with a lengthy statement of his own. He must be careful, however, to avoid using the same encouragers over and over again—after a while, that may indicate a lack of genuineness. Also, the worker should be aware that encouraging is not sufficient in itself to demonstrate understanding. More complete communications (i.e., active listening) are necessary for that.

The final dimension of listening involves remembering what the client communicates. Hearing and observing are skills without much inherent value unless the messages received can be retained. Remembering refers to the process of temporarily storing information in order that it may later be used, for example, to communicate understanding, make thematic connections between messages expressed at different times, prepare a written record, or develop an assessment.

■ Exercise 4-3: Listening

Recruit a friend or colleague to join you in a listening exercise. Inform him that the purpose of this exercise is to determine how well you can understand and remember what he says. If he agrees, tell him that you will tape record a conversation between the two of you and, following the conversation but before replaying it, you will attempt to write down, word for word, what he said. Then you will compare what you remember with what was recorded. Ask your partner to identify a topic of interest to him that the two of you might discuss for approximately ten minutes. As the listener, your tasks are to encourage him to discuss the subject, observe him carefully, comprehend his message, and remember what was said and done. Keep in mind that his perspective is paramount. Withhold your own opinions. It is your partner's time. Let him discuss the topic in his own way. Encourage him to express himself fully and try not to interfere with the flow of his communication. As your partner talks, listen attentively and observe carefully. At the conclusion of ten minutes, thank your partner and proceed with the following:

1. Ask your partner to rate on a scale of 0 to 10 (where 0 = did not listen and completely misunderstood and 10 = perfectly listened and completely understood) how well he thinks you listened and understood what he said. Ask him if he believes that you were truly interested in him and the topic. Thank your partner again and say goodbye. Record his rating below and make mental note of his other responses.

```
 |___|___|___|___|___|___|___|___|___|___|
 0   1   2   3   4   5   6   7   8   9   10
```

2. Now, before listening to the tape recording, get a notebook and (a) try to reconstruct from memory the words he said; (b) characterize your partner's speaking voice and speech in terms of modulation, volume, rate or pace, pitch, and common patterns (e.g., blockages, stammering, and frequent use of fillers); (c) prepare a physical description of your partner's clothing, hair and eye color, approximate height and weight, body build, and apparent physical condition; (d) describe his general facial expression and body position as well as any significant changes or gestures that occurred during the course of the conversation; and (e) based upon the above, characterize his overall mood and identify the primary emotions that were evident.

3. Now play the tape recording of the conversation. As you listen, compare it to the written transcript you reconstructed from memory. Approximately what percentage of his comments did you recall (e.g., ten, fifty, or seventy-five percent)? Record your rating below.

```
 |___|___|___|___|___|___|___|___|___|___|
 0%  10% 20% 30% 40% 50% 60% 70% 80% 90% 100%
```

Identify the factors that helped you to remember and those that hindered you. If your recall rating is less than seventy-five percent, develop a plan and a schedule for practicing these skills. Outline the major elements of your plan in the space below.

ACTIVE LISTENING

Active listening combines the talking and listening skills in such a way that the client feels understood and encouraged toward further self-expression. It is a form of feedback. The worker listens carefully and communicates his understanding of the speaker's message by reflecting or mirroring the client's statement back to the client. In essence, the worker paraphrases the client's message. Ideally, the worker's words should be completely equivalent to those of the client—they should be synonymous.

Active listening demonstrates that the worker has understood, or at least is trying to understand, what the client has expressed. It indicates that he wants to accurately and fully comprehend the client's message. Active listening shows to the client that the worker is curious about the client's views, feelings, and experiences. Because it conveys empathy and furthers understanding, there is no substitute for active listening. It constitutes a major element of the vital feedback loop between worker and client. Social workers who do not listen actively are more likely to miss part of the client's message and thereby misunderstand, distort, or misrepresent it. Furthermore, the worker who does not listen actively or does so in a consistently inaccurate fashion is likely to discourage the client from free and full expression and inhibit her investment in the relationship.

Active listening combines the talking and listening skills into three steps:

Step One: Inviting. Through the use of his body position, facial expression, voice, and speech, the worker shows that he is prepared to listen. Often he invites by asking a question such as, "Would you please tell me about . . . ?" However, it is not always necessary to ask a specific question. Many clients begin to talk about themselves and their concerns as soon as the social worker attends to them with his eyes, face, and body.

Step Two: Listening. When the client, responding to the invitation to speak, begins to talk, the worker attempts to hear, observe, encourage, and remember.

Step Three: Reflecting. When the client pauses at the conclusion of a message segment, the worker paraphrases the client's statement. For example, a client might say, "I'm really frustrated with my boss. He says he wants production, production, production! But then he comes down to my shop and spends hours shooting the breeze." In active listening, a worker could say in response, "You're annoyed with him because he tells you he wants something but then he interferes with you when you're trying to do it." By communicating an equivalent message, the worker demonstrates empathic understanding.

Active listening is, of course, useful when the social worker has accurately heard and paraphrased the client's message. However, it may even be helpful when he has not. Sometimes a message is misunderstood or part of it missed if the worker's attention wanders; or the client may misspeak or send an incomplete or confusing message. In such cases, the worker can initiate active listening by phrasing his response in the form of a question. For instance, suppose a client says, "Ever since I was seven years old, I felt fat and ugly. I had no friends. I would go to school and come back home as fast as I could. Then I'd watch TV and eat the cookies that my mother left for me. She was never home in the afternoons but she always left me with plenty to eat." A worker might say in response, "From the time of your childhood up to now, you have believed you are overweight and unattractive. Are you also saying that your mother gave you food instead of spending time with you?"

When a worker's response is an accurate reflection of his message, the client often spontaneously confirms that fact by saying something like, "Yeah, that's right." Then she usually expresses herself further. When the worker is not quite accurate but close enough to demonstrate that he heard much of the message and is genuinely trying to understand, the client may say, "Well, no. What I meant was . . . " Again, she is likely to continue to express herself on the topic at hand. However, when the worker is extremely inaccurate, perhaps reflecting a lack of interest or attention, the client may very well respond with an emphatic no and then become much less expressive. A similar phenomenon may occur when the worker does not active listen frequently enough. The worker who only talks or only listens and does not active listen is likely to discourage the client from free and full expression.

There are several common errors workers tend to make when first developing skill in active listening. These include: (1) using several of the same words as the client so that the worker's reflections sound like mimicry; (2) using the same lead-in repeatedly (e.g., "I hear you saying . . ." "It sounds like . . ."); (3) trying to be clever, profound, or interpretive—playing psychoanalyst tends to indicate that the social worker is listening to his own thoughts and speculations rather than the client's message; (4) reflecting only facts and thoughts or only feelings and emotions rather than active listening to all dimensions of the client's expression; (5) frequently interrupting in order to reflect the client's message; and (6) active listening following each short phrase or statement.

■ **Exercise 4-4: Active Listening**

In the spaces provided, write the words you might say if you were to active listen in response to the following statements:

1. *CLIENT:* My life is in shambles. My wife is divorcing me and she's going to take me to the cleaners.

2. *SUPERVISOR:* I'm disappointed that you didn't follow up on the Sanchez case. You know that those children are at risk.

3. *PROFESSOR:* I wonder if the match between your personal values and those of the social work profession is a good one. It appears to me that your attitudes are a whole lot different from those required of social workers.

4. *CLIENT:* My husband thinks I'm an alcoholic. I'm here because he made me come. Sure, I drink. I drink a lot. But he's the reason I drink.

5. *CLASSMATE:* I've missed the last three classes and don't know what's going on in here. Today is the day of the midterm exam and I know I'm going to flunk. I'm so uptight, I can't think straight.

6. *COLLEAGUE:* I have this case that is driving me up the wall. I know I have a problem here. I get so angry at this family for not trying to help themselves. I work so damn hard and they don't do a thing.

7. *CHILD:* Sometimes my mommy's boyfriend is mean to her. He hits her and she ends up crying a lot. I don't like him.

SUMMARY

The basic interpersonal skills of talking and listening are fundamental to all aspects of human interaction, including the phases and processes of social work practice. In order to talk and listen effectively, a social worker must be able to use skillfully his voice, speech, and body language in talking and must be able to hear, observe, encourage, and remember in listening. Additionally, he must be able to combine the talking and listening skills in the form of active listening. Active listening conveys empathy by demonstrating that the social worker is making a genuine effort to understand.

■ **Exercise 4-5: Summary**

The following exercises are intended to aid you in refining the talking, listening, and active listening skills.

1. With the consent of a friend or colleague, make a videotape (audiotape will suffice) recording of a fifteen-minute conversation. Indicate that you are trying to practice your interviewing skills and would like to interview him about his choice of career (e.g., social worker, homemaker, lawyer, bus driver, or secretary). Inform him that he need not answer any question about which he feels uncomfortable. Also, be sure to tell him that your professor and perhaps some of your classmates may review the tape in order to give you feedback about the quality of your interviewing skills. During the interview, explore with your partner how he came to make the career choice he did. Explore the factors that influenced and motivated him. Ask about his hopes and aspirations as well as his hesitations in regard to his career.

   During the conversation, encourage your partner to share as much as possible about his career decision. Use the skills of talking, listening, and active listening. At the conclusion of the interview, ask your partner for feedback concerning his thoughts and feelings about the experience. Make mental note of his responses. Also, ask your partner to rate on a scale of 0 to 10 (where 0 = did not listen and completely misunderstood and 10 = perfectly listened and completely understood) how well he thinks you listened and understood what he said. Ask him if he believes that you were truly interested in him and the topic. Thank your partner again and say goodbye. Record his rating in the space below and make mental note of his other responses.

0	1	2	3	4	5	6	7	8	9	10

2. Consider your own reactions to the interview. How did you feel about the exchange? What did you like and what did you dislike about your part in the conversation? What would you do differently if you were to engage in the conversation again? Summarize your reactions in the space below.

3. Next, play the tape. In a notebook, prepare a transcript so that it accurately reflects what was said by whom. Identify the talking and listening skills you used during the conversation. For example, identify as talking a statement you made or a question you asked that came from your frame of reference. Identify as active listening your attempts to communicate your understanding of your partner's expressions. Use the following format:

INTERVIEWER: (Record here what you said. Then identify which skill, if any, is represented.)

INTERVIEWEE: (Record here what he said.)

4. At the conclusion of the transcript, evaluate your use of the talking and active listening skills. How would you characterize this sample of your voice and speech? When you listen to the sound of your voice, what do you think and feel? How clear is your pronunciation? Is your speech modulated? What is the rate of speech? How about the pitch?

   In this conversation, do you speak more or less than your partner? Do you tend to interrupt or to be interrupted? What proportion of your words are factual or informational? What proportion reflect your feelings? Do you tend to use extraneous fillers, such as *uhh* or *you know*? Are there vocal indications of nervousness or tension? If so, what are they? Do your voice and speech reflect interest in what the other person has to say? Does the other person seem interested in what you have to say? If you would change anything about your voice, what would it be?

   How often do you active listen? Do you do so too often, not often enough? How accurate are you in your attempts to active listen? As you paraphrase, are your words equivalent to your partner's? Are there indications that he feels understood? Does your partner express himself fully and freely or is he inhibited in some ways at points during the interview? In the space below, summarize the major elements of your evaluation.

5. Consider your body position, body language, and facial expressions as reflected on the videotape (or as you recall from memory). It may be particularly enlightening to view the videotape with the sound turned off. Evaluate the nonverbal dimensions of your communication during this interview. How well do you physically attend to your partner? What do you think your body position and body language communicate to your partner? What emotions do your facial expressions convey? What is the nature and extent of your eye contact? How comfortable and confident do you appear? Summarize your self-assessment in the space below.

6. Observe your partner's nonverbal expressions as displayed on the videotape (or as you recall from memory). Note his facial expression, eye contact, body position and body language, body movements, and the rate and nature of his speech. Characterize his overall mood and energy level. What is your impression of his general attitude toward you and toward the topic of conversation? Would you say he is involved and interested? Active? Cooperative? Responsive? Summarize your observations in the space below.

7. Ask a colleague or instructor from the school of social work to evaluate your talking, listening, and active listening skills as reflected on the tape recording you made. Summarize his feedback in the space below. With which points do you agree or disagree?

8. Using the rating scales below (where 0 = no proficiency and 10 = complete proficiency), assess your current level of proficiency in the talking and listening skills.

The Talking Skills

Voice and Speech

0	1	2	3	4	5	6	7	8	9	10

Body Language

0	1	2	3	4	5	6	7	8	9	10

The Listening Skills

Hearing

0	1	2	3	4	5	6	7	8	9	10

Observing

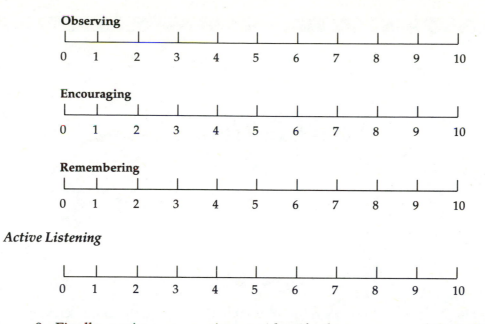

0   1   2   3   4   5   6   7   8   9   10

Encouraging

0   1   2   3   4   5   6   7   8   9   10

Remembering

0   1   2   3   4   5   6   7   8   9   10

Active Listening

0   1   2   3   4   5   6   7   8   9   10

9. Finally, review your ratings to identify those aspects of the talking, listening, and active listening skills in which you remain less proficient (e.g., a score of 7 or less). Then, in the space below, outline the steps you might take to improve your skills in those areas.

PREPARING

This chapter is intended to aid the student in developing the skills relevant for the preparing phase of social work practice. First meetings significantly influence the general direction and tone of subsequent interactions. In fact, the nature of the initial contact often determines whether a prospective client decides to attend future meetings. Adequate preparation can make the difference (Kadushin, 1983, pp. 123–141). The overall purpose of the preparing skills is to enable the worker to be personally and professionally ready to perform competently from the very first moment of contact.

Social workers commonly use the preparing skills before the first meetings with clients and other persons with whom the social workers interact as part of their professional responsibilities. In addition, social workers routinely use the preparing skills before each subsequent encounter. The preparing skills include: (1) preparatory reviewing, (2) preparatory exploring, (3) preparatory consulting, (4) preparatory arranging, (5) preparatory empathy, (6) preliminary planning, (7) preparatory self-exploration, (8) centering, and (9) recording during the preparing phase.

PREPARATORY REVIEWING

Preparatory reviewing is a skill that involves the examination and consideration of current information available to the worker and agency prior to an initial contact (Kadushin, 1983, pp. 136–137). For example, in instances where a prospective client has received service at the agency before, the worker will look over the relevant records that the agency has on file. When a telephone contact has preceded the first visit, any notes of the nature and substance of that interaction should be examined. In the case of first meetings with other persons, such as an agency director, a client's medical doctor, or a new supervisee, the worker should thoughtfully review relevant materials concerning the general purpose for the meeting and any topics likely to be addressed.

Reviewing enables the worker to have a good grasp of significant factual information. This reduces the possibility that the applicant, client, or other person will have to repeat information he has previously provided. It allows for more efficient use of time and helps the person feel that what he says is heard and remembered. In some instances, failure to review available materials could constitute professional negligence. For example, suppose a teenager with a history of making serious suicide attempts within days of breaking up with a girlfriend contacts the agency. He has been a client off and on over the past several years, and the pattern of previous suicide attempts is clearly reflected in his agency file. He requests an appointment for some time later that day, indicating that the reason for his call is that his girlfriend recently decided she wanted to date another boy. If the worker does not review the case record, she may decide to give him an appointment several days from now, not realizing that he is currently at serious risk of ending his own life.

Of course, in addition to the benefits of reviewing materials, there are some potential disadvantages as well. For example, some records contain hearsay or opinions that are expressed as if they were indisputed facts. Some workers may inadvertently accept at face value information contained in an agency record. In addition, some records contain personality profiles or psychiatric diagnoses that may lead a worker to reach fixed conclusions about a person before even seeing or talking with him. Such profiles and diagnoses may have been inaccurate when recorded or may now be out of date. In other words, the person, the problem, or the situation may have changed. In preparatory reviewing, workers must recognize that information contained in case records or other forms of written material may be inaccurate or incomplete. It is vital that the worker maintain an open mind during the preparatory reviewing phase.

■ **Exercise 5-1: Preparatory Reviewing**

CASE EXAMPLE: At 10:13 A.M., on Tuesday, an agency intake worker received a telephone call from a woman who reported that her name was Mrs. Nancy Cannon. The intake worker jotted a few notes concerning the call on a form entitled *Telephone Intake Report*. The intake worker later gave the report to you, the social worker assigned to conduct the initial face-to-face interview and, if appropriate, to provide the relevant social work services. Here is what was written on the intake report:

Telephone Intake Report

September 21, 1987, 10:13 A.M. Mrs. Nancy Cannon telephoned from her place of work (the XYZ Insurance company—phone 234-6213). She sounded concerned. She said that on the previous Saturday night, her fourteen-year-old daughter Amy had come home after her nine o'clock curfew and smelled of alcohol. She says that she has grounded her daughter but now wants to talk with a professional about the situation. Mrs. Cannon requested an appointment for herself alone, indicating that she wanted to sort things out with someone before she dealt further with her daughter.

Mrs. C. reported that this was the first such incident. She had "never had any trouble from Amy before." She stated that she had not sought professional help before and that this was her first contact with any social agency. She indicated that her husband, Amy's father, had recently filed for divorce and had left the home approximately six weeks ago. Mrs. C. wondered whether that might be connected with Amy's behavior over the weekend.

Disposition: An appointment was scheduled with Ms. Susan Holder, MSW, for Wednesday, September 23rd at 12:00 noon. Mrs. C. wanted to use her lunch hour for the appointment, if at all possible, in order to reduce the amount of time away from her job.

Demonstrate your use of the preparatory reviewing skill by examining the telephone intake report above. Using a pen or marker, highlight the information contained in the report which you, as the social worker, would want to remember for a first meeting with Mrs. Cannon.

PREPARATORY EXPLORING

The skill of preparatory exploring involves asking questions of the intake worker or the referring person about the prospective client and the situation. This is an important but often neglected skill. Physicians, judges, teachers, ministers, and, of course, family members often contact an agency on behalf of someone else. They may possess important information concerning the client system, the presenting problem and situation, and sometimes even the nature of the service needs.

Preparatory exploring may also be applicable in situations where a prospective client has previously been served by a colleague in the agency. For example, by reviewing agency files a worker may learn that a prospective client had been provided service by Ms. Castilla, another worker in the agency, some two years before. It may be extremely useful to ask Ms. Castilla about her recollections of the case.

The use of the preparatory exploring skill can lead to a much more positive and productive first meeting. However, as in the case of the reviewing skill, information gained through the preparatory exploring process may lead some workers inadvertently to stereotype clients or inaccurately anticipate the nature of a problem situation. These tendencies may be resisted by the worker who consciously distinguishes fact from opinion and recognizes that the views of one person are likely to differ from the views of another.

In preparatory exploring, the worker seeks information that may help her be a more effective and more efficient problem solver and service provider. Names and approximate ages of the persons involved are often helpful. So are phone numbers and addresses. Information concerning the nature, severity, and urgency of the problem is extremely important as are observations about how it has affected members of the client system.

■ **Exercise 5-2: Preparatory Exploring**

CASE EXAMPLE: At 3:15 P.M., October 10, you, a social worker at the social services agency, receive a telephone call from Father Julio Sanchez, a Catholic priest in a largely Hispanic parish. He indicates that a family of seven needs help. He says that the parents and older children are migrant workers. He reports that the family had been working in another part of the state and were traveling to another work site when their automobile broke down.

In the space provided below, write the questions you would ask and identify the information you would seek as you use the skill of preparatory exploring with Father Sanchez.

PREPARATORY CONSULTING

The skill of preparatory consulting involves seeking opinions and advice from a social work supervisor or colleagues concerning an upcoming first visit with a prospective client or other person. Commonly, the topics addressed involve identifying tentative objectives for an interview or discussing other related practice considerations. However, the specific nature of the consultation varies from situation to situation. On one occasion, the topic of discussion might involve determining the best location for the interview. In another, assuring that the worker has reasonable protection in a potentially violent situation might be the major area of concern. In still another, the prime focus might be the identification of agency policies or legal obligations that might apply in a particular case. The use of the consulting skill often enhances the quality of initial meetings.

■ **Exercise 5-3: Preparatory Consulting**

CASE EXAMPLE: You work in an agency serving an elderly population in the community. On Tuesday morning, a woman telephoned the agency and talked with you about her neighbor Mrs. Anderson. According to the caller, Mrs. Anderson is eighty-two years old and lives in an apartment by herself. The caller reported that Mrs. Anderson has not left her apartment in three days and would not answer her door or telephone. However, the caller did say that she could hear movement in the apartment.

Immediately following the phone call, you examined agency files and discovered that Mrs. Anderson had not previously received agency services.

In the space provided below, please identify the information you would seek and the issues you would address as you consult with your supervisor prior to taking any action concerning Mrs. Anderson.

PREPARATORY ARRANGING

The skill of preparatory arranging refers to the logistical preparation for a first meeting. It includes scheduling an appointment, ensuring that there is adequate time and privacy, and organizing the physical environment. It may involve securing an interview room or locating additional chairs. It includes considering the appropriateness of one's apparel and appearance. It may involve locating transportation for a client or securing temporary child care so that you can meet separately with a parent. When making visits outside your agency (Kadushin, 1983, pp. 141–148), you should consider the environment in terms of its significance for the client. For example, the worker would usually try to avoid scheduling a home visit during mealtime. She would also refrain from sitting in a client's favorite chair.

In agency contexts, preparatory arranging includes considering the potential effects of the physical environment. Do clients have a comfortable place to sit upon their arrival at the agency? Are interviewing rooms sufficiently soundproofed so that respect for persons' privacy may be maintained? When you have office space assigned to you, arranging involves the selection for display of pictures, posters, and other items such as college degrees and professional certificates. It may also include the selection of paints or wallpapers and the placement of furniture. The office environment can have a powerful impact upon clients. For example, a social worker who practices in areas of the country where firearms are widely owned would be unwise to place a "ban handguns" poster on her office wall. She would needlessly alienate many clients. Personal or political messages may interfere with clients' ability to experience the worker as unbiased toward and respectful of them.

In sum, preparatory arranging involves various considerations and activities that enable worker and client to meet and conduct their business in a manner that enhances communication and diminishes, to the degree possible, interference and distraction.

■ **Exercise 5-4: Preparatory Arranging**

CASE EXAMPLE: Assume that you are a social worker in a high-security, men's prison. You have been assigned an office, which you share with another worker. The office contains two desks, chairs behind and next to each desk, two bookcases, two telephones, and two file cabinets. In addition, there is a small area containing a sofa, two comfortable chairs, and a coffee table. You have a 10:00 A.M. appointment scheduled with a prisoner, Mr. Somes. The topic for conversation concerns the serious illness of his wife of twenty-three years and the new information you have just received. According to a report from her physician, it appears that Mrs. Somes will die sometime within the next few days.

As the appointment approaches, you notice that your social work colleague remains at his desk, actively engaged in paperwork. You had expected him to be out of the office, as he usually is during this time.

In the space below, discuss how you would use the skill of arranging in preparation for the meeting with Mr. Somes.

PREPARATORY EMPATHY

Preparatory empathy (tuning in) involves "putting oneself in the client's shoes and trying to view the world through the client's eyes" (Shulman, 1984, p. 22). Even before the first face-to-face meeting, the social worker engages in preparatory empathy in order to heighten her sensitivity to the prospective client's possible agenda, thoughts, feelings about himself, the presenting concern, and the situation; to issues and dynamics related to seeking or receiving service from a social worker; to the nature of his motivation and reason for the contact; to his thoughts and feelings about beginning a potentially vulnerable experience with a stranger who is also a professional and represents an authority figure; and to potential issues related to his stage of life-cycle development, culture, ethnic background, and gender.

In sum, preparatory empathy involves trying to imagine, on the basis of the limited information you possess, what the client may be thinking, feeling, and doing. Because preparatory empathy is done in advance of face-to-face contact, the social worker should realize that much of the time she will be off target. Therefore, she must recognize that preparatory empathy is always tentative; always preliminary and subject to immediate change based upon the client's communications. However, even when her preparatory empathy proves to be inaccurate, it is productive because it helps the social worker to be sensitive to actual expressions of the client when they do meet person-to-person.

Returning to the new client, Mrs. Nancy Cannon, a social worker engaging in preparatory empathy might review the telephone intake report and then go through a process such as the following:

> If I were in Mrs. Cannon's shoes, I might be feeling anxious, concerned about, and disappointed in my daughter. I would also love her a great deal. I might feel responsible and perhaps even guilty about my parenting behavior. I might feel uncertain about how to proceed. I could very well feel somewhat inadequate and maybe frightened. I would be concerned about what the future might hold for Amy and for me. I am aware that my husband's divorce petition and his recent departure from the home may have adversely affected my daughter, and I might feel angry at him. If I believed I could have been a better spouse or taken actions to prevent his departure, I might also feel guilty about the separation and upcoming divorce proceedings. I would feel a great deal of stress during this period. I would probably feel confused about the present and afraid of the future. I might be concerned about finances; about after-school supervision of Amy; about my ability to discipline Amy; about whether there is another person in my husband's life; about whether there ever will be someone else in my life; about my capacity to assume the roles of a single person and a single parent; about my ability to deal with my husband around parental issues concerning Amy; and about dozens of other

issues provoked by my husband's departure and Amy's recent behavior. I would probably feel enormously burdened and perhaps overwhelmed by the events of recent weeks. If sadness and grieving have not yet occurred, I might begin to experience them soon. It is also possible that I may have begun to anticipate that not only has my husband left the household but eventually Amy will also leave. After all, she is already fourteen.

■ Exercise 5-5: Preparatory Empathy

CASE EXAMPLE: Assume that you are a social worker in a general hospital. This morning, a physician contacts you and asks that you accompany her while she informs the mother and father of a twenty-three-year-old man that their son has AIDS. The physician wants you to provide support and social services to the family after she informs them of the diagnosis and prognosis.

Engage in the skill of preparatory empathy as if you were about to meet the parents of the AIDS patient in this situation. Record your thoughts and feelings in the space provided below.

PRELIMINARY PLANNING

Social workers engage in preliminary planning before meetings, contacts, and interviews. They do so by asking and answering questions such as, Why is this meeting occurring? What is its overall purpose? What do I, as social worker, hope to accomplish through this meeting—what are the desired outcomes? What is my function or role? Alfred Kadushin (1983, p. 21) suggests that the "general purposes of most social work interviews can be described as informational (to make a social study), diagnostic (to arrive at an appraisal), and therapeutic (to effect change). These are discrete categories only for the purpose of analysis; the same interview can, and often does, serve more than one purpose."

In information-gathering interviews, the social worker encourages the client to share his views and feelings about himself, the problem and goal, and the situation. In information-giving interviews, the social worker provides information relevant to the client's needs, problems, goals, or situation. In assessment-forming interviews, the social worker arrives at an assessment, diagnosis, evaluation, or recommendation. In change-making interviews, the social worker effects or helps to effect change.

It is often possible for the worker to identify, at least tentatively, which of the major purposes apply to a given interview. Once identified, the worker may proceed to sketch out a preliminary plan or tentative agenda for the meeting. For example, many first meetings have a primary purpose of gathering information. A worker might formulate a general but flexible plan concerning the kinds of information to seek and from whom. In many cases, the worker must decide whether to see all family members together at the same time or to see them separately. If the worker plans to see members separately, she must determine whom to interview first, second, and so forth. Sometimes the worker may decide to see various subsystems of a family unit (e.g., a mother-daughter dyad or perhaps the parental subsystem).

In the case of a client who had indicated in an earlier telephone message an interest in resolving a "family problem," a worker might plan to explore (1) the presenting problem that stimulated the phone contact; (2) the history and development as well as the consequences of that problem; (3) the identity and characteristics of the family or household members; (4) the resources available to the family; and (5) the means that the family has used in the past to address problems such as this.

This preliminary plan enables the worker to begin the interview in a coherent fashion and helps her formulate a tentative purpose to share with the client.

■ **Exercise 5-6: Preliminary Planning**

CASE SITUATION: Assume that you are a social worker who works in conjunction with a court that handles child custody disputes. You have

been assigned the responsibility of collecting information and formulating a recommendation concerning the placement of a twelve-
year-old boy whose parents are divorcing. Each parent wants custody
of the child.

Develop a preliminary plan by which to fulfill your professional responsibilities in this case.

PREPARATORY SELF-EXPLORATION

In addition to engaging in preparatory empathy, the social worker should also
engage briefly in preparatory self-exploration before meeting with clients or
prospective clients. Preparatory self-exploration requires the worker to be introspective in relation to the person, the presenting problem, and the situation.
She asks herself questions such as, How am I likely to feel about this person?
Given what I know about the problem and situation, what personal reactions
might I anticipate from myself? The purpose of this skill is to identify the
potential negative impact of the worker's personal characteristics, biases, emo-

tional tender spots, and behavioral patterns upon the client. Self-exploration involves the worker's conscious recognition of personal aspects that may constitute obstacles to the delivery of effective service to a particular client system.

Preparatory self-exploration also involves the identification of other personal factors that may affect the worker's readiness to provide service (e.g., headache, life stress, fatigue, or worries).

■ Exercise 5-7: Preparatory Self-Exploration

CASE SITUATION: Assume that you are a social worker in an agency that provides psychosocial counseling services to children who have been sexually abused. You have recently begun to work with Cathy, a seven-year-old who had been molested for a period of four years by her biological father. Approximately one month ago, Cathy's father forced her to perform fellatio. That incident led to his arrest and departure from the family home while awaiting further legal developments. You are about to interview Cathy's father for the first time. Your purpose for the interview is to gather information upon which to base a tentative assessment of his potential to benefit from a counseling program.

In the space provided below, please write what you discover about yourself as you engage in self-exploration before meeting Cathy's father.

CENTERING

When, through preparatory self-exploration, the worker has identified personal obstacles in her ability to serve a prospective client, she then attempts to manage or contain them temporarily in order to provide the most effective service to the person or persons involved. The worker asks herself, What can I do to ready myself before the meeting begins? Centering involves organizing one's personal thoughts, feelings, and physical sensations so that they do not interfere with professional obligations and activities. Depending upon the nature of the particular situation, centering includes various kinds of activities. Sometimes it involves brief stress-management exercises in order to reduce emotional upset. Among the useful stress-reducing activities are positive self-talk, visualization, muscular relaxation, journal writing, and brief meditation.

For example, a worker who had been sexually victimized a few years before is about to interview a client who has recently been raped. Through preparatory self-exploration, the worker recognizes that she remains tender about her own rape experience. She centers herself by taking a few deep breaths, engaging in a brief relaxation exercise, and compartmentalizing (putting into an enclosed area of oneself) her personal experience in order to provide full attention to the client. As part of the process, she says to herself: "I'm still tender about being raped but I'm able to manage my feelings of rage and guilt and fear so that they don't get in the way of my service to this client. However, since it is obvious that I still have some unresolved issues, I hereby commit myself to spend time addressing them at 11:00 o'clock when I have a free hour."

In centering it is important that workers do not deny or minimize personal issues and strong feelings. Rather, the worker temporarily manages them and plans to address them at another time in a more appropriate context.

■ **Exercise 5-8: Centering**

CASE SITUATION: Assume that you are scheduled to meet with a client in approximately ten minutes. While finishing a brief coffee break with a colleague, you learn that everyone else in the agency received a raise of seven percent. In spite of the fact that you have earned outstanding evaluations and were recently promoted, you know that you received only a three-percent raise.

In the space provided below, please describe the activities you would undertake in order to center yourself prior to meeting with the client.

RECORDING DURING THE PREPARING PHASE

The written recording that takes place during the preparing phase may take several forms. Many agencies use a telephone intake form upon which the worker makes relevant notations concerning the caller, the reason for the call, the substance of the conversation, and any plans that have been made. Although these notes are usually informal in nature, they provide valuable information to the worker who subsequently engages the person in face-to-face contact. Many workers develop, in rough and tentative form, brief notes concerning identifying characteristics of a person-problem-situation (e.g., name, gender, age, reasons for contact, description of concern or problem, occupation, family role, address, and phone number) and an outline of the preliminary plan for the initial meeting.

For example, the worker assigned to interview Mrs. Cannon (see Exercise 5-1) wrote the following notes in advance of the first meeting:

Mrs. Nancy Cannon—seems to prefer "Mrs."—presenting concern: fourteen-yr.-old daughter "Amy" alleged to have drunk alc. and come home after 9:00 P.M. curfew. First such incident; may be related to separation and filing for divorce by Mrs. C.'s husband (Amy's father). He left the home about six weeks ago. Mrs. C. wants noontime appointment to avoid time away from work. Could there be financial constraints or concerns about keeping her job?

Explore presenting problem re: Amy. What is Amy like now? What was she like prior to marital problems? What is Mrs. C. like? How did the separation and divorce petition come about? What are Mrs. C.'s feelings re: the divorce? What are Amy's reactions to the divorce? Explore current situation—finances; legal; housing; supervision of Amy; and arrangements re: father's parental responsibilities and visits with Amy, etc.

■ **Exercise 5-9: Recording During the Preparing Phase**

CASE SITUATION: Assume that you are a social worker in a Vietnam veterans' center. You receive a telephone message from Ms. Francine Rivera concerning her brother Hector. Ms. Rivera indicated that Hector is forty-five years old and completed two tours of combat duty in Vietnam during the period 1967 through 1970. She reported that he has had trouble keeping jobs; drinks alcohol (beer) every day; has nightmares at night; and occasionally has violent outbursts. She has become especially concerned lately because he has talked about ending "his own miserable life." She says that he won't go to an agency but he might be willing to talk with someone if a counselor came to the house. You, the social worker, have agreed to come for a first visit at 5:30 P.M. on the next afternoon.

In the space below, please write what you would include in your notes as you prepare for this initial visit.

SUMMARY

The use of the preparing skills enables the worker to be ready to provide professional social work services efficiently and effectively from the earliest person-to-person contact. The preparing skills are used extensively prior to initial interviews and are also commonly used in advance of later meetings as well.

The preparing skills include: (1) preparatory reviewing, (2) preparatory exploring, (3) preparatory consulting, (4) preparatory arranging, (5) preparatory empathy, (6) preliminary planning, (7) preparatory self-exploration, (8) centering, and (9) recording during the preparing phase.

■ **Exercise 5-10: Summary**

Assume that you are a social worker with an agency that offers a broad range of social services. Using the skills requested below, prepare for a first meeting with each of the following clients. Use the space provided to demonstrate your ability to execute each skill.

CASE SITUATION: Family of seven (two parents and five children—who range in age from one to seven) have been sleeping in their dilapidated

Chevy in a rest area on the interstate highway. En route to another state where they hoped to find work, they are out of money and food and nearly out of gas. A state patrolman referred them to the agency.

1. Engage in the process of preparatory empathy as you ready yourself to meet with this prospective client system. Describe the results below.

2. In the space below, prepare a recording that reflects the results of your preliminary planning as you prepare to meet the family.

3. Through preparatory self-exploration, identify those personal factors that might get in the way of helpful service to the family. Then describe how you might center yourself in order to diminish those potentially adverse responses.

CASE SITUATION: A thirty-three-year-old man who has been accused of molesting his girlfriend's thirteen-year-old daughter is required to undertake counseling in order to stay out of jail while the judge considers whether to proceed with felony charges. The man had been living with his girlfriend but has now been required to leave the house.

4. Engage in the process of preparatory empathy as you ready yourself to meet with this prospective client. Describe the results below.

5. In the space below, prepare a recording that reflects the results of your preliminary planning as you prepare to meet the man.

6. Through preparatory self-exploration, identify those personal factors that might get in the way of your helpfulness to the man. Then describe how you could center yourself in order to manage your reactions.

CASE SITUATION: You are a worker with Child Protection Services (CPS). You receive a telephone report from a neighbor of the Smith family that the parents have neglected and abused their two children (ages one and three). According to the neighbor, the mother sleeps while the children play in a filthy yard (which contains animal waste, junk, and potentially dangerous materials—glass and sharp metal objects). Also, the neighbor reports that the man in the house drinks heavily and beats both mother and children. Following the telephone call, you prepare to make a home visit to the family in question.

7. Engage in the process of preparatory empathy as you ready yourself to meet with this prospective client system. Describe the results below.

8. In the space below, prepare a recording that reflects the results of your preliminary planning as you prepare for the meeting.

9. Through preparatory self-exploration, identify those personal factors that might block your ability to be helpful. Then describe how you might center yourself in order to diminish your potentially adverse responses.

CASE SITUATION: A medical social worker on the cancer ward of a children's hospital receives a request from a physician that she join him while he informs the parents of an eight-year-old girl that their daughter has terminal leukemia.

10. Engage in the process of preparatory empathy as you ready yourself for this meeting with the physician and the parents. Describe the results below.

11. In the space below, prepare a recording that reflects the results of your preliminary planning as you prepare for the meeting.

12. Through preparatory self-exploration, identify those personal factors that might inhibit your effectiveness in this situation. Then describe how you might center yourself in order to diminish these potentially adverse responses.

13. Using the rating scales below (where 0 = no proficiency and 10 = complete proficiency), assess your current level of proficiency in the preparing skills.

Preparatory Reviewing

0	1	2	3	4	5	6	7	8	9	10

Preparatory Exploring

0	1	2	3	4	5	6	7	8	9	10

Preparatory Consulting

0	1	2	3	4	5	6	7	8	9	10

Preparatory Arranging

0	1	2	3	4	5	6	7	8	9	10

Preparatory Empathy

0	1	2	3	4	5	6	7	8	9	10

Preliminary Planning

0	1	2	3	4	5	6	7	8	9	10

Preparatory Self-Exploration

0	1	2	3	4	5	6	7	8	9	10

Centering

0	1	2	3	4	5	6	7	8	9	10

Recording During the Preparing Phase

0	1	2	3	4	5	6	7	8	9	10

14. Finally, review your ratings to identify those preparing skills in which you remain less proficient (e.g., a score of 7 or less). Then, in the space below, outline the steps you might take to improve your skill in those areas.

_____

BEGINNING

The beginning phase of social work practice commences when the prospective client and the worker initially come together and embark upon the process of mutual exploration. Because first impressions tend to be so important, the initial contact often affects the nature and extent of all future encounters. In addition, the beginning portion of each subsequent interview tends to influence the course of those sessions as well.

Competent use of the beginning skills helps to ensure that the early meetings are positive and productive. An effective beginning results when the worker and client accomplish the purpose for which they first meet (e.g., crisis intervention, assessment, information gathering, or information giving).

Typically, clients and workers make contact with one another in one of two ways (Compton & Galaway, 1989, p. 414): "(1) The individual, family, or group may reach out for help with a problem they have identified as being beyond their means of solution; or (2) a community source may identify an individual, a family, or a group as having a serious problem threatening the welfare of a vulnerable person or group and request that the social worker intervene to solve that problem."

In general, during the beginning of a first meeting, the social worker hopes to facilitate an exchange of introductions, establish a tentative direction or purpose for the meeting, outline the general expectations of clients, describe the policies and ethical principles that might apply during this and future encounters with the client, and ensure that the prospective client understands the conditions under which the interview takes place. This is an especially crucial part of the beginning process because it fulfills part of the legal and ethical obligations related to informed consent. Here the client is provided information concerning relevant agency policies as well as information about relevant laws and ethical principles. This enables the prospective client to understand the context within which the helping endeavors takes place. Frequently throughout the beginning phase, the worker seeks feedback from the client concerning information discussed. Often, clients need further clarification about various points or have questions concerning related topics.

The beginning skills are commonly used during the first few meetings with clients and other persons with whom social workers interact as part of their professional responsibilities. In addition, some of the beginning skills are used during the early portions of later encounters. The beginning skills include: (1) introducing oneself, (2) seeking introductions, (3) describing initial purpose, (4) outlining the client's role, (5) discussing policy and ethical considerations, and (6) seeking feedback.

INTRODUCING ONESELF

At the beginning of any first interview, the social worker identifies himself by name and profession and by agency or departmental affiliation. For example, at the beginning of a meeting in the agency where he works, a worker might say, "Hello [offers hand to shake], I'm Dan Majors. I'm a social worker here at the family service agency." At the start of a visit to the home of a prospective client, a worker might say, "Hello [offers hand to shake], I'm John Samples. I'm a social worker with the local school system." In most circumstances, a friendly facial expression and a warm, firm handshake are extremely useful ways to make human contact. Also, a few informal comments about such things as the weather, transportation to or time of the meeting, or other matters unrelated to the immediate problems of concern may help prospective clients warm up to the meeting and feel more at ease with the worker. However, the worker's introduction and informal remarks should be appropriate to the context. The other person fully realizes that the worker does not yet really know her as an individual. Therefore, pronouncements concerning the "great pleasure" which he has in meeting the client are premature. Sometimes, such effusive introductions are experienced by clients as disingenuous and unauthentic.

In addition to identifying himself, the worker sometimes provides formal identification. For example, John Samples may very well give a prospective client his business card, upon which is printed:

John Samples, MSW, ACSW
School Social Worker
Franklin County School System
1300 West Longview Drive
Franklin, Indiana
Telephone 317-274-6708

In office settings, the placement of the worker's university degrees and professional certificates upon a wall may also help in the introductory process. Clients may notice that he has a BSW or MSW degree, is licensed to practice social work in his state, or that he is a member of the Academy of Certified Social Workers (ACSW).

■ Exercise 6-1: Introducing Oneself

The following exercises are intended to provide you with an opportunity to practice the introducing skill. In the spaces provided, write the words you would say and describe the actions you would take in introducing yourself in the following circumstances:

1. Assume that you are a social worker in a residential nursing facility for elderly persons. You are scheduled to meet with family members concerning the possible placement in the residence of their eighty-five-year-old parent. What would you say and do in introducing yourself?

2. Assume that you have recently been employed as a social worker in a training center for developmentally disabled children and young adults. Today you are about to lead a small group of perhaps six or eight teenage residents. The students are already seated in the room when you arrive. Although a few of them may have seen you walking around campus, none of them know you and you do not know any of them. What would you say and do in introducing yourself?

SEEKING INTRODUCTIONS

A person's sense of self is often integrally associated with his name. Therefore, it is important to elicit from a client her name and to try to pronounce it correctly. The worker should then occasionally use the client's name throughout the interview. For example, after introducing himself, the worker might say, "And your name is . . . ?" Or if he already knows the name, "And you're Mr. Nesbit? Is that right? Am I pronouncing your name correctly?" Later, during the first meeting or in a subsequent interview, it may be useful to explore how the person prefers to be addressed (e.g., first name, nickname, or surname). Frequently, a person may share some additional form of identification during the exchange of introductions. For example, when a client introduces herself by saying, "I'm Mrs. Jones, I'm the mother of this mob of children," the worker might tentatively conclude that Mrs. Jones prefers to be addressed as "Mrs. Jones" and that a significant part of her personal and social identity is related to her role as parent. Depending upon the manner in which she expressed the phrase "mob of children," the worker may glean additional information concerning the nature of Mrs. Jones's experience as a parent.

In family and group contexts, it is useful to request members to "go around" and introduce themselves. Because initial group meetings can be quite anxiety provoking, it may be helpful to incorporate a stress-reducing dimension to the introduction process. For example, the worker might ask members to introduce themselves and share a few of their thoughts and feelings as they anticipated coming to this first meeting.

■ **Exercise 6-2: Seeking Introductions**

For these exercises, assume that you are a social worker with a family and children's counseling center. Respond in the spaces provided by writing the words you would say in each situation.

1. You are about to begin an interview with a recently divorced, fifty-five-year-old man. As you walk together to your office, you smell a strong odor of alcohol. How would you introduce yourself and seek an introduction from him? What else, if anything, would you do? Discuss your rationale for the approach you have taken.

2. You are about to begin an interview with a seventy-seven-year-old widow who has a hearing impairment. She can make out most words, if they are spoken clearly, distinctly, and at a low pitch. How would you introduce yourself and seek an introduction from her? What else would you do? Discuss your rationale for the approach you have taken.

3. You are about to begin the first interview with a family of seven members. You know that it is a blended family and that not all the children have the same last name. However, you do not know which children are from which relationships. How would you introduce yourself and seek introductions from the family members? What else would you do? Discuss your rationale for the approach you have taken.

4. You are about to begin an interview with a prospective client. As you introduce yourself and seek an introduction from her, you realize that she speaks neither English nor Spanish but another language, which you do not understand. What would you do? Discuss your rationale for the approach you have taken.

DESCRIBING INITIAL PURPOSE

It is important for the social worker to identify for himself a tentative general purpose (refer to preliminary planning in Chapter Five) for the meeting (W. Schwartz, 1976, pp. 188–190; Shulman, 1984, pp. 37–49) because the client will look to him, as the authority, for some indication of the purpose for the interview. If the worker does not know or does not share some beginning sense of direction or purpose, he is likely to end up with a client who is even more uncertain, anxious, and ambivalent about a process that is already extraordinarily difficult for her. If the worker shares with the other person a general purpose, it almost immediately lessens some of the anxiety experienced by the client. It also is likely to convey that the worker knows what he is doing.

In some instances, not only is the general purpose for the meeting clear but so is the role that the worker will assume in relation to that purpose. When such a strong degree of clarity exists, it is appropriate for the worker to also use the skill of describing the worker's role (W. Schwartz, 1976, pp. 188–190; Shulman, 1984, pp. 37–49). This skill involves expressing to the prospective client the worker's view of the role or roles that he expects to assume in working toward the purpose.

Among the more common social work roles are broker, educator, counselor, therapist, mediator, investigator, evaluator, and advocate. With persons who are visiting the social worker on an involuntary or nonvoluntary basis, both the purpose and the role of the worker warrant more complete and often more lengthy description. This is also the case in situations where clients seek a specific programmatic service offered through the agency. For example, an agency may sponsor an educationally oriented six-week group experience for teenagers who are considering marriage. Because it is a structured group that follows a predictable agenda, the worker's role as educator and facilitator in providing leadership is clear. The worker may safely describe to applicants his role vis-à-vis the group.

However, frequently the exact nature of the worker's role is unclear at the time of the first meeting. When that is the case, rather than speculating about the role, a tentative description of general purpose will suffice. This often occurs with voluntary clients who seek service from organizations that have several programs and serve a variety of functions.

The following represent a few examples of a social worker tentatively describing a purpose for a social work interview:

CASE SITUATION: The client is a young woman (age thirty) who had called the agency a few days previously asking for help with a troubled marriage. The worker and client have already exchanged introductions. The worker begins to describe her purpose. She says:

WORKER: When you telephoned the agency the other day, you said that your marriage is on the brink of collapse. You and your husband are fighting all the time. Is that correct? Yes? All right, during our meeting today I'd like to explore with you the problems and concerns that caused you to call. I hope that as we talk about your situation we'll both be able to gain a better understanding of the problem. Maybe then it will be possible to consider some means for addressing the difficulties.

CASE SITUATION: The divorcing parents of a nine-year-old boy are involved in a child custody proceeding. The social worker has been employed by the juvenile court to make recommendations to the judge about the placement of the child. The worker has just exchanged introductions with the father and describes his (the worker's) purpose and role as follows:

WORKER: Judge Bloom has asked me to meet with you, your former wife, and your son for the purpose of making a recommendation to her about the custody arrangements for Kevin. I'll be meeting with Ms. Brown [former spouse] this afternoon and with Kevin [son] tomorrow morning. After these three meetings I should have a fairly good understanding of the situation. At that time, should further meetings be needed, I'll let you know.

I certainly recognize that this is a difficult time for you and for everybody involved. You may feel a bit like you're on trial here. It may seem that way. I'll try my best to make it as reasonable a process as possible. However, you should know that your son Kevin will be fully considered in these processes. My efforts will be geared toward determining what is best for him, for his growth and well-being. I'm sure that you are also concerned about the consequences of the divorce and the upcoming court proceedings on your son, and you want what's best for him too. I hope that we can approach this interview with that in mind and can work together toward finding the best resolution of this difficult situation.

CASE SITUATION: First meeting of an educational group for persons arrested for driving under the influence (DUI) of alcohol. The participants range in age from sixteen to sixty-two and cross gender, ethnic, and socioeconomic class lines. The group experience involves twelve weekly meetings of approximately two hours each. Members participate in order to decrease the chance of a jail sentence. The worker and group members have exchanged introductions and engaged in some small talk. The worker now proceeds to describe his purpose and role in this manner:

WORKER: I have been asked by the county judge to lead this educational group for the next twelve weeks. It's my understanding that each of you is here because you were arrested for driving under the influence of alcohol and that you have chosen to participate in the group in order to reduce the chances of a term in the county jail. I imagine that you all have other places that you would rather be at this time. Some of you are probably pretty annoyed at having to be here and you may be angry at me. If I were in your shoes, I'd be feeling quite a bit of resentment and perhaps a bit of embarrassment too. It's my hope that, in spite of these feelings, the series of group meetings will increase your knowledge about drinking and driving and will be of use to you in the future.

CASE SITUATION: The interview setting is the front doorstep of the Frankel residence. It is a large home in an upper-middle-class neighborhood. The social worker has knocked on the door and it has been opened by a woman who appears to live there. The worker is employed by the Child Protection Division of the Department of Human Services. He is visiting the home unannounced because his agency has received a complaint indicating that Mrs. Frankel has severely beaten her four-year-old son. The worker has introduced himself and learned that the woman is indeed Mrs. Frankel. He says:

WORKER: Our department has the legal obligation to investigate all allegations of abuse or neglect of a minor child. We have received a complaint concerning the treatment of your four-year-old son. Let me show you my identification card to let you know that I am who I say I am. I'd like to discuss this situation with you further. May I come in?

■ **Exercise 6-3: Describing Initial Purpose**

Use the following case situations to practice the skill of describing your initial social work purpose and, where appropriate, your role. Please respond to each situation in the spaces provided.

1. Assume that you are a social worker in a public housing agency. You are currently in the process of interviewing all residents of a building in an effort to determine their social service needs. You have just knocked on the door of Mrs. Strong's residence. Mrs. Strong is a single mother with five children who range in age from nine years to six months. Write the words you would say to her as you describe an initial purpose for the meeting.

2. You are a social worker in the emergency room of a general hospital. Paramedics have just brought in an automobile accident victim. Doctors and nurses are providing lifesaving measures. Family members of the patient arrive. It is your function to provide them with a place to wait and to inform them in general terms about what is happening to the patient. You go up to the family, introduce yourself, and guide them to a more private waiting area. Write the words you would say in describ-

ing an initial purpose for the meeting. In this case your role is also likely to be fairly clear. Describe your role as well.

3. You are a social worker in a nursing residence for elderly persons. A new resident arrived over the weekend and you go to her room for a first visit. You intend to introduce yourself and get acquainted. You realize that you will need to complete a social history before the week is out and want to set the stage for that more lengthy interview. Write the words you would say in describing an initial purpose for the upcoming meeting.

4. You are a social worker for an agency that serves children who have been sexually abused. You lead groups for victimized girls seven to ten years of age. You are about to begin a new group, which has five members. You have met individually with each of the five before and have talked with them at length. However, this is the first time they have been in a group and they have not met each other before. You ask each girl to share her first name with the others. They do so—although several introduce themselves in soft and tentative voices. You want to begin the group in a warm, safe, and secure manner. Write the words you would say in describing an initial purpose for the meeting.

OUTLINING THE CLIENT'S ROLE

During the beginning phases of a professional helping relationship, clients often experience considerable uncertainty and anxiety about what is expected of them. Prospective clients are certainly concerned about the problems that have led to the contact, but they are also worried that they may not be able to do what is needed to improve or resolve the difficulties. In particular, prospective clients are often uncertain about how they may best help the worker to help them. Therefore, it is frequently useful to outline how the client may cooperate in the helping process (Garvin, 1987, pp. 72–74). For example, prior to the first meeting of a group for adolescents having school problems, a worker might describe the role of members by discussing the initial purpose for the group and then saying:

> We all have problems at some point in our lives. It's part of being human. We've found that talking about such problems with other people who are in similar situations tends to help resolve those problems. This group will provide you an opportunity to talk with one another about your problems and concerns as well as your hopes and dreams. Although you will not be required to say anything that you wish to keep to yourself, members are expected to express themselves to one another, to listen carefully to what others say, and to offer suggestions about how things could be better. Members are also expected to follow the rule of confidentiality. What that means is whatever is said within the group setting should remain here. It should not be repeated outside this room.

In attempting to outline the client's role to an individual, a worker might say:

> You can best help in this process by sharing your thoughts and feelings as freely and as fully as possible. You can help by asking questions when you do not understand and by giving me honest

126

feedback concerning what is helpful and what is not. Finally, you can be helpful in this process by trying as hard as you can to do the tasks that we devise together in our efforts to resolve the problems you identify.

In outlining the client's role, the worker should recognize that his expectations for clients necessarily vary according to the purpose for which they are meeting. Additionally, the expectations differ somewhat depending upon the agency, its programs, and upon the makeup of the client system, its size, and the ages, capacities, and motivations of its members.

■ **Exercise 6-4: Outlining the Client's Role**

Use the following case situations to practice the skill of outlining the client's role. Please respond to each situation in the spaces provided.

1. Assume that you are a social worker meeting for the first time with a couple who want help with marital difficulties. Mr. and Mrs. Koslow have been married for ten years, have two children (eight and ten years old), and an adequate income. You have introduced yourself, secured introductions from Mr. and Mrs. Koslow, and have identified as a purpose for this first meeting to explore the problems and concerns that led the couple to come to the agency. You now want to outline their role in this process. What would you say?

2. Assume that you are a social worker meeting for the first time with a family of four (a single parent and three children, ages eleven, thirteen, and sixteen). The eldest child, a daughter, has reportedly begun to use marijuana and to drink beer and wine. The mother is very concerned and has brought the entire family in for help with this issue. You have introduced yourself, secured introductions from each of the family members, and have described as a purpose for this first meeting to explore the problems and concerns that led the family to come to the agency. You now want to outline their role in this process. What would you say?

DISCUSSING POLICY AND ETHICAL CONSIDERATIONS

Another extremely important skill applicable to the beginning phase of work involves the discussion of potentially relevant policy and ethical factors. Understanding the "ground rules" is a critical element in the development of an authentic and honest relationship. It constitutes part of the informed consent process. For example, a client who assumes that absolutely everything he says to the social worker will always remain confidential is probably going to feel betrayed by the worker who reports to child protective services what he had said about an instance of child abuse.

Professional social workers are bound by certain guidelines in the performance of their duties. Some of these originate with the agency with which they are affiliated (e.g., agency policies and procedures), others are promulgated by the profession (e.g., the Code of Ethics of the National Association of Social Workers [NASW]), and still others are formulated by governmental bodies (e.g., state or federal laws and regulations, and court decisions). Clients have a right to be informed of the policies and ethical principles that may apply to them. Many agencies wisely provide prospective clients with publications describing relevant policies. However, some clients do not or cannot truly understand the intent of such written material. The worker should therefore discuss the major elements with each prospective client.

Figure 6-1 shows a sample document that social workers might provide to prospective clients and use in guiding the discussion of policy and ethical issues.

F I G U R E 6-1
Agency Policies

The agency operates on a "sliding fee" basis. This means that the cost of each individual or family session varies according to clients' ability to pay. The higher the family income the higher the cost—up to a maximum of thirty-five dollars per session. Group sessions are generally somewhat less. Reimbursement from insurance companies, where applicable, is the responsibility of the client. However, the agency will help clients to complete the necessary claim forms.

If a scheduled appointment must be cancelled, the client should inform the agency at least one day prior to the scheduled session.

As a general guideline, whatever clients say during sessions remains confidential among agency personnel. However, there are a few exceptions to that rule. As required by law, any information concerning possible child abuse or neglect will be reported to child protection authorities. Similarly, information indicating that a person represents a real and present danger to him or herself or to others will not be considered confidential. Action to protect the lives of the persons involved will be taken. In potentially life-threatening circumstances, the value of human life takes precedence over that of confidentiality. Finally, clients should be aware that in this state social workers are not granted the right of privileged communication (as is, for example, the case for lawyers). Therefore, if subpoenaed by a court of law, agency social workers would not have legal grounds for refusing to answer questions concerning the sessions.

In this agency, we have a procedure for expressing concerns about the nature and quality of the services you receive. If, for any reason whatsoever, you are not sure about or are unsatisfied with the service provided, please feel free to discuss it with your social worker. If you do not receive an adequate explanation or if the service remains unsatisfactory, please then contact our agency's client representative, Ms. Sheila Cordula in Room 21 (telephone 789-5432). She will be happy to explore your concerns with you.

In discussing relevant policy and ethical issues, the worker must, of course, be cognizant of the relative urgency of a situation and the timing of the use of this skill. It should be obvious that the worker attempting to comfort a parent whose child has just been killed in an automobile accident will defer discussion of policy and ethical issues. In such instances, the client's immediate needs take precedence. In fact, all the social work skills must be used within the context of a person-problem-situation assessment. Often, a skill applicable in one circumstance would be totally inappropriate in another. Social work practice is a professional, not a technical, endeavor. As such, workers must continually make judgments about and adaptations in the use of themselves and their skills.

■ **Exercise 6-5: Discussing Policy and Ethical Considerations**

Use the following case situations to practice the skill of discussing policy and ethical factors. Note that these are the same situations to which you responded above with the skill of describing initial purpose. Please respond to each situation in the spaces provided.

1. Assume that you are a social worker in a public housing agency. You are currently in the process of interviewing all residents of a building to determine their social service needs. You have just knocked on the door of Mrs. Strong's residence. Mrs. Strong is a single mother with five children who range in age from nine years to six months. Follow up your description of an initial purpose by writing the words you would say in discussing policy and ethical factors.

2. You are a social worker in the emergency room of a general hospital. Paramedics have just brought in an automobile accident victim. Doctors and nurses are in the process of providing lifesaving measures. The family members of the patient arrive. It is your function to provide them with a place to wait and to inform them in general terms about what is happening to the patient. You go up to the family, introduce yourself, and guide them to a more private waiting area. Follow up your description of an initial purpose and role by writing the words you would say in discussing policy and ethical factors.

3. You are a social worker in a nursing residence for elderly persons. A new resident arrived over the weekend and you go to her room for a first visit. You intend to introduce yourself and get acquainted. You realize that you will need to complete a social history before the week is out and want to set the stage for that more lengthy interview. Follow

up your description of an initial purpose by writing the words you would say in discussing policy and ethical factors.

4. You are a social worker for an agency that serves children who have been sexually abused. You lead groups for victimized girls seven to ten years of age. You are about to begin a new group, which has five members. You have met each of the five before and have talked with them at length. However, this is the first time they have been in a group and they have not met each other before. You ask each girl to share her first name with the others. They do so—although several introduce themselves in soft and tentative voices. You want to begin the group in a warm, safe, and secure manner. Follow up your description of an initial purpose by writing the words you would say in discussing policy and ethical factors.

SEEKING FEEDBACK

The skill of seeking feedback (W. Schwartz, 1976, pp. 188–190; Shulman, 1984, pp. 37–49) involves the worker encouraging the client or other person to react to and to comment about the purpose, the role, or other aspects of the worker-client interaction about which the worker has communicated. An important part of effective communication involves "checking out" one's expression in order to determine whether it has been accurately heard and understood. Seeking feedback serves this function. Although the social worker routinely seeks feedback throughout the working relationship, he must recognize that it is especially important during the beginning phase. By asking for feedback about his tentative description of purpose and role and his discussion of policy and ethical factors, the social worker has, in a real sense, initiated the process of contracting. He has also provided the other person with an opportunity and an invitation to express her lack of clarity or disagreement about the social worker's comments. He sends a message that this process has mutuality—that he is interested in what the other has to say about him and about what he has said, and that the other is expected to participate in the process.

Some of the more common ways to seek feedback about purpose, role, and policy factors include the questions: "How does that sound to you? What do you think about what I've said thus far? What questions or comments do you have?" Often, the client responds to seeking feedback by asking for further clarification. This provides the worker with an opportunity to explain in greater detail his view of the tentative purpose, role, or policy and ethical factors. The greater the level of understanding of these dimensions the more likely the client is to feel respected and informed.

■ Exercise 6-6: Seeking Feedback

Use the following case situations to practice the skill of seeking feedback. Please respond to each situation in the spaces provided.

1. You, a social worker in an agency that serves children and their families, are meeting for the first time with a thirty-two-year-old mother and her eight-year-old daughter. They have voluntarily sought help regarding some problems in the child's schoolwork. At this time, you do not know anything more about the school or family situation. You have introduced yourself and elicited introductions from the others. You have learned that Ms. Pomerantz prefers to be called "Joan" and that her daughter prefers "Emily." You have asked them to call you by your first name. You have also outlined an initial purpose for this first meeting by saying: "In today's meeting I hope that we will be able to gain a beginning understanding of the problems and concerns that led you to this visit. Once we have some understanding of the problems, I hope we'll be able to figure out some of the factors that contribute to their occurrence. After that, we'll try to plan some ways to resolve those problems and concerns."

    Write the words you would use in seeking feedback regarding purpose from Joan and Emily.

2. As you continue to interact with Joan and Emily, you state:

> Everything that you and Emily say during our meetings will be treated as confidential. No one outside the agency will have access to information you share. The only exceptions to this policy of confidentiality are when you specifically and in writing request that we provide information to someone else, when a person's life is in danger, or when there is evidence of child abuse or neglect. In such instances, we are required by law to report that evidence to state agencies charged with the responsibility of protecting children. Also, if subpoenaed by a court of law, for example when there is a divorce and a custody dispute occurs, we might be required to provide information to the court.

Write the words you would use in seeking feedback from Joan regarding policy and ethical factors.

3. You are a social worker in an agency that serves adults and children who have had child abuse problems. You are meeting for the first time with a twenty-two-year-old man who has been charged with severely beating his four-year-old son. He has come to this first meeting involuntarily. He is required to receive counseling as part of an adjudicated court agreement that, depending on the results of the counseling, may enable him to avoid incarceration. Thus far, you have introduced yourself and elicited an introduction from the man. You sense from the nature of his body position that you should address him as "Mr. Bosch." You inform him that he may call you by your first name if he prefers. You have also outlined an initial purpose for this first meeting by saying, "In today's meeting I hope that we will be able to gain a

beginning understanding of your current situation and identify some preliminary goals for our work together. It is my understanding that you are required by Judge Koopman to receive counseling once per week for a minimum of six months."

Write the words you would use in seeking feedback from Mr. Bosch concerning what you have said thus far.

4. As you continue to interact with Mr. Bosch, you say:

I hope that we will be able to identify some of the factors that have contributed to incidents of violence and that we will work toward eliminating any future violent actions. You should know that in situations such as this, where the court is involved, I will be providing regular reports to the judge. I will report to the judge the number of sessions that you attend, the degree of your cooperation in the process, my assessment of progress, and my estimate concerning the risks of further violence.

Write the words you would use in seeking feedback from Mr. Bosch concerning what you have said.

SUMMARY

During the beginning phase, the social worker introduces and identifies himself and seeks introductions from the prospective client. Following the exchange of introductions, the worker attempts to describe an initial purpose for the meeting, describes the role the client might assume in order to aid in the helping endeavor, and identifies relevant policy and ethical factors that might apply. Throughout this beginning process, the worker regularly seeks feedback from the client concerning her understanding of and reactions to what has been expressed. As a result of the use of the beginning skills, the worker helps to clarify the nature and boundaries of the helping process, to lessen somewhat the initial anxiety or ambivalence prospective clients often experience, and to establish a tentative direction for work.

■ **Exercise 6-7: Summary**

Assume that you are a social worker with a human service agency that offers a broad range of social services. Prepare for a first meeting with each of the following prospective clients. In the spaces provided, write the words you say and the actions you would take as you meet for the first time. Among the skills useful for this series of exercises are: introducing oneself, seeking introductions, describing initial purpose, describing the worker role, describing the client's role, and seeking feedback. Please identify the skills you use in each case situation.

1. Earlier in the day, a woman telephoned the agency and said she wants to talk with someone about an experience that occurred about one week before. A man she had met in a bar drove her home and raped her. She had thought that she would be able to manage her feelings about the incident but she now realizes that she needs help. She says she's "falling apart."

    An appointment has been scheduled for the present time. What would you do and say in beginning?

2. The agency receptionist informs you that in the waiting room there is a fifty-five-year-old man who says that he wants to kill himself. You are the social worker responsible for interviewing all persons who come to the agency without appointments. You ask him to accompany you back to your office. What would you do and say in beginning?

3. Recently, a fourteen-year-old black girl revealed to her school teacher that she is pregnant by her white boyfriend. She also told her that she needs to get an abortion quick or "her parents will kill her if they find out she's pregnant." The teacher urged her to talk with you, the school social worker, and secured the girl's permission to tell you about the situation. The teacher has done so and an appointment has been arranged for this time.

What would you do and say in beginning with the mother? With the child?

4. An eight-year-old girl who has been the victim of incest seems to be in a state of emotional shock. She hasn't spoken or expressed feelings since the incident was discovered. The child protection caseworker has tried to help but to no avail. The case has been referred to you, a social worker who specializes in work with victimized children.

   A home visit has been scheduled for the present time. You drive to the girl's home (where she still resides). The child's mother answers the door. What would you do and say in beginning?

5. A forty-two-year-old woman, beaten nearly to death by her husband several times over the past ten years, wants help in dealing with the situation.

   You have an opportunity to meet the woman while she stays temporarily at a shelter for battered women. What would you do and say in beginning?

6. Using the rating scales below (where 0 = no proficiency and 10 = complete proficiency), assess your current level of proficiency in the beginning skills.

Introducing Oneself

```
|___|___|___|___|___|___|___|___|___|___|
0   1   2   3   4   5   6   7   8   9   10
```

Seeking Introductions

```
|___|___|___|___|___|___|___|___|___|___|
0   1   2   3   4   5   6   7   8   9   10
```

Describing Initial Purpose

```
|___|___|___|___|___|___|___|___|___|___|
0   1   2   3   4   5   6   7   8   9   10
```

Outlining the Client's Role

```
|___|___|___|___|___|___|___|___|___|___|
0   1   2   3   4   5   6   7   8   9   10
```

Discussing Policy and Ethical Considerations

```
|___|___|___|___|___|___|___|___|___|___|
0   1   2   3   4   5   6   7   8   9   10
```

Seeking Feedback

0   1   2   3   4   5   6   7   8   9   10

7. Finally, review your ratings to identify those beginning skills in which you remain less proficient (e.g., a score of 7 or less). Then, in the space below, outline the steps you might take to improve your skill in those areas.

EXPLORING

Following the beginning phase, the worker and client commence the process of exploration. Exploration involves the worker encouraging the client to share his thoughts, feelings, and experiences regarding himself; those regarding the problems or concerns that led to the contact with the worker; and those regarding his situation. Through exploration, both the worker and the client derive a more complete and realistic perspective. This is a common result of publicly airing one's experience, since talking openly with another person involves hearing oneself. As the client shares thoughts, ideas, and feelings as well as facts, he not only experiences the reactions of the worker but he more fully experiences his own. Through the process of exploration, the worker and the client gather and consider information regarding the person, the problem, and the situation. This helps them understand the factors associated with the development and maintenance of the problem as well as those attributes and resources that may later be useful in working toward problem resolution. Such information, in conjunction with the worker's professional knowledge, leads to an assessment and plan for work.

The skills most applicable to the exploration phase include: (1) probing, (2) seeking clarification, (3) reflecting content, (4) reflecting feeling, (5) reflecting complex communications, (6) partializing, and (7) going beyond what is said. Applied to the person-problem-situation, these skills are used for *exploring the person*, *exploring the problem*, and *exploring the situation*.

In undertaking the exploration process, the worker often proceeds according to the sequence reflected in the exploration matrix shown in Figure 7-1. She first explores the problem as it is now, then traces its past history and development, and then seeks the client's view of the problem in the future. Next, she explores the person's present experience of himself, what he was like in the past, and his view of himself in the future. Finally, the worker encourages exploration of the present situation, the past situation, and the situation as envisioned in the

FIGURE 7-1
Exploration Matrix

In social work practice, many exploratory interviews proceed in the sequence shown in the matrix below. Usually, workers encourage clients to explore and express themselves in their own way and according to their own preference. However, social workers need certain information in order to develop a thorough understanding and to formulate a professional assessment. Therefore, if clients do not spontaneously address relevant information, workers encourage them to explore areas 1, then 2, then 3, and so on until the problem, person, and situation have been explored throughout the present, past, and future time dimensions.

	PRESENT	PAST	FUTURE
PROBLEM	1	2	3
PERSON	4	5	6
SITUATION	7	8	9

future. Of course, these nine dimensions overlap. As the problem is discussed, the client may share information about himself or his situation. While exploring the present, he may reveal material about the past. It is not necessary to interrupt him in order to keep in sequence—he should be allowed to share in his own way. The purpose for the exploration matrix is to provide the worker with a flexible guide for exploring with clients the person-problem-situation; the matrix should not be viewed as a fixed interview schedule.

Exploring the problem involves examination of the *present* status of the problem, its intensity, frequency, duration, and the context in which it tends to happen. The worker is also interested in what happens before, during, and following the occurrence of the problem. Additionally, the worker explores the problem's *past*. She traces the development of the problem from the time of its initial occurrence on through to the present. Included in the exploration is an examination of the client's attempts to resolve or avoid the problem. The worker wants to learn which attempts were successful, which were partially successful, and which were unsuccessful. As part of this exploration, the worker encourages the client to share any thoughts, feelings, and actions associated with the problem. Finally, the worker explores the problem's *future* as envisioned by the client. In this dimension, she explores what the future might be like if the problem were to remain as it is now. She also asks the client to imagine what would be different in the future if the problem were to be completely resolved.

Through *exploring the person*, the worker encourages the client to talk about himself as an individual. In this dimension, the worker is vitally interested in the *thinking*, *feeling*, and *doing* aspects of the client's experience. Within the dimension of thinking, the worker examines both the substance of the client's thoughts—whether they occur as beliefs (what people say to themselves) or as images (the mental pictures people experience)—and the process of his thinking (the means by which people move from one thought to another). Within the dimension of feeling, the worker is interested in the client's emotions (e.g., anger, fear, sadness) as well as his physical sensations (e.g., muscular tension, nausea, or light-headedness). Within the dimension of doing, the worker is interested in the client's actual, overt behavior (e.g., walking, speaking, hitting, looking) as well as omissions of behavior (those behaviors, such as assertive requests, that the client might use appropriately in a situation but, for whatever reasons, does not).

Exploring the situation involves examining the client's current and, when applicable, his past situational circumstances. The worker is particularly interested in social, economic, cultural, and environmental aspects of the situation as they may relate to the problem. Exploring the client's family, community, ethnic affiliation, religious involvement, housing, education, employment, and finances may be useful in certain case situations.

Usually, within one or two meetings, the worker and client have discussed the more pressing concerns and developed a beginning understanding of the nature of these concerns. At this point, the worker and client may be able to decide whether this particular worker and agency have the sanction, resources, and expertise necessary to help the client effectively address the problems that led to the contact. Often, in large part due to a lack of familiarity with the human service network, prospective clients contact an agency that is not well prepared to address their particular problems. As a result of a beginning exploration of the presenting concerns, the worker may be able to inform a prospective client that another organization in the community specializes in work with such problems and would probably be better able to provide help in this particular instance. Then, if the client concurs, the worker might contact the other agency to initiate the process of a professional referral. Of course, the referral process should be done with the utmost care so that the client does not feel that he is being rejected by the worker or the agency. Also, the referral agency's personnel should be treated with professionalism and courtesy. The nature of a worker's relationships with other community professionals often determines whether prospective clients receive a warm or a cold reception. Therefore, each social worker should relate to other professionals with the same kind of respect she shows clients.

When the presenting problems are congruent with the agency's function and range of services and fall within the worker's areas of expertise, the worker and client continue the helping process by undertaking a more complete exploration.

PROBING

When the beginning phase of the interview has been completed and the worker and client concur with an initial purpose for the meeting, the worker then proceeds to seek information concerning the problem or concerns that led to this encounter (Perlman, 1957, p. 88). Probes are the worker's statements or questions that attempt to elicit from the client knowledge, ideas, and feelings concerning the person, the problem, the situation, and potential means for resolution of the identified difficulties (Cournoyer, 1989, pp. 355–356). The process of probing yields information necessary to the worker and client for mutual understanding, assessment, contract formulation, movement toward problem resolution and goal attainment, and evaluation and ending.

The first use of the probing skill typically occurs after the worker and client have concluded the beginning phase. The parties have introduced themselves, reached some tentative understanding of their purpose for meeting, and, usually, have discussed the policies and ethical principles that may apply. The initial exploratory probe represents the first entry into the realm of the problem that led to the contact. Typically, the probe is phrased in such a way as to allow the client maximum opportunity to express himself freely. Probes may be expressed by the worker as questions or as requests. For example, a worker might ask, "What led you to contact us at this time?" Or she might say, "Please tell me about the difficulties that are troubling you." In the case of an involuntary client, she might say, "I understand that the judge has required you to come here for counseling. I know a little bit about the situation, but I'd like to hear the full story from you. How did this all come about?"

As you might expect, probing is a skill applicable at many points throughout the exploration phase. Probes are used to explore the circumstances surrounding the origin and maintenance of the problems and to encourage the client to discuss his family history and current living situation. A worker might ask any of the following questions: "How did these difficulties begin? Who was included in your family as you were growing up? What were your parents like? Who lives with you now?" Similarly, probes are used to elicit information concerning the client's thoughts, feelings, and actions: "What did you feel when she left? What were you thinking about when that happened? What would you like to be different? What did you do then?"

By and large, probes are phrased as questions. The nature of the questions derive from the worker's active pursuit of information regarding the person-problem-situation from the time the problem first occurred up through the present. There are two general types of questions. *Closed-ended questions* (Goodman & Esterly, 1988, pp. 123–127) are phrased in such a way as to elicit a short response, sometimes simply a yes or no. Closed-ended questions yield a great deal of information in a brief time. They are especially useful in crisis situations where vital information must be gathered quickly.

Here are a few examples of the closed-ended questions that a social worker might ask a client: "What is your phone number? Where do you live? Do you have a car? Do you live at home? When were you born? Who lives with you? Is there somebody there in the house with you right now? Which do you prefer? Have you taken some medicine? What drugs did you take? How many pills did you take?"

Usually, answers to such questions are quite short, which can be advantageous or not according to the nature and needs of the situation. Sometimes, at a particular point in time, the rapid collection of specific information is so important that the worker postpones the free and full exploration of an aspect of the person-problem-situation. However, too many closed-ended questions, one after another, may lead the person to feel more like a subject than a client. He may feel interrogated rather than interviewed, and the quality of the professional relationship may suffer. Therefore, unless the situation is immediately life threatening or otherwise highly urgent, it is usually wise to mix closed-ended with open-ended questions and active listening responses.

Open-ended questions (Goodman & Esterly, 1988, pp. 127–137) are expressed in a manner that tends to encourage the other person to share a more extensive response. Open-ended questions are designed to further exploration on either a deeper level or in a broader way. Often, they are phrased as *what* questions such as, "What is the nature of your concern? What happened then?" *What* questions can be expressed as closed- or open-ended questions. Most of the time, they tend to elicit a factual or ideational answer, unless a feeling response is specifically requested. For example, "What feelings did you experience when he left?" encourages the client to share emotions. *How* questions nearly always yield open responses from clients. Probes such as "How did that come to happen? How did he react? How do you feel right now? How do you think you came across in that situation?" also tend to elicit expansive expressions from clients. Other forms of open-ended questions include: "In what way did you . . . ? Would you talk more about . . . ? Please tell me about . . . . "

Why questions may generate defensiveness. A client may believe that the worker is judging him and may feel compelled to justify or defend some aspect of himself, his behavior, or the situation. Therefore, workers should be cautious in using *why* questions. However, they do not have to avoid them completely. For example, the defensive-eliciting quality may be moderated by qualifying the question with, "I wonder why (that might be)?" Or, "Why do you think that happens?" When asking *why* questions, workers should be especially alert to communicate nonverbally an attitude of warmth and acceptance.

During the exploration process, workers should intersperse their probes with active listening responses. Also, they should realize that probing questions, like statements, can suggest blame, evaluation, or advice—such questions are not always simply neutral requests for information. For example, "Have you talked with your mother about that yet?" might imply to a client that the worker expected and wanted the client to talk with her. "Have you completed that form yet?" conveys a similar message. Although it is sometimes useful to express a statement of opinion or preference in the form of a question, the worker must be aware that she is doing so. Phrasing a comment in the form of a question does not relieve the worker of responsibility for the substance of the message. She should try to avoid asking several questions, multiple-choice fashion, at the same time. For example, "Are you still going with Jackie or have you given up on her and are now dating only Jill? And what about Cathy?" leaves the client uncertain. He does not know whether to respond to the worker's first, second, third, or fourth question.

During the exploration phase, probes can be extremely useful for providing a sense of coherence and continuity to the interview. The worker helps the client to express himself about himself as a person, the problems of concern, and the situational context in which he functions. When the client jumps around too much or avoids or only briefly touches upon issues and content areas likely to be of importance, the worker may select probes to help the client focus on the person-problem-situation aspects of the interview. However, as is the case with respect to the other exploratory skills, the worker must be cognizant of the client's psychological and interpersonal defenses. When a client is especially fragile concerning a process or content issue, the worker may wish to postpone probing that particular dimension until the relationship becomes more established. Then, when the client feels more secure, the worker may probe areas requiring further exploration.

Probes are obviously relevant to the exploration phase. Indeed, they are of great utility throughout all phases of practice.

■ Exercise 7-1: Probing

For these exercises, assume that you are a social worker with a family and children's counseling center. In the spaces provided, write the words you would say in each situation.

1. You are in the midst of the first interview with Mr. K., a recently divorced, fifty-five-year-old man. You have introduced yourself and have addressed the other aspects of the beginning phase of practice. You are now ready for your initial exploratory probe. At this point, you have no idea of the nature of Mr. K.'s concern—it may or may not be related to the divorce. Therefore, you are interested in encouraging him to identify the problem that led him to contact the agency. Write the words

you would say in making this first probe. After you have written it, determine whether your probe is open or closed ended. Discuss your rationale for choosing this particular probe. How do you think such a client would react to this probe?

2. As an outreach worker for elderly persons, you have begun an interview with Mrs. O., a seventy-seven-year-old widow who lives alone. The interview is taking place in her small apartment. Although you are not aware of any problems and Mrs. O. has not requested that you visit, your function with the agency is to identify needs and resources (e.g., transportation, meals-on-wheels, or in-home medical services) that may be helpful to the elderly population, so you have initiated the contact. You have introduced yourself and addressed other dimensions of the beginning phase. Now write the words you would say in making your initial exploratory probe. After you have written your probe, determine

whether it is open or closed ended. Discuss your rationale for choosing this particular probe. How do you think Mrs. O. would react to this probe?

3. You have begun the first interview with the S. family, a seven-member, blended family. You have gone through the introductions and addressed other aspects of the beginning phase. As your initial probe, you asked, "What do you see as the issues within the family that led you to contact the agency?" The father responded to this question first, then the mother answered, followed by other family members. Although the specific nature of the responses varied somewhat, there appeared to be considerable agreement that the problem involves the relationship between the two teenage boys (biological children of the father) and their father's wife (their stepmother). This relationship seems to contain a great deal of conflict and anger. As the social worker, you now wish to probe the origin and development of these difficulties. Write the words you would say in doing so. After you have written your probe, determine whether it is open or closed ended. To whom is it directed— the boys, the other children, Mrs. S., Mr. S., or the entire group? Discuss your rationale for choosing this probe and for selecting the person or

persons you decided to address it to. What do you anticipate would be the boys' reaction to this probe? What might be Mrs. S.'s response?

Assume that you were to continue to explore the problem, the family, and the situation. Write the words you would say in formulating five additional exploratory probes. For each one, determine whether it is open or closed ended. Also, identify whether each probe addresses the person, family, problem, or situation aspect of the case.

4. You have begun to interview a prospective client of Hispanic background who fluently speaks both Spanish and English. You have completed the introductions, addressed the policy and ethical factors, and established a tentative purpose for the meeting—which is to explore the concerns Mrs. F. has about her two children, ages seven and nine years. It appears that they are the only Hispanic children in their school and have been subject to harassment from white boys. Mrs. F. is worried that her children might be in physical danger and that their attitude toward school might be negatively affected by these experiences.

As the worker, you are now ready to explore the problem further. Write the words you would say in asking an exploratory probe. Follow that by writing the words you might say in expressing five additional exploratory probes concerning the problem, the children, Mrs. F., the family system, or the school situation. Briefly discuss your rationale for the probes you have selected. Determine whether each is closed or open ended and predict the reaction that Mrs. F. might have to each question.

SEEKING CLARIFICATION

Sometimes, in response to an exploratory probe or at other points during an interview, a client makes a statement that remains unclear: he may communicate in an apparently contradictory fashion, skim over a relevant issue, or entirely neglect an aspect of himself, the problem, or the situation that appears to be materially significant to the exploration process. Since such indirect, unclear, or incomplete messages often concern important aspects of the person's experience, the manner in which the worker responds may significantly affect the nature of the relationship, the direction of the work, or the outcome of the helping endeavor. In such instances, it may be appropriate to respond to an unclear, subtle, indirect, unfinished, or nonverbal expression by seeking clarification. To do this, the worker attempts to elicit a more complete expression of the meaning contained in the words or gestures. During the early portion of a relationship, the purpose for seeking clarification is usually not to increase the client's self-awareness or insight but rather to address potential obstacles to the development of a working relationship and a thorough understanding of the person-problem-situation. For example, during the early part of a first meeting, a black client might say to a white worker, "Do they have any black social workers at your agency?" This may be an indirect communication (Shulman, 1984, pp. 20–28) by a client who wonders whether this white worker has the capacity to understand and to value him and his culture. He might have a preference for a black worker. He may have had a negative experience with a white worker in the past. A white worker might respond to this by saying something like, "Yes, we have several black social workers although not have as many as we should. I wish we had more. Since you ask that question though, I wonder, how do you feel about having a white worker?"

Client communications are not always entirely clear and understandable to the worker. Sometimes, this is because the social worker is not listening well. At other times, it is because the client is not certain what it is he actually does think and feel. Occasionally, it is because the client is sending a subtle or indirect message that he hopes the worker will notice. Because of the difficulty many people have in asking for help and because of the emotion-laden nature of many of the concerns discussed with social workers, indirect and unclear communication by clients is common. The social worker must be sensitive to indirect expressions, whether they occur in the form of hints, nonverbal gestures, or mixed messages. The worker should be aware that the meaning behind the indirect message may be fraught with anxiety for the client. Because he may not be fully aware of nor comfortable with that aspect of his thinking or feeling, or because he may be somewhat frightened about the nature of the worker's response to a message, he sends the message indirectly.

In responding to such communications, the worker typically moves carefully toward a greater degree of directness and clarity in communicating by asking for further information concerning the unclear, incomplete, or indirect message. For example, during a first meeting a fifty-eight-year-old prospective client says to a worker in her middle twenties, "I've never had much luck with social workers in the past. They all are so young and innocent." The worker might respond to such a statement by saying, "I'd like to hear more about the kinds of things that previous workers did that weren't helpful. In what ways were they unhelpful?" Later, the worker might come back to this topic in an even more direct manner by asking, "Do you feel that I might be too young and inexperienced to help you deal with these problems?"

Seeking clarification may also be used to elicit greater specificity (Shulman, 1984, pp. 60–61) concerning aspects of a thought, feeling, action, or situation. People often communicate in vague or general terms—they often use words such as *always*, *every*, *never*, which tend to convey a sense of the universal or absolute nature of a situation or phenomenon. Seeking specificity can enable both the client and the worker to appraise and understand more realistically the nature of an experience. For example, a client might say, "My spouse and I just don't get along. We haven't for years. The relationship stinks."

Although the client probably understands what he means by "don't get along" and "stinks," it is unlikely that the worker does. In seeking specific clarification, she might say, "Your marriage is really in trouble. It has been for a long time and you feel lousy about it. Can you be more specific about what makes the relationship so bad?" Or, "What bothers you most about the relationship?" Or, "Could you tell me more about what happens between you and your wife that leaves you feeling so bad?"

As is the case with most of the other exploratory skills, seeking clarification is applicable throughout the helping process. It is especially relevant during the problem-definition and goal-setting phases, the work phase, and during evaluation and ending processes. Often, the worker precedes her request for clarification with an active listening response.

■ Exercise 7-2: Seeking Clarification

For these exercises, assume that you are a social worker with a family and children's counseling center. Respond in the spaces provided by writing the words you would say in seeking clarification in each situation.

1. You are in the midst of the first interview with Mr. K., a recently divorced, fifty-five-year-old man. You have introduced yourself and have addressed the other aspects of beginning. You are in the midst of exploring the person-problem-situation. Mr. K. says, "I hurt so bad. I miss her terribly. I'm not sure I can go on." Write the words you would say in seeking clarification of what he has said. After you have written your response, discuss your rationale for the words you have chosen. How do you think he might react to this question? Now try preceding your clarification seeking with an active listening response. What effect does that have?

2. As an outreach worker for elderly persons, you are in the midst of an interview with Mrs. O., a seventy-seven-year-old widow who lives alone. The interview is taking place in her small apartment. Although you are not aware of any problems and Mrs. O. has not requested that you visit, your function with the agency is to identify needs and resources that may be helpful to the community's elderly population, so you have initiated the contact. At one point in the conversation, Mrs. O. abruptly stops talking and looks blankly away. For perhaps forty-five seconds, she does not respond to any of your questions. Then, suddenly, she shakes her head slightly and redirects her attention to you. Write the words you would use in seeking clarification in this situation. After you have written your response, discuss your rationale for the words you have chosen. How do you think Mrs. O. might react to this question?

3. You have begun the first interview with the S. family, a seven-member, blended family. You are in the midst of exploring the nature and development of the problem when one of the teenage boys (biological children of the father) angrily refers to their father's wife (their step-mother) as a "home wrecker." In reaction, Mrs. S. lowers her eyes and becomes very quiet. Write the words you would say in seeking clarification from the teenager. Discuss your rationale for the words you have chosen. How do you think the teenager who made the reference might react? How might Mrs. S.? Mr. S.? Other members of the family? Now write the words you would say in seeking clarification from Mrs. S. concerning her reaction to the term *home wrecker*. How do you think she and the other family members might react to your request for clarification from Mrs. S.?

4. Assume that you are in the midst of exploring problems with Mrs. F., who is of Hispanic background and fluently speaks both Spanish and English. Mrs. F. is concerned about her two children, seven and nine years old, who, as the only Hispanic children in their school, have been harassed by several white boys.

   During the course of the problem exploration, Mrs. F. says angrily, "Whites control this whole country and do not care about us at all." Write the words you might say in seeking clarification. Discuss your rationale for the words you have selected. How do you think Mrs. F. might react to your question? Now write three other ways in which you might seek clarification in this situation.

REFLECTING CONTENT

Reflecting content (Carkhuff, 1987, pp. 95–97) refers to the empathic skill of communicating to the other person an understanding of the factual or informational part of his expression. Along with the other reflecting skills, it is a more precise form of active listening. Commonly, reflecting content involves paraphrasing the client's words and expressing them back to him. The reflecting skills demonstrate that the worker has heard the information that the other is trying to convey.

Although the worker may wish to use lead-in phrases, such as, *You're saying . . . , If I understand you correctly, you mean that . . . , I hear you saying . . .* , the repeated use of such phrases may begin to sound artificial and mechanical. As much as possible, the worker should try to use her own words to reflect the message the client has expressed. If she accurately reflects the content of the person's message, such lead-in phrases are usually unnecessary. Here is an example of an exchange in which the worker responds by reflecting content:

CLIENT (MR. C.): About two years ago, I lost my job with General Motors. There was a huge layoff. Most of my buddies and I were let go. Since then, my wife has gone to work part-time and that keeps some food on the table. My unemployment compensation payments have run out and the union contributes only fifty dollars per month, so we have been unable to pay the mortgage on the house for the last six months. I think the bank is going to foreclose on us soon.

WORKER: You haven't had an adequate income for a long time. It's beginning to look like you may lose the house.

Although it is extremely likely that Mr. C. is experiencing a lot of emotion while he expresses himself, he has not actually used "feeling" words. In using the skill of reflecting content, the worker stays with the unemotional content of the message. Sometimes, even when a client expresses both feelings and information in a statement, a worker might choose to reflect only the content portion of the message. She might do so when the urgency of a situation requires that factual information be elicited quickly or when she is helping the client to maintain emotional control. Of course, at other times a worker may appropriately go beyond the actual words of the client in order to share her understanding of the unstated feelings behind the factual message. In general, however, during the early stages of the exploration process, the worker would be wise to be especially respectful of the defensive and coping mechanisms that clients reflect. She should follow their lead. For example, Mr. C. may be maintaining control of his emotions by expressing himself in a matter-of-fact, businesslike fashion. He may not yet trust the worker or himself enough to risk full and free expression of his feelings. The worker can develop the relationship a bit further by accurately reflecting the content of Mr. C.'s stated message before she encourages him to express feelings.

■ Exercise 7-3: Reflecting Content

For these exercises, assume that you are a social worker with a family and children's counseling center. Respond in the spaces provided by writing the words you would say in reflecting content in each situation.

1. You are in the midst of problem exploration with Mr. K., a recently divorced, fifty-five-year-old man. He says, "She left me about three weeks ago. She told me that she had had enough of my constant criticism of her and she was getting out. She's already filed for divorce." Write the words you would say in reflecting the content of what he has said. After you have written your response, discuss your rationale for the words you have chosen. How do you think he might react to your reflection?

2. You are in the midst of an interview with Mrs. O., a seventy-seven-year-old widow who lives alone. Following an episode in which she appeared to lose awareness of her surroundings, Mrs. O. says, "I occasionally have these blackouts. I seem to almost lose consciousness but I don't pass out or fall down or anything. I just kind of wake up after a period of several minutes." Write the words you would use in reflect-

ing the content of Mrs. O.'s message. After you have written your response, discuss your rationale for the words you have chosen. How do you think Mrs. O. might react to this question?

3. You are in the midst of an interview with the seven-member, blended S. family. During the course of the exploration, Mrs. S. says, "I fell in love with Hank [Mr. S.], and when we married I hoped that his children and mine would come to love one another as brothers and sisters. I also wanted his kids to know that I would love and treat them as if they were my own children." Write the words you would say in reflecting the content of Mrs. S.'s message. Discuss your rationale for the words you have chosen. How do you think Mrs. S. might react to your response? Now write two other ways in which you might reflect the content of her message in this situation.

4. You are interviewing Mrs. F., a Hispanic mother of two children who have been harassed at school by several white boys. During the course of the problem exploration, Mrs. F. says, "I have talked to the teachers and the guidance counselor. They listen politely but don't understand or care about what this does to my children. They don't do a thing about it." Write the words you might say in reflecting content. Discuss your rationale for the words you have selected. How do you think Mrs. F. might react to your response? Now write two other ways in which you might reflect the content of Mrs. F.'s message.

REFLECTING FEELING

Reflecting feeling (Carkhuff, 1987, pp. 99–110) is another of the empathic, active listening skills and usually consists of a fairly brief response that communicates the social worker's understanding of the feeling or feelings expressed by the client. Some of the more effective responses often constitute a simple sentence with only one feeling word. For example, "You are really hurting" can be a powerful empathic reflection of feeling. In spite of its brevity and apparent simplicity, reflecting feeling is not a skill that all social workers find easy to learn or to use. Reflecting emotions requires that the worker, at least to some extent, feels them herself. Empathy can be uncomfortable, even painful. Partly because of such discomfort, some workers inadvertently convert feeling reflections to content reflections by neglecting to use actual feeling words. For instance, a client says, "I am devastated." A worker might reflect the feeling by saying, "You're crushed." However, if she responds by saying, "It feels like you've been hit by a freight train," the feeling is merely implied. The message conveys an idea rather than a feeling. Although "hit by a freight train" is an apt phrase to amplify the feeling of devastation, it is most effective when used in conjunction with one or more feeling words. For example, "You feel crushed. It's like you've been hit by a freight train" includes both the feeling word and a powerful idea implying the feeling. Workers should realize that lead-in phrases, such as *You feel like . . .* , tend to be followed by a content reflection rather than a feeling message. Therefore, at least for training purposes, workers should use expressions like the following: "You feel [followed by a feeling word]. That leaves you feeling _____. Are you feeling _____? It's got you feeling _____." When two feelings are in evidence, the worker can respond to both, for example: "You feel _____ and _____." However, it is often possible to identify a single word that communicates both feelings. For example, *burdened* and *discouraged* might be reflected as *overwhelmed.* Here are some examples of feeling reflections:

CLIENT: (His former wife remarried about a year ago. Last month she and her current husband left the state with the client's five-year-old son. They moved two thousand miles away. The client tried to stop their relocation by filing a motion with the court but his former spouse won.) I just can't stand it. I miss my son terribly. I know that he'll gradually lose interest in me and I can't do a thing about it.

WORKER: You feel sad and powerless.

CLIENT: (sixteen-year-old girl who wanted desperately to be selected to the school's cheerleading team but was not chosen) It's awful. I can't go back to school. I can't face them. I wanted to be on the team so bad. It hurts. It really hurts.

WORKER: You feel rejected and unwanted.

Usually, especially in the early stages of relationships with clients, workers reflect the feelings that are expressed verbally. However, after establishing a base of accurate reflections or when the nonverbal, emotional message is very clear, a worker may reflect what she perceives to be the unspoken feeling message. Nonverbal messages in the form of facial expressions, body positions and movements, tone of voice, and so on are important means for communicating emotions. They should not be ignored. However, when a worker reflects the feeling suggested by nonverbal behavior, she must recognize that she is taking a modest risk. Her interpretation of the feeling behind the nonverbal expression is less likely to be accurate when feeling words have not been used. Also, a client may not be ready to acknowledge his feelings. Therefore, the worker must be cautious in reflecting the unstated message, particularly while establishing the working relationship. When she does so, she should be tentative in her reflection and prepared to return to content reflection or seeking clarification skills if the client indicates that the worker is premature or off target.

In order to use feeling reflections effectively, social workers need to possess a large vocabulary of terms that connote emotions or feelings. To convey different levels of intensity, they must be familiar with a range of feeling words—otherwise, they will have difficulty paraphrasing or reflecting accurately the feelings expressed by clients. For example, anger is an emotion everyone experiences in varying degrees. A person who is feeling annoyed or irritated would probably not feel understood by a worker who responds by saying, "You feel enraged." The words the worker uses should match both the kind as well as the intensity of the feeling expressed by clients.

■ Exercise 7-4: Reflecting Feeling

Active listening generally and the skill of reflecting feeling specifically require that you have a well-developed vocabulary of feeling words. Without such a

Feeling Vocabulary

Happy   *Hurt and Loss*   *Anxiety and Fear*   *Sad*   *Anger*   *Guilt*

164

vocabulary, it is extremely difficult to paraphrase the emotions experienced and expressed by clients. In order to begin to develop a feeling vocabulary of your own, please review the six categories of emotions listed in the table on page 164. Underneath each, identify at least ten feeling words that connote some degree of the emotion specified above.

For example, under the happiness category you might include the word *content*; under the anxiety category you might list *stress* as an associated term. When you have completed the list of ten words within each category, rate them in terms of their relative intensity (1 = mild; 2 = moderate; 3 = strong).

Following completion of this exercise and throughout the remainder of this course, enlarge your feeling vocabulary by adding words to the different emotional categories. As you become more sophisticated with the language of feelings, you might decide to revise this group of emotions by adding others or separating one category into two.

Now that you have developed initial familiarity with a range of feeling words, you can practice some feeling reflections. Assume that you are a social worker with a family and children's counseling center. In the spaces provided, write the words you would say in reflecting feeling in each situation.

1. In the midst of your first interview with Mr. K., a recently divorced, fifty-five-year-old man, you are exploring the person-problem-situation. He says, "I am absolutely lost. There is no reason to go on. I feel like someone reached into my gut and wrenched out my insides." Write the words you would say in reflecting the feelings contained in what Mr. K. has said. After you have written your response, discuss your rationale for the words you have chosen. How do you think he might react to your reflection? Identify two alternative feeling reflections that might also apply in this situation.

2. In the midst of an interview with Mrs. O., a seventy-seven-year-old widow who lives alone, she says, "I feel just fine. Sure, I have my low points, but everybody does. I still cook my own meals and care for myself. I'm proud of that—but, with these blackouts, I'm afraid I won't be independent much longer." Write the words you would use in reflecting the feelings contained in Mrs. O.'s message. After you have written your response discuss your rationale for the words you have chosen. How do you think Mrs. O. might react to your reflection? Identify two alternative feeling reflections that might also apply in this situation.

3. You are interviewing the seven-member, blended S. family. Mrs. S. has just said, "I fell in love with Hank [Mr. S.], and when we married I hoped that his children and mine would come to love one another as brothers and sisters. I also wanted his kids to know that I would love and treat them as if they were my own children." Following her statement, she hangs her head as tears fall down her cheeks. Mr. S.'s eyes are also watery. Although specific feeling words were not used, write the words you would say in reflecting the feelings suggested by Mr. and Mrs. S.'s nonverbal messages. Discuss your rationale for the words you have chosen. How do you think Mrs. S. might react to your response? Identify two additional ways in which you might reflect the feelings suggested by their behavior in this situation.

4. You are interviewing Mrs. F. She is of Hispanic background and is concerned about the safety of her two children because they have been harassed at school by several white boys. During the course of the problem exploration, Mrs. F. says, "I'm so angry. Talking with the teachers and the guidance counselor doesn't help. It's so frustrating having to fight so hard for fair treatment. My kids deserve to be protected." Write the words you might say in reflecting feeling. Discuss your rationale for the words you have selected. How do you think Mrs. F. might react to your response? Now write two other ways in which you might reflect the feelings indicated by Mrs. F.'s message in this situation.

REFLECTING COMPLEX COMMUNICATIONS

Reflecting complex communications (Carkhuff & Anthony, 1979, pp. 78–82) is a skill representing one of the more complete forms of active listening and empathic communication. It conveys both feeling and content elements of a message. For training purposes, workers can use a format such as, "You feel _____ because _____"; "You feel _____ and _____"; "You feel _____ but/yet/however _____."

Complex reflections, like their content and feeling counterparts, stay with (reflect) the client's feelings and meaning. The worker still does not take much liberty in going beyond, in guessing, or in interpreting what the client thinks, does, and feels. In particular, when a client conveys his view of the cause for or the meaning associated with the feelings he has, the worker reflects that perspective even though she might believe it to be incomplete or inaccurate. Often, the meaning conveyed by the client will suggest that external or situational factors are the primary causes for his feelings. At other times, the client will assume that aspects of himself (e.g., attitudes, habits, psychological patterns, fears, or physiological conditions) influence how he feels. However, whether the meaning associated with the feelings is externalized or internalized, the worker using the skill of complex reflection stays with the client's experience and does not add much to or alter the meaning of the message. Here are two examples of complex reflections:

CLIENT: (fifty-five-year-old man who has just lost his job after thirty-five years of employment) I have nowhere to turn—no job—no income—no nothing. They just let me go after thirty-five years of pain and sweat for them.

WORKER (reflecting complex communication): You feel angry and lost because they turned your life upside down. [Or] You feel desperate because the company has turned you out after so many years of service and it doesn't look like you'll be able to find something else. [Or] After thirty-five years of dedicated labor, the company just dumps you. You end up feeling worthless—like a nobody.

CLIENT: I'm a wreck. I can't sleep or eat; I can't concentrate. I know my head is really messed up.

WORKER (reflecting complex communication): You feel awful; you're anxious and confused. Right now you know you're not thinking straight.

■ Exercise 7-5: Reflecting Complex Communications

For these exercises, assume that you are a social worker with a family and children's counseling center. In the spaces provided, write the words you would say in reflecting the complex communication in each situation.

1. In the midst of your first interview with Mr. K., a recently divorced, fifty-five-year-old man, you are exploring his feelings about his situation. He says, "I was so used to her being there. I needed her but never told her. Now that she's gone, I realize just how much she meant to me." Write the words you would say in reflecting the complex message contained in what Mr. K. has said. After you have written your response, discuss your rationale for the words you have chosen. How do you think Mr. K. might react to your complex reflection? Identify two alternative complex reflections that might also apply in this situation.

2. You are in the midst of an interview with Mrs. O., a seventy-seven-year-old widow who lives alone and occasionally has blackouts. During the conversation, she says, "I'm afraid of being a burden to somebody. I'd rather be dead than be treated like a small child who cannot care for herself." Write the words you would use to reflect the complex message contained in Mrs. O.'s statement. After you have written your response, discuss your rationale for the words you have chosen. How do you think Mrs. O. might react to your response? Identify two alternative complex reflections that might also apply in this situation.

3. You are interviewing the seven-member, blended S. family. Following a moment when both Mr. and Mrs. S. had begun to cry, one of the teenage boys (Mr. S.'s biological children) says, "Well, it just seems that she has come into the house and expects to be *Mom*. She'll never be my mother, and I resent it when she tries to be." Write the words you would say in reflecting the complex message contained in his statement. Discuss your rationale for the words you have chosen. How do you think he might react to your response? How might Mr. S.? Mrs. S.? Identify two additional ways in which you might reflect the complex message suggested by his words.

4. You are interviewing Mrs. F. While exploring the problem, Mrs. F. says, "I'm frustrated with the whole system! This goddamn society is racist to the core! Money and power are the only things they respect." Write the words you might say in reflecting this complex message. Discuss your rationale for the words you have selected. How do you think Mrs. F. might react to your response? Now write two other ways in which you might reflect the complex message indicated by Mrs. F.'s words.

PARTIALIZING

Partializing (Perlman, 1957, pp. 144–149; Shulman, 1984, pp. 80–81) is frequently very helpful during the exploration phase of practice. Partializing is the process of breaking down several problems, issues, concerns—complex phenomena—into more manageable units in order to address them more easily. For example, a client might say, "My whole life is a mess. My husband is a drunk. He's out of work—again! My teenage son is a drug addict; he's just been expelled from school. And my doctor won't give me any more Valium." A worker and client who attempt to deal with all these concerns simultaneously are likely to end up confused. There are simply too many topics here. The use of the partializing skill helps to organize the process. The worker might say, "You sure have a lot to deal with. It sounds like everybody in the family has their share of problems to work on. I wonder, since there are so many concerns to look into, could we start by looking at them one at a time? Okay. Which one concerns you most right now?"

■ **Exercise 7-6: Partializing**

Assume that you are a social worker with a family and children's counseling center. In the spaces provided, write the words you would say in using the skill of partializing in each situation.

1. You are interviewing Mr. K., a recently divorced, fifty-five-year-old man. He says, "I think I'm on the brink of a nervous breakdown. I can't do my work. I can't sleep at night. I don't eat. All I do is think of her. I wonder what she's doing and whether she ever thinks of me. It's affecting my job. I think my boss is getting tired of my mistakes. I've also forgotten to pay some bills. Creditors are calling all the time. My whole life is a mess." First, separate and identify each of the elements in the client's message. List them in outline fashion. Which do you think is most important? Now write the words you would say in attempting to partialize what Mr. K. has said. After you have written your response, discuss your rationale for the words you have chosen. How do you think Mr. K. might react to your partialization?

2. You are in the midst of an outreach interview with Mrs. O., a seventy-seven-year-old widow who lives alone. During the conversation, Mrs. O. says, "Sometimes I get so lonely. All my friends have moved away or died. And my children don't visit me any more. One of them lives in town, but he doesn't even telephone me. I don't get birthday cards from them. It's like I'm already dead. And these blackouts. I don't know what's going to happen to me." First, separate and identify each of the elements in the client's message. List them in outline fashion. Which do you think is most important? Now write the words you would use in attempting to partialize Mrs. O.'s statement. After you have written your response, discuss your rationale for the words you have chosen. How do you think Mrs. O. might react to your response?

3. You are interviewing the seven-member, blended S. family. During the course of the exploration, Mr. S. says, "Since we married, we've had troubles with both my teenagers and her children. They dislike each other, they seem to hate us, and lately my wife and I have begun to fight. Finances have become a problem, and there's no time for anything. I don't think I've had a single minute to myself in six months. My wife and I haven't been out of the house on a weekend evening since our wedding." First, separate and identify each of the elements in the client's message. List them in outline fashion. Which do you think is most important? Now write the words you would say to partialize the complex message communicated by Mr. S. Discuss your rationale for the words you have chosen. How do you think Mr. S. might react to your response?

4. You are interviewing Mrs. F. During the conversation, Mrs. F. says, "I've had troubles since I moved into this community. The school system is insensitive to the Hispanic population. My kids have begun to disrespect me and berate their own heritage. The neighbors all are white and haven't even introduced themselves to us. My mother is seriously ill in Peru, but I don't dare leave the children here while I feel they're in danger." First, separate and identify each of the elements in the client's message. List them in outline fashion. Which do you think is most important? Now write the words you might say in partializing this message. Discuss your rationale for the words you have selected. How do you think Mrs. F. might react to your response?

GOING BEYOND WHAT IS SAID

Going beyond what is said (Hammond, Hepworth, & Smith, 1977, pp. 137–169) involves the worker extending somewhat the client's stated expression. Instead of reflecting what the client has overtly communicated, the worker uses her knowledge, experience, and intuition to add slightly to the feelings or meanings actually communicated by the other. Through a process called additive empathy, the worker takes a small step ahead of the client, often bringing into greater awareness or clarity information that the client already knows at some level. As Hammond, Hepworth, and Smith (1977, p. 137) suggest, the worker's responses "go beyond what the client has explicitly expressed to feelings and meanings only implied in the client's statements and, thus, somewhat below the surface of the client's awareness. Consequently, these . . . add implicit material that the counselor infers from the client's message."

Going beyond what is said sometimes involves combining what was expressed by the client verbally with what was hinted at nonverbally. However, in doing so the worker remains congruent with the client's general direction and perspective. Although departing somewhat from his actual statement, the worker continues to try to reflect the general frame of reference of the other. The worker is not attempting to initiate a new agenda. Rather, she is trying to build upon the client's own agenda.

For example, a client might say, "I've been depressed for months. I've been down in the dumps ever since my son died in that terrible motorcycle crash. I feel so ashamed. Just before he drove off that morning, I yelled at him for not picking up the dirty clothes in his room. Why did I have to say anything? My last memory is of me nagging at him." In going beyond what is said, the worker might say, in a very gentle manner, "You feel guilty about the last words you said to your son before he died—almost as if your words caused him to have the accident?"

Going beyond what is said is not psychoanalytic interpretation nor is it wild speculation. Rather, it involves putting into words those thoughts and feelings that a person whose experience you have begun to understand might think and feel but which have not yet been expressed verbally. For example, a twelve-year-old girl who was sexually molested by her mother's male friend says, "My mother loved him very much and now he's gone." A worker, in going beyond what is said, might say, "Do you sometimes feel that somehow it's your fault that he's gone?"

■ **Exercise 7-7: Going Beyond What Is Said**

For these exercises, assume that you are a social worker with a family and children's counseling center. Respond in the spaces provided by writing the words you would say in using the skill of going beyond what is said in each situation.

1. You are interviewing Mr. K., a recently divorced, fifty-five-year-old man. You are in the process of problem exploration when he says, "I guess I'm a real wimp! I want so bad for her to come back home. All I do is think of ways to get her back. I make these plans about how to contact her; how to persuade her to change her mind. I constantly wonder what she's doing and whether she ever thinks of me." Write the words you would say in going beyond what Mr. K. has said. After you have written your response, discuss your rationale for the words you have chosen. How do you think he might react to your response? Identify two other ways you might go beyond what he said.

2. You are in the midst of an outreach interview with Mrs. O., a seventy-seven-year-old widow who lives alone. Mrs. O. says, "Oh, I guess all children forget about their parents when they get old. They have so much to do, what with their work and their own children. They're busy. I know that. I should be grateful for what I do have." Write the words you would use in attempting to go beyond Mrs. O.'s statement. After you have written your response, discuss your rationale for the words

you have chosen. How do you think Mrs. O. might react to your response? Identify two alternative means for going beyond what she said.

3. You are interviewing the seven-member, blended S. family. During the course of the exploration, Mrs. S. says, "Things are so bad between my kids and his kids that I've begun to wonder whether it's worth trying to continue like this. Maybe my children and I should just leave. We made it on our own before, we can do it again." Write the words you would say in going beyond what Mrs. S. has said. Discuss your rationale for the words you have chosen. How do you think Mrs. S. might react to your response? Identify two additional ways in which you might go beyond what she said.

4. You are interviewing Mrs. F. At one point, she says, "Maybe it's not worth fighting this racist system. Maybe I should just accept things as they are. I'm just one person—just one woman—what can I do?" Write the words you might say in going beyond this message. Discuss your rationale for the words you have selected. How do you think Mrs. F. might react to your response? Now write two other ways in which you might go beyond Mrs. F.'s statement.

SUMMARY

During the exploration phase of social work practice, the worker encourages the client to share thoughts, feelings, and experiences regarding the problems that led to the contact. Through the process of exploration, the worker and the client gather information regarding the person, the problem, and the situation. This material is useful to both the worker and the client as they attempt to better understand the development and maintenance of the problem. When combined with the worker's professional knowledge and the client's input, the information leads the worker and client to an assessment and plan for work.

Several of the skills applicable to the beginning phase (e.g., seeking feedback) are also relevant to the process of exploration. In this chapter, several skills considered especially pertinent as the worker explores the thinking, feeling, and doing aspects of the person, problem, and situation were addressed, including: (1) probing, (2) seeking clarification, (3) reflecting content, (4) reflecting feeling, (5) reflecting complex communications, (6) partializing, and (7) going beyond what is said. The exploring skills are functional throughout the entire helping process. They are used again and again as the worker and client examine the complex interplay of human and environmental phenomena.

■ **Exercise 7-8: Summary**

Assume that you are a social worker with a human service agency offering a broad range of social services. You are actively exploring various aspects of the person-problem-situation. For each of the cases below, write the words you would use and describe the actions you might take in using the requested skills.

> CASE SITUATION: You are in the midst of the first interview with a teenage couple (a black male and white female) who have sought counseling in advance of their forthcoming marriage. She says, "I know there are going to be lots of difficulties and that's why we're

here. We don't want all the problems to get in the way of our feelings for each other."

1. Write the words you would say in reflecting the content of her statement.

2. Formulate an exploratory probe to follow her statement.

3. Write the words you would say in seeking clarification of her expression.

Following your response, she says, "One of the biggest problems has to do with my parents. My mom is fit to be tied and my dad is even worse. He's ready to kill Johnnie and he doesn't even know him. I'm afraid they won't even come to the wedding. That would really hurt."

4. Write the words you would say in reflecting the complex communication contained in her message.

5. Demonstrate how you would use the skill of going beyond what is said in response to her expression.

CASE SITUATION: You are interviewing a family of seven (two parents and five children, ranging in age from one to seven) who have been sleeping in their dilapidated Chevy out in a rest area on the interstate highway. En route to another part of the country where they hoped to find work, they are out of money and food and nearly out of gas. A policeman referred them to the agency.

During the interview, Mrs. Z. says, "We don't want charity—just enough money and food to make it there."

6. Write the words you would say in seeking clarification following her statement.

7. Write three exploratory probes that might yield useful information in your effort to understand and help the family.

Following one of your probes, Mrs. Z. says, "The baby hasn't been eating well, she's sleeping an awful lot and has a fever. Yesterday she vomited three times."

8. Write how you would seek clarification following her statement.

9. Then write the words you would say in asking three additional exploratory probes concerning the baby's health.

CASE SITUATION: You are interviewing for the first time a man, Mr. T., who has been accused of molesting the thirteen-year-old daughter of his woman friend. Mr. T. is required to receive counseling in order to stay out of jail while the judge considers whether to proceed with felony charges. He had been living with the girl's mother but has been required to leave the house during this period. During the interview, Mr. T. says, "I don't know why she said that I did those things. It really hurts me. I've been good to her and her mother. She's just lying and I don't know why. Maybe she's jealous."

10. First, write the words you would say in seeking clarification concerning his message.

11. Write three exploratory probes that might follow his statement.

12. Reflect the content of his statement.

13. Reflect the complex communication contained in his message.

14. Demonstrate how you might use the skill of reflecting feeling in response to his statement.

15. Write three ways in which you might go beyond the words he has said.

CASE SITUATION: You are serving a child protection function during an initial interview with Mrs. D. Recently, your agency received a telephone call in which the caller alleged that Mr. and Mrs. D. have neglected and abused their children (ages one and three). According to the caller, the mother sleeps while the children play in a filthy yard (which contains animal waste, junk, and potentially dangerous materials—glass, sharp metal objects, etc.). Also, the caller reported that Mr. D. drinks heavily and beats both mother and children.

Mrs. D. has permitted you to enter the house, and the two of you have begun to talk. Mrs. D. says, "I know who made the complaint. It's that nosy neighbor from down the street. She's always poking into things that are none of her business."

16. Which of the exploring skills would you use in responding to Mrs. D.'s message? Discuss the rationale for your choice. Write the words you would say in using that skill.

17. Write five exploratory probes you would want to ask at some point during the interview.

■ Exercise 7-9: Supplement

Now that you have had some beginning practice in using the exploring skills, it is time to attempt an interview. Recruit a colleague from the school of social work. Inform her that you are practicing some social work skills and would like her to assume the role of client while you practice the role of social worker. A classmate in this course or a student who has already completed it might be receptive to your request. Inform her that you would appreciate a few hours of her time over the course of the next several weeks. Indicate that she would be expected to serve in the role of "client" and would be asked to behave "as if" she were voluntarily seeking help from a social worker concerning some aspect of herself or her situation. Tell her that she would be expected to identify at least one problem or concern for exploration. However, be sure to indicate that you will only meet together a few times. She should understand that you will probably not be of any actual help with the concerns, except to the extent that talking about them might be beneficial.

You might mention, however, that it is often professionally useful for social work students to take the client role. By assuming the role of clients, social workers may become more sensitive to the experience of seeking help—it is not always easy to ask for and receive assistance. Being a client can also significantly heighten the worker's awareness of what she might do or not do in her own social work practice. It often leads to greater understanding of how to be an effective social worker.

Inform your colleague that the meetings will be audiotaped or videotaped and that you will prepare a written recording based upon the interviews for your social work instructor's review. Indicate that you might discuss the interviews with your social work instructor but that you will not reveal her identity without her permission. Mention that, as the client, she may read your written records when they are completed, if she wants. Assure your colleague that in your notes about the interview, her identity will be disguised in order to protect her privacy. Also, ask her to use only her first name or a nickname while she is being taped during the interviews. Inform her also that she will not have to discuss any aspect of her life that she prefers to keep to herself. If you were to address a topic that she does not want to talk about, she may simply say, "I prefer not to talk about this." Notify her that this is an entirely voluntary exercise. It is perfectly all right to decline. Finally, advise her that you are still learning about social work and have not perfected the social work skills. You will probably make mistakes. Therefore, she should realize that you may not *really* be of help to her. The primary purpose of the exercise is to practice your skills.

Request that the problem or concern she identifies as the focus of the meetings be a genuine one for which she might conceivably seek service from a social worker. However, ask her to make sure it is one that is reasonably under control—one that she has addressed before and has found to be manageable. The problem should not reflect an immediate crisis situation nor should it be one with the potential to overwhelm her coping mechanisms. Students who are dealing with such pressing concerns would be wise to avoid using them as the focus for these exercises or to decline participation in the exercise altogether. After all, you are practicing skills here, not actually providing social work services.

If your colleague understands what is requested of her and she consents, arrange for a time and place during the next week to meet *privately* for approximately thirty minutes. Inform her that you will assume the role of social worker during that period. Remind her that she will be asked to identify a problem or concern and that she should assume the role of client from the moment you come together at the time of the scheduled meeting.

At the time of the interview and with her consent, tape record the interview. The overall purpose of the interview should be the exploration of your colleague's problem or concern as well as those aspects of the person and situation that may have relevance to the identified problem. Limit the interview to the exploration phase only. Do not attempt to assess, contract, or in any way try to work toward change or resolution of the problem. At the conclusion of the meeting, arrange for a second thirty-minute meeting in approximately one week.

1. At the conclusion of the interview, ask your partner for feedback concerning her thoughts and feelings about the experience. Request completely candid reactions to the following questions: (a) Did she feel comfortable and safe with you? Did she trust you? (b) Did she feel that you were sincerely interested in her and in what she had to say? (c) Did she feel that you understood what she was trying to communicate? If not, explore with her what led her to believe that you did not understand? (d) Did she enjoy the experience? (e) Does she have any suggestions for you concerning how the interview could have been better or more satisfying for her? Summarize your partner's feedback in the space below.

2. In the space below, note your own reaction to the conversation. How did you feel about the interview? What did you like and what did you dislike about it? What would you do differently if you were to have a chance to conduct the interview again?

3. Play the audio or videotape. In a notebook designated for use in this course, prepare a transcript so that it accurately reflects what was said by whom. As part of the transcript, identify where you used specific skills. For example, if you responded to a statement of your partner by asking a question concerning her current situation, identify that response as a probe. If you requested further information about a statement she has made, indicate that as seeking clarification.

   The format might look something like this:

   CLIENT: I'm just so tired all the time.

   WORKER: You're simply exhausted [reflecting feeling].

   CLIENT: Yes. I can barely get to class each day.

   WORKER: When did you first begin to feel this way? [probing—the problem's past and its development].

4. Using the exploration matrix reproduced on page 194, indicate the degree to which you have explored the various dimensions of the person-problem-situation. Use approximate percentages to reflect the extent of exploration within each category. For example, if you have fully discussed the problem as it exists at the present time, write 100 percent in that box. If you have not talked at all about the person as she views herself in the future, place 0 percent in that category.

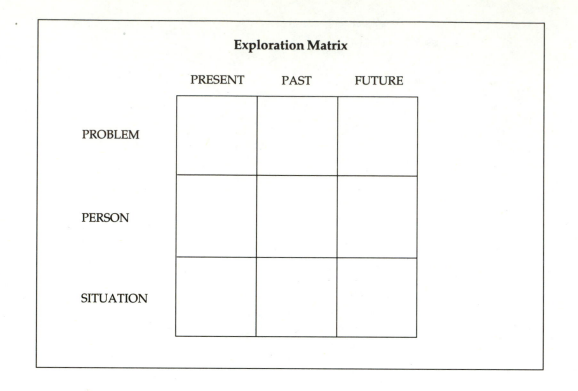

In the space below, write three probes for each matrix category needing further exploration.

5. Based upon your performance in the interview, use the rating scales below (where 0 = no proficiency and 10 = complete proficiency) to assess your current level of proficiency in the exploring skills.

Probing

```
|__|____|____|____|____|____|____|____|____|____|
0   1    2    3    4    5    6    7    8    9    10
```

Seeking Clarification

```
|__|____|____|____|____|____|____|____|____|____|
0   1    2    3    4    5    6    7    8    9    10
```

Reflecting Content

```
|__|____|____|____|____|____|____|____|____|____|
0   1    2    3    4    5    6    7    8    9    10
```

Reflecting Feeling

```
|__|____|____|____|____|____|____|____|____|____|
0   1    2    3    4    5    6    7    8    9    10
```

Reflecting Complex Communications

```
|__|____|____|____|____|____|____|____|____|____|
0   1    2    3    4    5    6    7    8    9    10
```

Partializing

```
|__|____|____|____|____|____|____|____|____|____|
0   1    2    3    4    5    6    7    8    9    10
```

Going Beyond What Is Said

```
|__|____|____|____|____|____|____|____|____|____|
0   1    2    3    4    5    6    7    8    9    10
```

6. Finally, review your ratings to identify those exploring skills in which you remain less proficient (e.g., a score of 7 or less). Then, in the space below, outline the steps you might take to improve your skill in those areas.

ASSESSING

Assessment is a fundamental element in all social work practice (Richmond, 1944; Ripple, 1955; Perlman, 1957, pp. 164–203; and Compton & Galaway, 1989, pp. 443–454). When exploration of the person-problem-situation has progressed well, the worker and the client have a great deal of information available to them. They can then attempt to understand how the person and situation influence the problem and vice versa. The understanding gained through assessment provides the worker and client with a direction in which to proceed. The assessment represents the foundation on which a contract for work is negotiated.

Two primary social work skills are involved in the assessment process: (1) organizing descriptive information and (2) formulating a tentative assessment.

Although social work assessment is an ongoing process rather than a finished product, it does typically result in a written recording. However, the assessment frequently changes, sometimes dramatically, during the course of work with a client system. Also, it is a professional as opposed to a technical activity. As such, social work assessments are not undertaken in exactly the same way with all clients. Rather, the nature of the assessment varies with the unique characteristics of the person system, the problem system, and the situation system, as well as with the worker and agency systems. For example, a social worker serving in a crisis intervention and suicide prevention program conducts a significantly different assessment than a worker who performs hospital discharge planning for elderly patients seeking quality nursing care. A worker who meets with whole families formulates assessments differing from those of a worker who serves individual clients. A worker who specializes in helping children conducts assessments that vary substantially from a worker who serves adults. Similarly, a worker who approaches practice from a psychodynamic perspective is likely to undertake an assessment process considerably different from that of a task-centered social worker. However, because most professional social workers adhere to certain common conceptual premises and practice principles, there are similarities as well as differences in the nature of all social work assessment processes.

Through assessment, the worker, in conjunction with the client, comes to a tentative understanding of the elements, subsystems, factors, and forces within the person-situation system that affect and maintain the problems of concern. He determines the primary client system and other persons who may need to be contacted. He begins to identify potential targets for change (i.e., those aspects that, if altered, might alleviate the problem). He predicts probable consequences if things do not change, assesses risk, and determines the urgency with which intervention must be undertaken. He identifies potential resources, means, and avenues for change as well as probable obstacles to change. In addition, he identifies intervention modalities, strategies, tasks, activities, and techniques that might be applicable to a resolution of the problems of concern. He develops a means for evaluation and identifies a time frame for work.

Assessing is a process of many dimensions and many purposes. In general, it leads the worker and client to a better understanding of the reasons or causes for the problem and the factors that may aid or hinder its resolution.

There are many ways to structure a social work assessment and record the results. The Description, Assessment, and Contract (DAC) presented in Figure 8-1 is one of many that social workers may consider.

F I G U R E 8-1
Description, Assessment, and Contract (DAC)

I. Description
   A. Client Identification Information
   B. Description of Person System, Family/Household/Primary Social System, and Ecological System
      1. Person System
      2. Family/Household/Primary Social System
      3. Ecological System
   C. Presenting Problems and Goals
   D. Strengths and Resources
   E. Referral Source and Process; Collateral Information
   F. Social History
      1. Developmental
      2. Interpersonal/Familial/Cultural
      3. Instances of Trauma, Violence, Suicidal Attempts, Victimization, Oppression, or Discrimination
      4. Sexual
      5. Alcohol and/or Drug Use

As the title suggests, the DAC includes three major parts. First, the information gained through the exploration process is organized into a description. Second, the worker's thoughts concerning the case are formulated into a tentative assessment. Third, the contract for work as negotiated between the worker and client is summarized.

This chapter addresses the description and assessment parts of the DAC. Chapter Nine explores the contracting portion.

Description provides a means for organizing a great deal of information about a client, her situation, and the problems of concern. Assessment provides a means by which the worker's synthesis and analysis of the descriptive data may be structured. At first glance, the DAC may appear exhaustingly inclusive. Although it *does* cover a great many areas, several of these may not be applicable for work with all clients or all problems. Also, the DAC may be readily adapted to fit the particular needs and functions of many contemporary social work settings. Additionally, there are numerous alternate schemes available to social workers. Ultimately, the worker must determine the utility of any assessment format for his particular circumstances.

ORGANIZING DESCRIPTIVE INFORMATION

Most social work interviews do not occur in so logical or coherent a fashion that a transcript or process recording of the interaction between worker and client would represent a cogent description of the available information. Therefore, the first step in the assessment process is to organize the information gained through exploration into some sensible structure to allow for efficient retrieval and examination. Usually, the worker arranges the information in accordance with certain categories or dimensions that are considered theoretically or pragmatically significant.

Regardless of the structural format used in presenting and recording information, the worker should clearly distinguish between fact and opinion and between reported or observed information and that which is the result of speculation or hypothesis. Organizing descriptive information allows the worker to present in a coherent manner that which is reported to or personally observed by him. This kind of data may be organized within the description part of the DAC in accordance with the following guidelines.

I. Description
   A. Client Identification Information
      In this section, the social worker provides information that helps to identify the client and other relevant members of the person and situation systems. Such data as names, ages, home addresses, places of work, telephone numbers, and dates of interview may be included.
   B. Description of Person System, Family/Household/Primary Social System, and Ecological System
      1. Person System
         In this section, information that helps the worker to further describe the prospective or identified client is presented. Information such as height and weight, race and ethnicity, physical appearance, striking or characteristic features, speech patterns, and clothing may be included.
      2. Family/Household/Primary Social System
         In this section, description of the client's family, household or primary social system is provided. If not included elsewhere,

names and ages of persons involved are presented. Among the more useful tools for quickly organizing this data are the family genogram and the household eco-map. One or both of these may be entered here.

3. Ecological System

In this section, a description of the ecological system within which the identified client functions is presented. Systems such as school, work, medical, recreational, religious, neighborhood, and friendship affiliations are identified. A useful tool for organizing and presenting this information is the eco-map. It may be included within this section.

C. Presenting Problems and Goals

In this section, the worker describes the client's view of the problems and goals. Here the worker describes the origin and development of the concerns and summarizes the reasons that social work services are sought or required at this time. It is important that the worker also record the desired outcome of the social work service as envisioned by the client.

D. Strengths and Resources

In this section, the worker includes information concerning the strengths and resources available within the client or situation systems. The kind of resources indicated may range from a concerned relative or an insurance policy to good physical health. The worker identifies strengths and resources in order to provide a balanced picture—one that is not solely characterized by problems, concerns, and deficiencies. In addition, the strengths and resources will become useful during the planning and intervention phases of work.

E. Referral Source and Process; Collateral Information

This section is typically used to summarize the information concerning the source of the referral (who suggested or required that the identified client make contact with the worker) and the process by which the referral occurred. Any information provided by sources other than the identified client or the client system (e.g., family member or a close friend) may be presented here.

F. Social History

This section includes summary information about the identified client's social history. Frequently, this section contains some of the following subsections:

1. Developmental
2. Interpersonal/Familial/Cultural
3. Instances of Trauma, Violence, Suicidal Attempts, Victimization, Oppression, or Discrimination
4. Sexual
5. Alcohol and/or Drug Use

6. Medical/Physical
7. Legal
8. Educational
9 Employment (including military)
10. Recreational
11. Religious/Spiritual
12. Prior Psychological or Social Service
13. Other

The following illustrates how a social worker might organize and record information about the case of Mrs. Lynn Chase into the description part of the DAC.

I. Description
  A. Client Identification Information
    Date of Interview: 6-14-89 and 6-20-89
    Persons Interviewed: Lynn B. Chase, white, female, thirty-four years old
    Residence: 1212 Clearview Drive, City
    Home phone: 223-1234
    Employment: Assembler at Fox Manufacturing Co., phone 567-5678
    Household Composition:
      Richard S. Chase, thirty-five years old, husband, carpenter with Crass Construction Co., phone 789-7890
      Robert L. Chase, twelve years old, son, sixth-grade student at Hope Middle School
    Referral Source: Sandra Fowles (former client of this agency)
  B. Description of Person System, Family/Household/Primary Social System, and Ecological System
    1. Person System
      Mrs. Chase (prefers to be addressed as "Mrs.") is of Irish-American heritage. She was raised as a Roman Catholic. Her maiden name was Shaughnessy. She is approximately five feet six inches tall and of medium build. On this date, she is attired in slacks and blouse. Her facial expression reflects tension, worry, and perhaps sadness. She appears tired. She walks slowly and sits down with a sigh. She speaks in an accent common to this area—although in a slow fashion. She is articulate and deliberate in her statements. Her speech is interrupted with thoughtful pauses and she sighs occasionally while talking.
    2. Family/Household/Primary Social System
      The household of the Chase family is composed of Lynn, Richard, Robert, and a mongrel dog, "Sly." Richard and Lynn Chase were married thirteen years ago in March 1976. Lynn became pregnant with Robert a few months after marriage. The

couple had met at a party hosted by mutual friends. They dated for two years before marrying. Mrs. Chase describes the marriage as a good one. "We've always been one another's best friend."

Mrs. Chase describes their family life as busy. During the week, both parents are employed from 8:00 A.M. to 5:00 P.M.. One parent, usually Mrs. Chase, drops Robert at his school en route to work. After school, Robert takes the bus home, arriving at about 3:45 P.M. The parents arrive home at about 5:45 P.M. Mrs. Chase indicates that Robert and his father have a very positive relationship. They go to sporting events together and both enjoy fishing. Robert has been on a Little League baseball team and his dad went to every game.

Mrs. Chase comes from a family of five. [Refer also to Figure 2-1, page 13, in Chapter Two]. Her mother and father married while in their late teens. Her mother became pregnant right away. Mrs. Chase is the eldest sibling. She has a brother who is thirty-three years old and a sister who is twenty-eight. Her parents are alive and remain married. Mrs. Chase reports that during her childhood her father was a workaholic ("still is") who was rarely home. She describes her mother as an "unstable, angry, and critical woman who never praised me for anything and always put me down." Mrs. Chase says that she "raised her younger sister" because, at that time, her mother was drinking all the time. Mrs. Chase says that her mother has refrained from drinking alcohol for the past three years and now goes to Alcoholics Anonymous meetings. She describes the relationship between her mother and father as strained. "They didn't divorce because of us (the children) and because they're Catholic." Mrs. Chase says that her mother disapproved of her marriage to Richard (because he had been married once before) and wouldn't attend the wedding. She says that her mother continues to berate Richard and "frequently criticizes the way I am raising Robert."

Mrs. Chase reports that she rarely sees her mother, who lives out of state, but she does visit with her sister about once a month. Her sister frequently needs emotional support, advice, and sometimes requires financial assistance. Mrs. Chase says that her sister had formerly abused alcohol and drugs, but Mrs. Chase thinks that the problem is now under control.

Mrs. Chase says that her husband's family was "even more messed up than mine—if that's possible." She indicates that Richard also came from a family of five. She reports that his father abandoned the family when Richard was nine and his sisters were ten and seven. Mrs. Chase says that Richard's father had a serious drinking problem and that Richard remembers his father beating his mother and him too. Mrs. Chase says that Richard grew up in very destitute circumstances and learned to value money. She reports that he closely watches how the family's money is spent.

Mrs. Chase says that the family members are in good physical health. They have not had any major medical problems. Robert broke his collarbone a few years ago but it has since healed properly. Richard's health is quite good. He doesn't exercise but his work is physically challenging. Mrs. Chase reports that about eight years ago she had an enlarged cyst removed from her uterus. Since that time, she has been unable to become pregnant. She and her husband had hoped to have at least one more child but have now concluded that it is not going to happen.

3. Ecological System

The Chase family is involved with several other social systems. [See Figure 2-2, page 18, in Chapter Two.] Mrs. Chase reports that the family attends the First Methodist Church regularly, although not every week. She says that she helps out occasionally with bake sales and the like. Robert goes to Sunday school. Richard is not really involved in many social activities. Mrs. Chase says that he doesn't really have close friends. "Robert and I are his friends." He attends Robert's baseball games and goes fishing with him. Most of the time, Richard works on the house or in the yard. He has a workshop in the basement and constructs furniture for the home.

Mrs. Chase reports that Robert has generally been a good student at his school. Teachers report that he is somewhat shy. When called upon, he speaks in a quiet and hesitant voice. But, they say, he usually has thoughtful answers to questions. Mrs. Chase indicates that Robert is a good baseball player on the Little League team. He has played in every game and the coach thinks highly of him. He has two or three close friends in the neighborhood.

Mrs. Chase reports that the family lives in a middle-class neighborhood. Racially, it is minimally integrated. Crime is reported to be low and the neighbors friendly. Homeowners tend to maintain their property carefully. The Chases are friendly with several families in the neighborhood and perhaps once every two or three weeks will get together for dinner or a cookout with them.

Mrs. Chase reports that her job is "okay". She says that her husband truly loves his work. "Being a carpenter is what he's made for."

C. Presenting Problems and Goals

Mrs. Chase says that she has been concerned lately because she and her son have been getting into arguments "all the time." She doesn't know what's causing the trouble, but she finds herself becoming critical and angry toward him at the slightest provocation. She doesn't believe that Robert is misbehaving. She thinks that it's really her own problem. She noticed that about six months ago she began to become more irritable with Robert and, to some extent, with Richard as well. She reports that she doesn't sleep as well as she once did and has lost about ten pounds. She says that she took up smoking again after quitting some five years ago and has begun to have frequent headaches. Mrs. Chase believes that the problem began about the time that she took the job at Fox Manufacturing. Prior to that, she had remained at home to care for Robert and the household.

Mrs. Chase hopes that as a result of services provided, she will feel less angry and irritable, sleep better, stop smoking, and have fewer arguments with her son and husband.

D. Strengths and Resources

Mrs. Chase acknowledges that she has an above-average intellect and a capacity to consider thoughtfully various aspects and dimensions of issues and problems. She reports that she is extremely responsible (she says, "At times, too much so.") and dependable in fulfilling her various roles. Mrs. Chase says that the family has sufficient financial resources. They live in a middle-class neighborhood and have a nice home. She indicates that her job is secure. She feels that the employer highly values her work and colleagues enjoy her company. Mrs. Chase reports that she has friends who provide her with support and understanding, although most of the time she is the one who provides support to them. She feels loved by her husband and indicates that both her husband and son would be willing to do anything for her.

Mrs. Chase reports that although in the past she has found great pleasure in gardening, during the last year or so she has discontinued that activity. However, she believes that she could probably regain a sense of satisfaction were she to resume gardening.

E. Referral Source and Process; Collateral Information

Mrs. Chase was referred to this agency by her friend and neighbor, Sandra Fowles. Ms. Fowles is a former client of this agency. In making the referral, she indicated that Mrs. Chase is "an incredibly kind and thoughtful woman who would give you the shirt off her back. She may be too kind for her own good." Ms. Fowles contacted the agency on behalf of Mrs. Chase and asked that an appointment be scheduled for her.

F. Social History

Mrs. Chase reports that her childhood development was not a happy one. She remembers feeling "different" from other children. She says she was shy, often afraid, and easily intimidated by other children. She frequently felt guilty and ashamed when parents or teachers criticized or corrected her. She states that she always tried to be "good" and, for the most part—at least until her teenage years—she was. She received excellent grades in school, although she was sometimes taunted by other children who called her the "teacher's pet." She was slightly overweight during her childhood years and always thought of herself as "fat." She had only a few friends during her younger years. She recalls one or two close friends and describes them as "shy and unattractive too." She remembers several occasions when other children she had hoped would become friends rejected her. She remembers feeling sad and depressed on many occasions throughout her childhood.

She described an incident that occurred when she was about twelve years old. A boy that she liked said she was "ugly" in front of a group of her peers. She was humiliated and "stayed at home and cried for days." She also recalled a time when she was about fourteen or fifteen. She had begun to explore her body and experimented with masturbation. She found it pleasurable but believed that such activity was sinful. She discussed it with a priest during a regular confession. Mrs. Chase says that the priest became very angry at her and told her in a forceful way to "stop abusing herself in that disgusting way." She felt horribly guilty and ashamed. The experience was a major reason that she later left the Catholic church.

Mrs. Chase reports that she did not date until her senior year in high school when she went out with one boy a few times. It was in this relationship that she "lost her virginity." She met her future husband about two years after graduation from high school.

Mrs. Chase reports that she has never been the victim of rape or any other violent crime. However, she does recall several occasions when a male relative (maternal uncle) attempted to kiss her and fondle her breasts. Each time, she pushed him away but remembers feeling disgusted and dirty. She was approximately twelve or thirteen years old at the time and never told anyone about what had happened.

Mrs. Chase states that she does not now have an alcohol or drug use problem but does remember drinking heavily as an eighteen year old. After graduation from high school, she ran around with a crowd that "partied a lot," and she drank a lot at that time. She says that she sometimes drank in order to "belong" and feel comfortable in sexual relations with boys.

Mrs. Chase reports that she has not had any major medical or physical problems other than the cyst mentioned above. She says that she got control of her weight problem during the early years of her marriage. She went to Weight Watchers and has maintained her appropriate weight since that time. She indicates that she occasionally feels extremely fatigued, doesn't sleep very well, and has periodic headaches. She has not talked with a physician concerning these problems.

Mrs. Chase has a high school education and has taken approximately two years of college courses. Recently, she discontinued an evening course in order to "be at home more."

Mrs. Chase became inactive in the Catholic church at the age of eighteen when she graduated from high school. She did not attend any church until the birth of her child. She and her husband then decided that they wanted their children to be brought up with some religious involvement. They therefore joined the Methodist church where they continue as members.

Mrs. Chase has not sought or received social or psychological services before. She does report that her mother has been in "therapy" for approximately four years.

■ **Exercise 8-1: Organizing Descriptive Information**

For this exercise, assume that *you* are your own client. In your course notebook, draft the description section of a written record as if you had, as a social worker, learned what you know about yourself as a person. Identify one or two problems or issues for which you might conceivably consult a helping professional. As do all human beings, social workers also confront obstacles, difficulties, and dilemmas as they proceed through life—it's inevitable. Therefore, build upon the self-awareness exercises that you undertook in Chapter Two by organizing information about yourself and your situation into a descriptive record. Use the DAC format to prepare the description portion of your own case record.

FORMULATING A TENTATIVE ASSESSMENT

When the available information has been described within the structure of an organizing framework, the worker then begins to formulate a tentative assessment through analysis and synthesis—the primary cognitive skills involved in assessment. Analysis involves examining various pieces of information from the person-problem-situation in fine detail. For example, consider the case of a thirty-year-old woman who "feels anxious in the presence of men." Commonly, a worker would analyze how the different dimensions of anxiety interact. What does the client think, feel, sense, imagine, and do when she experiences anxiety?

A worker might piece together the precise sequence of events leading up to and following the feelings of anxiety. In this instance, analysis might reveal that the anxious feelings usually occur in the presence of men who are of her own age or older, men who are confident and appear successful, and men who are eligible for romantic consideration. Further analysis might uncover that the client does not feel anxious when she interacts with men in business or professional contexts, men who are married or men who are gay, men who are much younger, or men who are less successful than she is. The worker may also discover that the client, when she first notices the early signs of anxiety, immediately begins to say to herself such things as, "I must not become anxious right now; if I become anxious, I will not say what I want to say and I will embarrass myself."

Analysis leads the worker to pinpoint crucial elements from among the various pieces of information. These become cornerstones in the formulation of a tentative assessment.

Synthesis builds upon what is gained from analysis. It involves placing significant pieces of information into a coherent whole by relating them to one another and to elements of the worker's theory, knowledge, and experience base. For example, a worker may take the client's problem of anxiety in the presence of the other gender and understand it in relation to his own experience growing up without sisters and attending boys-only grammar and high schools and later a men's college. These associations reflect the synthetic process of placing various data together with other bits of information. Sometimes, the synthesis is atheoretical but usually the worker applies elements of theory in selecting which pieces of information to place with others and in understanding their relationship as part of a unifying theme.

There are dozens of theoretical perspectives that social workers may find useful. For example, social learning theory may lead the worker to select prior family and educational experiences for consideration in relation to the presenting concern. Systems and ecological theories may lead a worker to consider how change or stress in one subsystem affects other subsystems. Ego-psychology might enable the worker to consider the defense mechanism of repression when attempting to understand certain individual human behavior (e.g., a client's blocked memory in response to a question about whether she has ever been raped, sexually molested, or physically abused). Fundamental concepts within role theory—role ambiguity, role change, and role conflict—may also be considered in relation to signs of frustration and stress. Crisis theory may help during tragic circumstances and times of sudden change. Knowledge of family systems theory may enable a worker to ponder the possible communication and interpersonal value or function of a particular behavior pattern. Understanding of individual, family, and organizational development theories may allow a worker to identify tasks necessary for further growth. A plethora of useful theories may inform the worker as he seeks to understand and synthesize significant information about the person-problem-situation.

In the early stages of work with a client system, the analysis and synthesis processes of assessment *must* be considered tentative and speculative, because the worker usually does not have conclusive support or confirmation for his ideas. In fact, analysis and synthesis typically yield a series of hypotheses or questions that guide the worker in collecting additional information. The worker must resist the temptation to conclude that he has *the* key to understanding and explaining the person-problem-situation. In addition to important hypotheses and questions, analysis and synthesis usually leads the worker to identify critical events and significant themes, patterns, and issues for further consideration.

As he does with descriptive data, the worker must organize the results of his analysis and synthesis into some coherent structure. The particular format used varies from agency to agency, program to program, and even worker to worker. However, all social work assessment schemes refer in one way or another to various theoretical dimensions and include consideration of the person, problem, and situation. The organizing structure may be derived from a single theoretical perspective or, eclectically, from several.

Guidelines for using the assessment part of the DAC to organize social work assessments are presented below. When prepared in written form, the assessment follows the description portion of the Description, Assessment, and Contract.

II. Tentative Assessment
   A. Person
      1. Identity and Structure
         Within this dimension, the worker considers the problem as it relates to the person's identity and self-structure. He determines the client's view of herself, the strength of her self-concept, and the degree of self-esteem. He notes her primary role identities and considers the extent of congruence among them. He observes her sociocultural affiliations and personal value systems. He determines the relative flexibility or rigidity of her personal boundaries. He notes whether she tends to refer to inner or outer resources when decision making.

         The worker recognizes the nature of the person's defensive and coping processes and assesses their relative strength and functionality. He determines the strength of the client's capacities for coping with stress and change, her ability to manage desires and impulses, and her vulnerability to personality decompensation. He identifies her personal, interpersonal, and life-style characteristics and determines how adaptive and congruent they are in relation to the identified problem.
      2. Mood and Emotion
         In this section, the worker assesses the person's mood and emotional state in relation to the identified concerns. He identifies feelings that are apparent and questions whether there might be other emotions that are hidden. He also considers the relative

conguence between verbal and nonverbal expressions of emotion.

3. Life-Cycle Development

Here the worker considers the problem in terms of the person's phase of life-cycle development. He identifies the developmental tasks and issues with which she may now or may soon be dealing and assesses the congruence between chronological and developmental age.

4. Competence

In this section, the worker considers the problem in relation to the person's relative level of competence to fulfill age- and situation-appropriate roles and tasks. He assesses whether the person is currently capable of caring for herself and determines the degree to which she can participate in the helping process.

5. Risk

Here the worker determines the relative degree of risk to the person's life and well-being as well as the potential danger to other people. He assesses the risk of suicide, homicide, violence, abuse, and neglect as it relates to the particular circumstances of the case.

B. Family/Household/Primary Social Systems

1. Identity and Structure

In this section, the worker considers the problem in relation to the system's identity and structure. He identifies the system's ethnic, religious, and cultural traditions. He considers its history and its expectation for the future. He determines the degree of energy, cohesion, and adaptability of the systems and recognizes the needs and aspirations of its members. He characterizes the operating procedures, the distribution of power and the availability of resources, the assignment of roles, the boundaries between members and subsystems, and the processes of decision making.

The worker also assesses the problem in relation to the nature and extent of communication and interaction among members of the system. He determines the form of communication and its relative degree of simplicity and directness.

2. Mood and Emotion

Here the worker considers the problem in relation to the dominant emotional climate within the system. He identifies feelings that are disguised or expressed indirectly and assesses the degree of affection and support that members give and receive from one another.

3. Life-Cycle Development

In this section, the worker classifies the system in terms of its life-cycle phase. He views the problem in relation to the issues that might apply to a system in this phase and points out the developmental tasks that may need to be undertaken.

    C. Ecology/Environment

        1. Resources

In this section, the worker assesses the problem in relation to the extent and sufficiency of resources within the ecological environment. He determines the relative availability of basic resources such as money, shelter, food, clothing, and social and intellectual stimulation. He characterizes the sociopolitical and economic environment. He highlights potential resources and opportunities and identifies deficiencies and obstacles within the ecology.

        2. Sociocultural

Here the worker considers the problem within the context of the sociocultural values and traditions of the ecological environment. He determines their relationship to the identified concerns and identifies how they might be utilized in meeting needs and addressing problems.

    D. Summary Assessment

In this section, the worker provides a narrative summary of the assessment of the problem in relation to theoretical dimensions within the person, primary, and ecology systems. He considers the legal and ethical implications of the case. He assesses the effects of the problem upon the person and situation and speculates upon the possible functions the problem may serve for both systems. He also makes projections concerning the potential benefits as well as the risks that might result from problem resolution.

The Chase case can provide an example of a tentative assessment organized as part of the DAC.

  II. Tentative Assessment

    A. Person

        1. Identity and Structure

Mrs. Chase views herself primarily as wife and mother. She also appears to assume the role of "big sister" with her siblings. She seems open to input from others, including this worker, and has a well-established sense of personal identity in relation to family roles. She seems less clear and secure, however, when it comes to roles outside the family system. In these other areas, she appears more uncertain and less inner directed.

Questions: Who is Lynn Chase when she is not wife, mother, daughter, or sibling? What are her personal life goals apart from raising a family? How does she see herself as an individual person? What does she see as her major personality characteristics?

Mrs. Chase reflects a coherent and integrated personality. Her life-style has been stable and congruent. She appears to feel a strong sense of obligation and responsibility toward others, especially her son and husband. Her thinking capacities are well developed. However, she appears less comfortable when it comes to permitting herself time for free and spontaneous play or recreation. In the past, she has enjoyed gardening, a productive avocation, but she seems reluctant to allow herself time for "unproductive" leisure and relaxation. She may have a tendency to assume disproportionately high levels of personal responsibility. As a result, guilty feelings are common.

Questions: How similar is Mrs. Chase to her father in terms of a workaholic, or compulsive, approach to life? How critical is she of herself? What happens when Mrs. Chase takes time for herself alone? Does she begin to feel anxious or uncomfortable without a specific worthwhile and "productive" goal?

Mrs. Chase has well-developed coping skills and defense mechanisms that have served her well over the years. Presently, however, she experiences sleep loss, headaches, heightened anger and irritability, and frequent arguments with her son and, to a lesser degree, her husband. These are indications that her coping capacities are diminishing somewhat. The patterns are also somewhat reminiscent of Mrs. Chase's description of her own mother, whom she described as "unstable, angry, and critical." Mrs. Chase indicates that the problems seemed to occur at a time when she went to work outside the home. This may be related to the fact that she views her father as "a workaholic who was never at home."

Questions: Does Mrs. Chase feel ambivalent—perhaps guilty—about working outside the home and being less available to her son and husband? Does she have feelings of anger of which she is unaware or which she does not directly express? If so, at whom or what is she angry? What does she think about when she lies awake at night?

2. Mood and Emotion

    Mrs. Chase looks sad. She may be depressed. There are also signs of some anxiety or stress. Over the past several months, she has experienced frequent feelings of anger and irritation. She does not recall having such feelings to this degree of intensity or frequency at any previous time in her life.

    Questions: Is she angry that she's working outside the home? Disappointed or sad that her son is growing up? Resentful that her husband is happy in his work? Does anger associated with mother and father remain unexpressed? Is there any indication that depression may run in the family? Is she sad that she cannot have another child? Is she ambivalent and anxious about her employment? Might there be stress as a result of role strain and conflict?

3. Life-Cycle Development

At thirty-four, Mrs. Chase may be considered to be in the middle of the adulthood phase of the human life cycle. She has expended much energy over the past twelve or thirteen years in child rearing and homemaking activities. Relatively recently, she took a job outside the family home. At this point, it is not certain that this work is or will be as satisfying to her as child rearing and homemaking have been. There may be role strain or conflict between the family and work roles. She and her husband had wanted more children; however, her medical condition (the cyst) appears to prevent that from happening. Questions: What led her to seek employment outside the home? How well does she really like the work? Is it congruent with her long-term, personal life goals? What thoughts and feelings does she have about her twelve-year-old son in relation to her employment? How does her husband feel about her working? Has she successfully resolved the disappointment concerning her inability to have more children?

4. Competence

Mrs. Chase reflects a high level of competence. She has coped well with life transitions and problems. In spite of the current concerns, she continues to function well in several important social roles.

5. Risk

Although reporting feelings of depression, Mrs. Chase does not currently represent a danger to herself or others. In response to a question concerning suicidal thoughts and actions, she indicated that she has never taken any self-destructive action and does not have suicidal thoughts. Similarly, she reported that she has never experienced thoughts nor taken actions intended to hurt another person.

B. Family/Household/Primary Social Systems

1. Identity and Structure

The Chase family system appears to be structured in such a way that Mrs. Chase is the primary executive or manager. She has responsibility for the bulk of the family's activities. She relieves Mr. Chase of both household and parenting duties. She is the primary housekeeper and parent. She plans and prepares meals, does the shopping, coordinates transportation for Robert, and pays the bills. In several ways, Mrs. Chase cares for both the males in the family system. Until Mrs. Chase began work outside the home, the family rules and role boundaries had been clear. Mrs. Chase sought ideas and input from Richard and Robert, but she made and implemented most decisions. Now that she is home less often and there are increased demands upon her, some of the rules and roles may be in flux. At this point, it seems that Mrs. Chase is trying to maintain her previous family duties while adding occupational responsibilities.

Questions: If Mrs. Chase were forced to choose between the two, would she prefer to work outside the home or remain as the primary parent and manager of the home? If she were to continue to work outside the home, what changes would she, Richard, and Robert need to make in order to lessen the extent of her household and family responsibilities? Would they be willing to make such changes? What would it be like for her to decrease her responsibility for and control of family and household duties?

Members of the Chase family appear to have adopted many of the stereotypes of men, women, and children projected by the dominant American culture. Mrs. Chase's adolescent experience and the shame she felt during the confession to a priest may continue to affect her today in relation to her son, Robert. She may wonder about his unfolding sexuality and be concerned about how he will deal with adolescent changes. Should Mrs. Chase and her family desire to change their family rules, roles, and communication patterns, it may be useful to explore with them some of their gender- and age-based assumptions and expectations.

Generally speaking, it appears that communication patterns within the Chase family are relatively open and direct. They seem to like each other. Sometimes, however, the male family members appear to hint at their preferences and Mrs. Chase responds to such indirect expressions by guessing what those wishes might be. For example, at a family dinner recently, Robert "made a face" when he was served his meal. Mrs. Chase then asked, "What's the matter?" Robert said, "Nothing." Mrs. Chase asked, "Don't you like the meal? I'll get you something else." Robert said, "Don't bother, this is okay." Mrs. Chase said, "No, I'll get you something else to eat." Robert said, "Oh, okay. Thanks." At this point, Mrs. Chase interrupted her own meal, got up, and prepared something Robert wanted to eat.

Questions: Are the communication patterns in the family such that Mrs. Chase enables the male family members to avoid responsibility for fully and directly expressing themselves? Does she try to "read their minds?" Do Richard and Robert realize that they sometimes communicate indirectly through facial expressions and bodily gestures? What might be the consequence of more direct and full verbal expression within the family system? What would each family member stand to gain or lose?

The family system appears capable of making adaptive changes. However, Robert's adolescence and Mrs. Chase's outside employment probably represent the most significant stressors the family system now faces. It remains uncertain whether the system can tolerate Mrs. Chase's employment outside the home.

Questions: Would Mrs. Chase be willing to let her husband and son assume greater responsibility for household and family tasks? Would they be willing to do so? How would the family members anticipate coping with the inevitable stress that accompanies change? What stress-reducing mechanisms do the family members have?

2. Mood and Emotion

Mrs. Chase appears to have the affection and support of her husband and son. Her mother, father, and siblings do not appear to provide much in the way of interest, understanding, or support. She does have several friends who care a great deal about her. However, in these relationships as in most others, she seems to "give more than she receives" and "knows more about others than others know about her." However, she strongly believes that both her husband and son would be willing to do anything they could to help her feel better.

3. Life-Cycle Development

As a system, the Chase family is moving into a phase when an adolescent child stimulates a number of issues and decisions for the youth, the parents, and the family system as a whole. According to Mrs. Chase, Robert is beginning to experience bodily changes and has become more self-conscious and self-centered. These changes may be affecting the nature of the relationship between Robert and Mrs. Chase and perhaps that with his father as well. Mrs. Chase, directly or indirectly, may be uneasy and unclear concerning her parenting role during this time. It is not certain how Mr. Chase is responding to Robert's adolescence.

Questions: What specific issues and dilemmas, if any, is Robert confronting? Is Mrs. Chase comfortable with an increase in her son's autonomy and personal responsibility? Is Mr. Chase involved with his son and available during this time? What hopes and dreams do Mr. and Mrs. Chase have for Robert's future? What doubts and fears do they have about him? What were the adolescent years like for Mr. and Mrs. Chase? Are they experiencing feelings reminiscent of their own adolescence?

C. Ecology/Environment
   1. Resources
      There are sufficient resources within the ecological environment of the Chase family. They have adequate opportunities to meet their needs and aspirations. They have not been subject to oppression or discrimination.

      Mrs. Chase does report being concerned about "teenage boys" in the neighborhood. She wonders whether Robert might be influenced by "bad boys" and get into some trouble. Questions: Might Mrs. Chase believe that she is less able to protect Robert from the influence of the neighborhood boys now that she works outside the home? Does she feel an obligation to keep Robert entirely away from negative influences? Does she suspect that Robert might be especially susceptible to such influence and that he might be unable to make responsible decisions? Might she be associating Robert's adolescence with her own teenage experience?

   2. Sociocultural
      There appears to be a favorable match between the sociocultural affiliation and traditions of the Chase family and the surrounding community. They are well accepted within the community.

D. Summary Assessment
   Mrs. Chase and her family have a lengthy history of competent functioning. The family members individually and as a system appear to be coherent and stable. However, Mr. Chase, Robert, and especially Mrs. Chase have begun to experience strain associated with changing demands upon them. These demands were initiated by two important events. First, about six months ago Mrs. Chase began to work outside the home. This has significantly increased the extent of her responsibilities and has caused her considerable stress. It appears that she has tried to continue to "do it all." The other family members are reacting to her increased stress and perhaps anticipate that they may have to change themselves. Second, Robert is beginning to undergo early adolescent changes.

   There are several factors that may have relevance to the identified problems. First, Mrs. Chase comes from a family of origin where she assumed parentlike responsibilities from an early age. She reports that her mother abused alcohol and her father was a workaholic. It is possible that Mrs. Chase tends to assume substantial responsibility for others—perhaps especially family members—because she was socialized to do so from an early age. Working outside the home may represent a major psychosocial conflict for her. One part of her (like her father) may be strongly tempted to invest a great deal of time and energy into her employment. Another part may feel much anxiety and uncertainty when she is away from the home. She is so familiar with the role of caretaker for her husband and son that she may sometimes feel anxious when she is working and unable to meet their needs. Second, Mrs. Chase wanted to have more children, but a medical condition has prevented that. She may not, as yet, have fully explored and grieved for the loss of her hope for additional children. She may also invest greater energy in her son Robert since "he's my only child." Third, Robert, as an early adolescent, may be troubled by physical, psychological, and social changes he is undergoing. This, along with Mrs. Chase's employment, is probably causing considerable systemic stress within the family. As a person emotionally attuned to the family, Mrs. Chase is understandably affected during this transition period. She may be confronting the limitations of her family-centered role identification.

If the problems of sadness, anxiety, and irritation were magically to disappear, it is likely that Mrs. Chase would continue to work outside the home while maintaining responsibility for most of the child and home care. The symptoms may be a signal that she's trying to do or be too many things. Perhaps it's time to reconsider her primary role identifications and her attitudes concerning family, employment, and leisure.

Questions: Are the needs of Robert such that by working outside the home Mrs. Chase believes that she is not providing him what he needs to develop into healthy adolescence and adulthood? Has he had special needs that she feels she is neglecting? Has her husband expressed concerns or indicated discomfort with her employment? What is her view of the ideal way to spend free time? If the family system were to regain its previous level of equilibrium by Mrs. Chase terminating her outside employment and returning to her traditional family and household roles, what would be the advantages and disadvantages to her, to Mr. Chase, to Robert, to the family system as a whole? If she maintains her employment, what might be other means through which the family could regain a sense of reasonable equilibrium?

■ **Exercise 8-2: Formulating a Tentative Assessment**

For this exercise, please review the information that you organized into the description section of your own case record as part of Exercise 8-1. Based upon what you know about yourself and what you included in the description, proceed to formulate a tentative assessment through analysis and synthesis of the available data. Record it in your course notebook. In conducting your assessment, however, remember that much of what you determine *remains* tentative and speculative. These are ideas or hypotheses that await later support and confirmation. Formulate your ideas in accord with the format provided above in Section II, Tentative Assessment, of the Description, Assessment, and Contract.

SUMMARY

During the assessment phase of social work practice, the worker attempts to "make sense" of the data gathered during the exploration phase. The assessment provides the worker and the client with a perspective from which to initiate the process of contracting. Two skills are especially pertinent to the assessment phase: (1) organizing descriptive information and (2) formulating a tentative assessment.

■ **Exercise 8-3: Summary**

Building upon the first interview you had with your social work student colleague (see Exercise 7-9), conduct a second interview. Ensure that the interview setting is private and again tape record the meeting. Using the exploring and other relevant skills addressed thus far, interview her with a view toward formulating an assessment. At the conclusion of the meeting, arrange for another meeting in about one week.

1. At the conclusion of the interview, ask your partner for feedback concerning her thoughts and feelings about the experience. Ask her for a totally honest reaction to the following questions: (a) Did she feel comfortable and safe with you? Did she trust you? (b) Did she feel that you were sincerely interested in her and in what she had to say? (c) Did she feel that you understood what she was trying to communicate? If not, identify what led her to believe that you did not understand. (d) Did she enjoy the experience? (e) Does she have any suggestions for you concerning how the interview could have been better or more satisfying for her? Summarize your partner's feedback in the space below.

2. In the space below, record your own reaction to the conversation. How did you feel about the interview? What did you like and what did you dislike about it? Do you believe that you used all the relevant skills during the interaction? What information did you gain that will be helpful in your assessment? What additional information would be useful? What would you do differently if you were to redo the interview?

3. In your notebook, *organize* the relevant information from both the first meeting (review your earlier transcript) and this second interview according to the format provided in the description section of the Description, Assessment, and Contract.

4. Using the information that you organized into a description, proceed to formulate a tentative assessment through analysis and synthesis of the available data. Record it in your course notebook. Remember to continue to disguise the identity of your colleague. Also, recall that much of what you determine *remains* tentative and speculative. These are ideas or hypotheses that await later support and confirmation. Formulate your ideas in accord with the format provided above in Section II, Tentative Assessment, of the Description, Assessment, and Contract.

5. After you have completed the description and assessment portions of the case record, play the audiotape or videotape. Study the tape for two purposes. First, make note of significant information that you neglected to include in your description and assessment. Add it to the appropriate sections of your DAC. Second, based upon your performance in the interview, use the rating scales below (where 0 = no proficiency and 10

= complete proficiency) to assess your current level of proficiency in the individual social work skills.

Probing

| | | | | | | | | | | |
| 0 | 1 | 2 | 3 | 4 | 5 | 6 | 7 | 8 | 9 | 10 |

Seeking Clarification

| | | | | | | | | | | |
| 0 | 1 | 2 | 3 | 4 | 5 | 6 | 7 | 8 | 9 | 10 |

Reflecting Content

| | | | | | | | | | | |
| 0 | 1 | 2 | 3 | 4 | 5 | 6 | 7 | 8 | 9 | 10 |

Reflecting Feeling

| | | | | | | | | | | |
| 0 | 1 | 2 | 3 | 4 | 5 | 6 | 7 | 8 | 9 | 10 |

Reflecting Complex Communications

| | | | | | | | | | | |
| 0 | 1 | 2 | 3 | 4 | 5 | 6 | 7 | 8 | 9 | 10 |

Partializing

| | | | | | | | | | | |
| 0 | 1 | 2 | 3 | 4 | 5 | 6 | 7 | 8 | 9 | 10 |

Going Beyond What Is Said

| | | | | | | | | | | |
| 0 | 1 | 2 | 3 | 4 | 5 | 6 | 7 | 8 | 9 | 10 |

6. Review your ratings to identify those individual skills in which you remain less proficient (e.g., a score of 7 or less). Then, in the space below, outline the steps you might take to improve your skill in those areas.

7. Now that you have completed these exercises, use the rating scales below (where 0 = no proficiency and 10 = complete proficiency) to conduct a summary evaluation of your proficiency in the assessing skills.

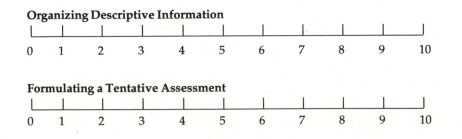

Organizing Descriptive Information

0   1   2   3   4   5   6   7   8   9   10

Formulating a Tentative Assessment

0   1   2   3   4   5   6   7   8   9   10

8. Finally, review your ratings to identify those assessing skills in which you remain less proficient (e.g., a score of 7 or less). Then, in the space below, outline the steps you might take to improve your skill in these areas.

CONTRACTING

The contracting process follows integrally from the assessment and yields clearly identified problems, specific goals for work, a change program through which the goals may be pursued, and, often, one or more discrete action steps. Usually, the worker and client also identify a means by which progress toward goal attainment may be evaluated.

During the contracting phase, the social worker clearly defines problems and goals for work and, on the basis of the assessment and in conjunction with the client, develops plans by which to achieve the goals. These processes typically occur during or shortly after the assessment process. Skills especially applicable to this phase of practice include: (1) reflecting the problem, (2) sharing worker's view of the problem, (3) specifying problems for work, (4) establishing goals, (5) developing a program for change, (6) identifying action steps, (7) planning for evaluation, and (8) summarizing the contract.

REFLECTING THE PROBLEM

Through the use of the skill of reflecting the problem, the worker demonstrates to the client that she understands *his* view of the problem. Reflecting the problem is a pivotal form of empathic reflection. It is a crucial outcome of active listening in that it constitutes the beginning of the contracting process.

Particularly in voluntary situations with adults, the client usually shares his view of the problem quite readily. In some cases, however, he may need a good deal of support, guidance, and encouragement in order to do so. In other circumstances, for example with many involuntary and some nonvoluntary clients, the worker assumes the major responsibility for both problem specification and goal determination.

Regardless of the context, the worker should not assume that the problem the client first identifies will necessarily remain the focus for work. It may.

However, as a result of exploration with an attentive worker, clients often identify concerns that are more pressing or more fundamental than those they initially mentioned.

As students begin to practice the skill of reflecting the problem, they can use the format outlined below. As they become more proficient, they can experiment with alternate forms.

As you see it, the problem is _____.

Example:

CLIENT: My wife left me—sure, for very good reasons—but I'm really down about it. She has left me before but always came back. This time I know she won't. She's gone for good and I don't know what to do. I can't go on the way things are. I'm so sad and lost without her.

WORKER (reflecting complex communication; reflecting the problem): You know now that your wife is gone and the relationship is over. You have accepted that as fact. But, as you see it, you are left with two major problems. First, you feel terrible. You're lonely and depressed and it's awfully hard to function well when you feel that way. Second, you're unsure of how to get on with your life without her. Would you say that these are the two major problems you want to work on here?

■ Exercise 9-1: Reflecting the Problem

For these exercises, assume that you are a social worker with a family and children's counseling center. In the spaces provided, write the words you would say in reflecting the problem as the client sees it.

1. You are interviewing Mrs. O., a seventy-seven-year-old widow who lives alone. At one point in the conversation, Mrs. O. says, "I feel just fine. Sure, I have my low points, but everybody does. I still cook my own meals and care for myself. I'm proud of that—but, with these blackouts, I'm afraid that I won't be independent much longer. I'm worried about that." Write the words you would use in reflecting the problem as Mrs. O. sees it.

2. You are in the midst of an interview with the seven-member, blended S. family. During the course of the exploration, Mr. S. says, "Since we married, we've had troubles with both my teenagers and her children. They dislike each other, they seem to hate us, and lately my wife and I have begun to fight. Finances have become a problem, and there's no time for anything. I don't think I've had a single minute to myself in six months. My wife and I haven't been out of the house on a weekend evening since our wedding." Write the words you would say in reflecting the problem as Mr. S. sees it.

3. You are interviewing Mrs. F. At one point during the conversation, she says, "I've had troubles since I moved into this community. The school system is insensitive to the Hispanic population. My kids have begun to disrespect me and diminish their own heritage. The neighbors all are white and haven't even introduced themselves to us. The whites in this town seem to all be prejudiced against Hispanics." Write the words you might say in reflecting the problem as Mrs. F. sees it.

SHARING WORKER'S VIEW OF THE PROBLEM

On the basis of the exploration of the person-problem-situation, the worker may identify one or more problem areas that the client has not mentioned. At other times, the worker will see a problem that the client has identified in a different way. For example, a client may identify his "wife's nagging" as the problem. After gaining a substantial understanding of the nature of what the client views as nagging, the worker may wonder aloud, "Might what you call nagging be a sign of a more basic problem? Could it be that the two of you have general trouble communicating with one another and discussing your opinions and preferences?"

Sometimes, the worker assumes primary responsibility for problem (and goal) definition. When the situation is immediately life threatening (e.g., suicidal behavior) or the client is involuntary (e.g., required to seek counseling or face felony charges for child abuse), the worker may define the problem *for* the client. Then the client decides whether or not to participate in the process. Even when the situation is neither life threatening nor involuntary, however, the worker frequently shares her view of the problems. The tentative assessment may lead the worker to suggest additional problems for joint consideration or to define one in a new way. She may have professional knowledge or previous practice experience that leads her to believe that a problem area not previously discussed ought to be examined. For example, a worker who hears a client describe feelings of constant fatigue, difficulty sleeping, loss of appetite, decreased interest in pleasurable activities, and diminished social involvement would be likely to wonder whether he is under considerable stress, has a physical illness, or suffers from depression.

Social workers frequently identify problems that may play a significant part in the present situation. Often, the worker shares this opinion with the client. However, the manner in which she identifies or redefines problems is consistent with the way in which she shares all her professional opinions—that is, she communicates them as opinions, not as indisputable facts, and provides the client with the freedom to agree or disagree. As a part of this process, the worker will reach for feedback from the client concerning these newly identified or redefined problems.

In practicing this skill, students may follow the format outlined below.

As we have talked about you and your concerns, I have been wondering about _____. What do you think? Is that a problem we should work on?

■ Exercise 9-2: Sharing Worker's View of the Problem

For these exercises, assume that you are a social worker with a family and children's counseling center. In the spaces provided, write the words you would say in sharing your view of the problem.

1. You are interviewing Mrs. O., a seventy-seven-year-old widow who lives alone. At one point in the conversation, Mrs. O. says, "I feel just fine. Sure, I have my low points, but everybody does. I still cook my own meals and care for myself. I'm proud of that—but, with these blackouts, I'm afraid that I won't be independent much longer. I'm worried about that." Write the words you would use in sharing your view of the problem.

2. You are in the midst of an interview with the seven-member, blended S. family. During the course of the exploration, Mr. S. says, "Since we married, we've had troubles with both my teenagers and her children. They dislike each other, they seem to hate us, and lately my wife and I have begun to fight. Finances have become a problem, and there's no time for anything. I don't think I've had a single minute to myself in six months. My wife and I haven't been out of the house on a weekend evening since our wedding." Write the words you would say, as the worker, in sharing your view of the problem.

3. You are interviewing Mrs. F. At one point during the conversation, she says, "I've had troubles since I moved into this community. The school system is insensitive to the Hispanic population. My kids have begun to disrespect me and diminish their own heritage. The neighbors all are white and haven't even introduced themselves to us. The whites in this

town seem to all be prejudiced against Hispanics." Write the words you might say in sharing your view of the problem.

SPECIFYING PROBLEMS FOR WORK

Specifying problems for work constitutes the first definitive indication that the client and worker agree to work toward resolution of certain problems. It is a fundamental component of the social work contract. Usually, the specified problems for work are derived from those problems the client identified, those the worker identified, or some negotiated combination or compromise of the two. Whatever their source, however, the specified problems for work provide basic guideposts for all worker-client activities. The problems for work should be stated in clear and understandable terms. They may be recorded within the contract portion of the Description, Assessment, and Contract (DAC).

The skill of specifying problems for work follows upon exploration of the person-problem-situation. Usually, the worker has used the skills of reflecting the problem and sharing her view of the problem before she specifies problems for work. Specifying problems for work results in an agreement of understanding—a contract—that these problem areas will be the primary focus of the worker and client's work together. In practicing this skill, students may follow the format outlined below.

> I think we agree about the problems to work on. I'd like to review them and to write them down so we can use them as the basis for our work together. First, there is the problem of _____.
> Second, . . . Third, . . . Does this seem like an accurate list to you?

When prepared in written form, the specified problems for work are included within the contract section of the DAC (see "Summarizing the Contract" later in this chapter).

Example:

CLIENT: My wife left me—sure, for very good reasons—but I'm really down about it. She has left me before but always came back. This time I know she won't. She's gone for good and I don't know what to do. I can't go on the way things are. I'm so sad and lost without her.

WORKER (reflecting problem; seeking feedback): You know now that your wife is gone and the relationship is over. You have accepted that as fact. But as you see it, you are left with two major problems. First, you feel terrible. You're lonely and depressed and it's awfully hard to function well when you feel that way. Second, you're unsure of how to get on with your life without her. Would you say that these are the two major problems you want to work on here?

CLIENT: Yes, that's right. I really am depressed and totally uncertain about what to do with my life.

WORKER (sharing worker's view of the problem): As we have talked about you and your concerns, I have been wondering about suicidal thoughts. How about it—have you been having thoughts of ending your life? Is that a problem we should work on?

CLIENT: Well, yes. I've been thinking that maybe everybody would be better off if I were dead and buried. I don't think I'd actually do it, you know—kill myself—but I've been thinking that if I were dead it would be a great relief.

WORKER (specifiying problem for work; seeking feedback): It sounds like the suicidal thoughts occur frequently enough that we should add suicidal thinking as a problem for our work together, is that right?

CLIENT: Yes.

WORKER (specifying problems for work; seeking feedback): Okay, I think we agree about the problems. I'd like to review them and to write them down so we can use them as the basis for our work together. How do these sound to you? First, there is the problem of sadness and depression. Second, there is the problem of confusion and uncertainty in terms of a direction for your life from here on out. And, third, there is the problem of suicidal thinking. What do you think—is this a pretty accurate list?

CLIENT: Yes.

■ **Exercise 9-3: Specifying Problems for Work**

For these exercises, assume that you are a social worker with a family and children's counseling center. Review your responses to Exercises 9-1 and 9-2 and then, in the spaces provided, write the words you would say in specifying problems for work.

    1. You are interviewing Mrs. O., a seventy-seven-year-old widow who lives alone. At one point in the conversation, Mrs. O. says, "I feel just fine. Sure, I have my low points, but everybody does. I still cook my own meals and care for myself. I'm proud of that—but, with these blackouts, I'm afraid that I won't be independent much longer. I'm worried about that." Write the words you would use in attempting to specify the problems for work.

2. You are in the midst of an interview with the seven-member, blended S. family. During the course of the exploration, Mr. S. says, "Since we married, we've had troubles with both my teenagers and her children. They dislike each other, they seem to hate us, and lately my wife and I have begun to fight. Finances have become a problem, and there's no time for anything. I don't think I've had a single minute to myself in six months. My wife and I haven't been out of the house on a weekend evening since our wedding." Write the words you would say in specifying the problems for work.

3. You are interviewing Mrs. F. At one point during the conversation, she says, "I've had troubles since I moved into this community. The school system is insensitive to the Hispanic population. My kids have begun to disrespect me and diminish their own heritage. The neighbors all are white and haven't even introduced themselves to us. The whites in this town seem to all be prejudiced against Hispanics." Write the words you might say in specifying the problems for work.

ESTABLISHING GOALS

Following the specification of problems for work, the worker encourages the client to participate in the process of establishing goals. Setting specific final or outcome goals is a fundamental element of the contracting process. It is a vital step toward change. The goals represent envisioned aims toward which cognitive, emotional, behavioral, and situational actions are directed. As the title of a popular book by David Campbell suggests, *If You Don't Know Where You're Going, You'll End Up Somewhere Else* (1974). Without clear and specific goals, clients and workers are indeed likely to end up somewhere other than where they intend.

Gerard Egan (1982b, pp. 212–218) outlines the following characteristics of effective goals: First, effective goals are described as *accomplishments* rather than *processes*. "To lose weight" is a process; "to achieve a weight of 125 pounds and maintain that weight for six months" is an accomplishment. Second, effective goals are *clear* and *specific*. They are not vague resolutions or mission statements. "Securing employment" is unclear. "Within six months of today, to secure employment as a short-order cook in a restaurant" is more clear and specific. Third, effective goals are stated in *measurable* or *verifiable* terms. The criteria for success are understood by both client and worker. "To feel better" is not sufficiently clear and measurable. "To feel better as indicated by sleeping the night through (at least seven hours per night on at least five nights per week), completely eating three meals daily, and by at least fifteen percent higher scores on the Beck Depression Inventory" is much more measurable. Fourth, effective goals are *realistic*. They must be achievable given the motivations, capacities, and resources of the person-situation systems. A goal "to get all straight *A*s would not be realistic for a student who has *never* before received a single *A*. Fifth, effective goals are *adequate*. A goal is adequate to the degree that its accomplishment would significantly improve the problem situation. Sixth, effective goals are *congruent with the client's value and cultural systems*. Unless there is a life-threatening situation, clients should not be asked nor expected to violate their fundamental values. Seventh, effective goals are described in terms of a *time frame*. The people involved need to know *when* the goals are to have been achieved.

Although specifying goals in a manner consistent with Egan's criteria represents the *ideal* form, it is not always desirable or feasible to do so. The worker should not become fanatical in attempting to define goals in measurable terms. Some clients are in such a state of uncertainty and confusion that to push them too hard toward specificity would exacerbate their state of distress. Therefore, on occasion, the worker purposely postpones this step and, instead, outlines a more general goal or direction. When the confusion and ambiguity subside, the worker resumes encouraging the identification of clear and precise goals.

Whether stated in specific or general terms, goals should follow logically from and relate directly to the identified problems for work. Consistent with the values of the profession, the goals that are established are usually negotiated with the client and have his consent. The skill of establishing goals enables the worker to express in a precise way these mutually agreed upon goals for work. Typically, clients are capable of active participation in the process of goal setting. As part of that process, the worker requests the client to identify a goal for work on a particular problem. However, she does so in a special way.

Clients tend to respond to direct questions such as "What is your goal for resolving this problem?" in vague and general terms. The worker encourages clearer and more precise goal definitions by asking questions that require the client to describe specifically *how he will know when* the problem *is* resolved. In addition to furthering the purposes of goal setting identified above, these questions serve another extremely important function. They encourage the client to envision, in considerable detail, a future in which *the problem has been resolved*. In so doing, the client almost always begins to feel better and to experience greater energy and motivation. However, to yield these results, the questions must be phrased in certain ways.

The exploring skill of *seeking clarification* is adapted in such a way as to both set a goal *and* to move the client to imagine a future in which the problem no longer exists. Questions phrased in the following manner tend to yield these dual results:

Specifically, how will you know when the problem of _____
_____ is solved? [Or] What will indicate to you that you have
resolved this problem?

Example:

WORKER: Now that we have a pretty clear list of the problems, let's try to
establish specific goals for each one. The first problem we've identified is
that your fourteen-year-old son skips school two or three days each week.
Now, let's imagine that it is some point in the future and the problem has
been resolved. How will you know that it is no longer a problem?

CLIENT: Well, I guess I'll know when Johnny goes to school every day and his
grades are better.

WORKER (reflecting goal; seeking feedback): When Johnny goes to school daily
and improves his grades, you will feel that it's no longer a problem. Is that
right?

CLIENT: Yes.

WORKER (seeking specificity; feedback): Okay, now let's try to be even more
specific. I assume that when you say "Johnny will go to school every day"
you also mean that he will attend all his classes and that you don't expect
him to attend school when he's sick, is that accurate?

CLIENT: Yes.

WORKER (seeking specificity): What do you think would be a reasonable time
frame for accomplishing this goal?

CLIENT: Well, I don't know. I'd like him to start now.

WORKER (sharing opinion; seeking feedback): That would be great progress! But
I wonder if that might be expecting a bit too much. Let's see, it's now one
month into the school year. As I understand it, Johnny skipped school some
last year too and this year he is skipping even more. What do you think
about a two-month time frame for accomplishing the goal?

CLIENT: That sounds really good.

WORKER (establishing goal): Okay, let's establish this as our first goal: "Within
two months from today's date, Johnny will attend school every day except
when he's sick enough to go to a doctor." Let me take a moment to write
that down for us. . . . Now about the grades. As I understand it, he is
currently failing most of his courses. How will you know when that is no
longer a problem?

As should be apparent from the above example, the worker is quite active
in encouraging specificity in goal definition. She consistently says things like,
"How *will* you know *when* it *is* no longer a problem? What *will* be the indications?" To avoid implying that the problem might not be resolved, the worker
does not say things like, "*If* the problems *were* gone . . . "

Often, in response to the worker's questions, a client will formulate a precise goal with which the worker can concur. When this occurs, the worker may simply reflect the goal as the client expressed it in a format such as:

As you see it, one goal for our work together is _____
_____.

Reflecting goals is an application of the skill of empathically communicating your understanding of a client's views. As are all reflecting skills, it is a specific form of active listening. Reflecting goals demonstrates that you have heard and understood the goals that the client has tried to convey. However, in reflecting goals, the worker tries to phrase her response so that it meets the criteria for effective goals cited above. In so doing, she must occasionally go slightly beyond the client's actual statement.

Sometimes, in spite of the worker's active encouragement, a client cannot or will not establish a goal. In such instances, the worker may defer goal setting and reengage in additional exploration of the person-problem-situation. Alternately, she may appropriately propose a tentative goal, which the client may accept, reject, or modify. In sharing her view of the goal, the worker may adopt a format such as:

Now that we have a pretty clear understanding of the problems and a sense of the direction we'd like to go, let's establish specific goals for our work together on each of the problems. The first problem is _____ _____. Would it make sense to establish this as our goal for resolving the first problem: _____?

The following is another example of how the process of setting goals may proceed:

Example:

CLIENT: Yes. It does feel like I've lost everything I had hoped for. I guess it's normal to feel sad when a marriage fails.

WORKER (reflecting content; sharing educated opinion): Your dreams for the future of your marriage have been shattered. As I see it, it's a sign of health to feel a sense of loss and sadness when a marriage ends. Wouldn't it be awful to feel nothing?

CLIENT: Yes, that would be worse. Like it all meant nothing. My marriage meant a lot to me.

WORKER (seeking a final goal): I wonder if it might be possible for us to establish a specific goal in relation to these feelings of sadness and depression. When it's no longer a problem, what will be the indications?

CLIENT: Gee, I don't know exactly. I guess when I'm finally over her I'll feel a lot better.

WORKER (reflecting content; seeking goal specificity): So, it will be a positive sign when you begin to feel better. And what will be the indications that you're feeling better?

CLIENT: I guess once I'm over this, I'll be able to sleep and eat again and not think about her so much, and I might even be dating someone else.

WORKER (reflecting content; establishing goal; seeking feedback): So, when you begin to eat and sleep better, and you think about her less, we'll know that things have taken a positive turn. Let's make the goals even more specific so that we will know when you have completely achieved them. How about this: "Within six months from this date I will be (1) sleeping six or more hours per night at least five nights per week, (2) regaining the weight that I have lost, (3) thinking at least seventy-five percent of the time about things other than my wife or the marriage, and (4) going out on at least one date." How does that sound to you?

CLIENT: Real good. Right now I probably think about her ninety-five percent of the time, and the idea of going on a date sounds just awful. If I were thinking about other things, doing other things, and dating someone else, I'd know that I was over her.

WORKER (establishing goal): Good. Let me jot that down so we can remember it.

■ **Exercise 9-4: Establishing Goals**

For these exercises, assume that you are continuing in your role as a social worker with a family and children's counseling center. In the spaces provided after each case below, complete two tasks. First, write the words you would say in seeking final goals from the client. Second, prepare goal statements that might reasonably follow from the problems you specified in Exercise 9-3. Of course, the nature of this exercise does not allow you to interact with the clients in the negotiation of final goals. Therefore, simply formulate questions and then suggest goals to match the problems. Our primary purposes here are to practice asking goal-related questions and preparing effective goal statements.

1. You are in the midst of an outreach interview with Mrs. O., a seventy-seven-year-old widow who lives alone. At one point in the conversation, Mrs. O. says, "I feel just fine. Sure, I have my low points, but everybody does. I still cook my own meals and care for myself. I'm proud of that—but, with these blackouts, I'm afraid that I won't be independent much longer. I'm worried about that." Using the formats above as guides, write the words you might use to ask, in two different ways, questions that might lead the client to specify a goal. Then formulate two distinct final goals that you believe might be applicable to Mrs. O.'s situation.

2. You are in the midst of an interview with the seven-member, blended S. family. During the course of the exploration, Mr. S. says, "Since we married, we've had troubles with both my teenagers and her children. They dislike each other, they seem to hate us, and lately my wife and I have begun to fight. Finances have become a problem, and there's no time for anything. I don't think I've had a single minute to myself in six months. My wife and I haven't been out of the house on a weekend evening since our wedding." Using the formats above as guides, write the words you might use to ask, in two different ways, questions that might lead the client to specify a goal. Then formulate two distinct final goals that you believe might be applicable to this situation.

3. You are interviewing Mrs. F. At one point during the conversation, she says, "I've had troubles since I moved into this community. The school system is insensitive to the Hispanic population. My kids have begun to disrespect me and diminish their own heritage. The neighbors all are white and haven't even introduced themselves to us. The whites in this town seem to all be prejudiced against Hispanics." Using the formats above as guides, write the words you might use to ask, in two different ways, questions that might lead the client to specify a goal. Then formulate two distinct final goals that you believe might be applicable to this situation.

4. When you have completed the above exercises, review the final goals you have set and ask yourself the following questions: Are the goals described as accomplishments rather than processes? Are the goals clear and specific? Are they measurable or verifiable in some way? Are they realistic given the circumstances? Are they adequate? Do they appear to be consistent with the fundamental values and the cultural preferences that you might expect of these clients? Finally, are the goals logically congruent with the specified problems identified in Exercise 9-3? In the space below, summarize the results of your review of the final goals you have established.

DEVELOPING A PROGRAM FOR CHANGE

When the final goals have been established, the worker begins to engage the client in the process of developing a program for change. Here the worker relies a great deal upon the information and the hypotheses generated during the description and assessment processes. Planning a program for change involves a great many determinations. The worker attempts to foster a flexible, creative, "brainstorming" atmosphere in which all sorts of ideas are identified and examined. Several skills are applicable during this process. Probing, reflecting, and going beyond what is said are three of the more pertinent.

There are many ways to resolve problems and achieve goals. Some programs involve changes in the person; others encompass changes in the situation. Many programs incorporate both. Changes such as increasing one's knowledge about parenting or increasing one's skill in communicating assertively are examples of person-focused change. In social work practice, change programs are not limited to the person alone. Changes within the situation are often necessary. Whenever a social worker serves as an advocate, a broker, or a mediator, she is working toward situational change. For example, an unemployed client's situation is likely to be dramatically changed when a social worker intercedes with a prospective employer to help the client secure a new job. Or consider the example of a client who lives with an abusive spouse. With the help of a social worker, several situational changes might be possible. Her spouse could be encouraged to join in marital or family counseling in hopes of decreasing the risk of future violence or be asked to participate in a program for abusive men. The client might file a criminal complaint with the police and courts, or she might leave the household for a safe shelter. All these involve changes within the situation. And all would affect the person as well. Although the goal in any given case may be primarily person-focused or primarily situation-focused, workers should be aware of the following systemic principle: changes in one dimension of the person-situation system nearly always result in changes in other dimensions.

In planning a change program, the worker and client must identify *who* will meet with the worker and *who* or *what* will be the target for change. They must also determine *who* will be involved in the change efforts and *how* the efforts might affect others. For example, consider a case in which the mother of an eight-year-old boy expresses concern about his "disobedience and aggression." The worker and client must determine who will meet with the social worker and in what context. Will it be the mother and boy together; mother separately; boy separately; sometimes one; sometimes the other; sometimes both; the boy in a group with other boys; or the mother in a group with other mothers? In addition, the worker must determine *what* role or roles she will play (e.g., advocate, mediator, broker, educator, or counselor) and *what* approach or strategy she will adopt in providing help to this client in relation to the established goals. For example, should the worker serve as counselor and adopt a task-centered approach, a sociobehavioral approach, a family systems approach, a psychosocial approach, or some combination thereof? The worker and client must determine *how* to implement the change efforts. How active should the worker be? Should she let the client take the lead or should she herself take the lead? She and the client must decide how fast to proceed with change efforts and how to approach other persons who could or should be involved. The worker and client must decide *where* to hold their meetings and *where* the change efforts will occur. Sometimes, it is easier or more effective to meet in the client's home than in an agency office. Often, change efforts are more successful when they are attempted in a neutral location. The worker and client must determine *when* the meetings and change efforts will occur, how often, and how long. They usually establish a time frame for their work together. Will they work together toward these goals for six weeks, three months, two years? In addition, the worker and client together identify potential obstacles and potential resources that might affect the outcome of the change program.

In planning a program for change, the worker and client consider a number of factors and begin to reach a sense of general direction for their work together. The following is an example of how a change program description might be succinctly recorded as part of the contract portion of the DAC:

> We, Carol Johnson and Susan Holder, agree to meet together for weekly one-hour sessions over the course of the next eight weeks. Our purpose is to work together toward achieving the final goals identified above. We will approach this work as a cooperative effort with each party contributing ideas and suggestions and undertaking actions intended to yield progress toward the goals. Sometimes we will meet in the agency and sometimes in Ms. Johnson's home. If agreeable

to Ms. Johnson, we may ask Mr. Johnson (her husband) to join us for one or two meetings. Throughout the eight-week period, we will monitor the rate and degree of progress. At the end of that time, we will determine whether to conclude our work, consult with or refer to someone else, or to contract with each other for further work together.

■ **Exercise 9-5: Developing a Program for Change**

For these exercises, assume that you are continuing your work with the clients described in the previous exercises. Review your responses to Exercises 9-3 (specifying problems for work) and 9-4 (establishing goals). Then, in the spaces provided below each vignette, describe change programs that might be applicable to each. Of course, they should be congruent with the identified problems and goals and consistent with the dimensions discussed above.

1. You are in the midst of an outreach interview with Mrs. O., a seventy-seven-year-old widow who lives alone. At one point in the conversation, Mrs. O. says, "I feel just fine. Sure, I have my low points, but everybody does. I still cook my own meals and care for myself. I'm proud of that—but, with these blackouts, I'm afraid that I won't be independent much longer. I'm worried about that." Plan a change program that might be applicable to Mrs. O.'s situation. Record it as if it were to be included in the contract portion of the DAC.

2. You have begun the first interview with the seven-member, blended S. family. During the course of the exploration, Mr. S. says, "Since we married, we've had troubles with both my teenagers and her children. They dislike each other, they seem to hate us, and lately my wife and I have begun to fight. Finances have become a problem, and there's no time for anything. I don't think I've had a single minute to myself in six months. My wife and I haven't been out of the house on a weekend evening since our wedding." Plan a change program that might be applicable to this situation. Record it as if it were to be included in the contract portion of the DAC.

3. You are interviewing Mrs. F. At one point during the conversation, she says, "I've had troubles since I moved into this community. The school system is insensitive to the Hispanic population. My kids have begun to disrespect me and diminish their own heritage. The neighbors all are white and haven't even introduced themselves to us. The whites in this town seem to all be prejudiced against Hispanics." Plan a change program that might be applicable to this situation. Record it as if it were to be included in the contract portion of the DAC.

4. When you have completed the above exercises, review the change programs you have formulated and ask whether each describes who is to be involved in meeting with you; who or what are the targets of change; when and how long the meetings are to occur; how active you are to be; what role or roles you are going to assume; what strategy or approach is to be used; and what the time frame for the program is to be. In addition, ask whether the change program appears to be consistent with the fundamental values and the cultural preferences that you might expect of these clients. Finally, determine whether the change program is logically congruent with the specified problems identified in Exercise 9-3 and with the final goals identified in Exercise 9-4. In the space below, summarize the results of your review and specify those aspects of change program planning you need to develop further.

IDENTIFYING ACTION STEPS

Often, the goals formulated by worker and client are too large to be accomplished in a single action, and it would be unrealistic and impractical to implement the change program all at once. When this is the case, the social worker engages the client in planning small action steps consistent with the change program and leading to goal accomplishment. Action steps are a form of subordinate goals. Like final goals, action steps should also conform to Egan's criteria for effective goal statements (1982b, pp. 212–218).

Taking action steps eventually leads to the achievement of final goals. Because they represent smaller goals, they tend to have a higher probability of success than would be the case if the final goal were to remain undivided. For example, suppose someone was fifty pounds overweight and wanted to lose that much in order to improve his health. In the absence of surgery, it is impossible to lose fifty pounds in a single effort. However, reducing by one pound, then another, and then another is conceivable. It is similar to the "one day at a time" notion of Alcoholics Anonymous (AA). "Abstaining from alcohol for the rest of one's life" is indeed a large order for any person who has regularly drunk alcohol for many years. Abstaining for one day, for one hour, or even for one minute is more manageable. By putting together and accomplishing several subordinate goals, a large, final goal may be successfully achieved.

The skill of identifying action steps, however, involves establishing subordinate goals that connote "doing something." They constitute steps, tasks, or activities that the client, and sometimes the worker, may take in moving toward goal accomplishment.

In identifying action steps, the worker and client engage one another in generating a first step toward the final goal. The worker initiates this process by asking questions such as: "What would represent a first step toward achieving this goal? What needs to change in order for you to be able to make a small step toward achieving this goal?" If the client cannot or will not respond to the question, the worker may tentatively suggest an action step for the client to consider. She might use a format such as:

As a first step toward achieving your goal, what would you think about (doing) _____?

There is an emphasis on identifying an activity that might be taken. The focus is upon doing something to move toward goal achievement. The client is encouraged to identify steps leading toward change in himself (e.g., thoughts, feelings, or behaviors) or change in the situation that might favorably affect the problem and attain the goal.

Questions such as the following often yield useful information in the identification of action steps: "What *will be* the first sign that you are beginning to make progress toward this goal? What *will be* the very first indication that there is progress in this matter?" Or, "What *will be* the very first indication that you are taking steps to reach your goal?" Such questions, as do those used in setting final goals, tend to increase a client's optimism and motivation. They do so by bringing the near future into the client's present thinking. He is asked to imagine or visualize the situation being somewhat improved and to identify the signs of that improvement. These signs are often indicative of specific action steps that might be taken in order to facilitate progress toward goal attainment.

During this phase, the worker's questions are intended to yield small and manageable tasks or actions. As the client and worker come to consensus concerning initial action steps, the worker empathically reflects them in clear terms.

In reflecting action steps, a worker might use a format such as:

So, the first step which you (or I, as social worker) are going to take on/by (date) is _____. Let me jot that down so we can remember it.

With the reflection of the first action step, the contract for work is firmly established.

The following are some examples of a worker establishing action steps:

Examples:

WORKER (reflecting final goal; seeking an action step): Your first goal is to improve your sleeping patterns. Right now, you sleep the night through only about one day per week and you want to be able to do so at least five days per week. Going from one to five nights is a pretty large jump. It might be helpful to start with something a bit smaller. What would represent a good first step toward achieving the goal?

WORKER (reflecting final goal; tentatively suggesting action step): Your first goal is to improve your sleeping patterns. Right now, you sleep the night through about one day per week and you want to be able to do so at least five days per week. Going from one to five nights is a pretty large jump. It might be helpful to start with something a bit smaller. As a first step toward reaching that goal, how about sleeping the night through on two nights by the end of next week?

WORKER (reflecting final goal; seeking action steps): We have established as your first goal the improvement in your sleeping patterns. Right now, you sleep the night through about one day per week and you want to be able to do so at least five days per week. What will be the first signs that you are beginning to sleep better?

■ **Exercise 9-6: Identifying Action Steps**

Continuing with the cases described above, review your responses to Exercises 9-4 (establishing goals) and 9-5 (developing a program for change). Then, in the spaces provided, write the words you would say in planning action steps in each of the following situations.

1. You are in the midst of an outreach interview with Mrs. O., a seventy-seven-year-old widow who lives alone. At one point in the conversation, Mrs. O. says, "I feel just fine. Sure, I have my low points, but everybody does. I still cook my own meals and care for myself. I'm proud of that—but, with these blackouts, I'm afraid that I won't be independent much longer. I'm worried about that." Using the formats above as guides, write the words you might use to ask, in two different ways, questions that might lead the client to identify an initial action step. Then formulate one distinct action step that you believe might represent progress toward achieving the final goal identified for this case in Exercise 9-4.

2. You are in the midst of an interview with the seven-member, blended S. family. During the course of the exploration, Mr. S. says, "Since we married, we've had troubles with both my teenagers and her children. They dislike each other, they seem to hate us, and lately my wife and I have begun to fight. Finances have become a problem, and there's no time for anything. I don't think I've had a single minute to myself in six

months. My wife and I haven't been out of the house on a weekend evening since our wedding." Using the formats above as guides, write the words you might use to ask, in two different ways, questions that might lead the client to identify an action step. Then formulate one distinct action step that you believe might represent progress toward achieving the final goal identified for this case in Exercise 9-4.

3. You are interviewing Mrs. F. At one point during the conversation, she says, "I've had troubles since I moved into this community. The school system is insensitive to the Hispanic population. My kids have begun to disrespect me and diminish their own heritage. The neighbors all are white and haven't even introduced themselves to us. The whites in this town seem to all be prejudiced against Hispanics." Using the formats above as guides, write the words you might use to ask, in two different ways, questions that might lead the client to an action step. Then formulate one distinct action step that you believe might represent progress toward achieving the final goal identified for this case in Exercise 9-4.

4. When you have completed the above exercises, review the action steps identified and ask yourself the following questions: Are the steps described as accomplishments rather than processes? Are the steps clear and specific? Are they measurable or verifiable in some way? Are they realistic given the circumstances? Are they adequate? Do they appear to be consistent with the fundamental values and the cultural preferences that you might expect of these clients? Finally, are the action steps logically congruent with the specified problems, the final goals, and the change program identified in Exercises 9-3, 9-4, and 9-5? In the space below, summarize the results of your review and specify those aspects of action step identification you need to develop further.

PLANNING FOR EVALUATION

All professional social workers are responsible for evaluating progress toward resolution of the problems and achievement of the goals mutually established by the worker and client. Regardless of the nature of the agency setting, the presenting problems, or the client's circumstances, it is possible to create *some* method by which progress toward achievement of the final goals may be evaluated or measured. Sometimes, such evaluation is quite subjective. At other times, it can be more objective. Nonetheless, social workers *must* somehow evaluate progress.

Social workers have several means through which to measure progress toward goal attainment. In fact, one of the more applicable methods is actually called *goal attainment scaling* (Kiresuk & Sherman, 1968). It is particularly well suited to social work practice because the dimensions for measurement are not predetermined as, for example, is the case with standardized testing instruments. In goal attainment scaling, the dimensions for assessment evolve from the goals negotiated by worker and client and are therefore specific to that unique person-problem-situation. Compton and Galaway (1989, pp. 671–674) and Kagle (1984, pp. 74–76) provide useful summaries of goal attainment scaling procedures. The major thrust is the generation of a series of predictions concerning the possible outcomes of work toward goal achievement. The worker, alone or with the client, identifies five possible outcomes for each final goal. The levels (from worst to best) are classified (from Kiresuk and Sherman's scale [Compton & Galaway, 1989, p. 672]): (1) "most unfavorable results thought likely," (2) "less than expected success," (3) "expected level of success," (4) "more than expected success," and (5) "most favorable results thought likely." The predictions provide the worker and client with "markers" upon which to base their evaluation of progress.

Among the other means for evaluating progress toward goal achievement are *counting* and *subjective rating*. Counting refers simply to the process by which a client, a worker, or another person in the client's environment keeps track of the frequency of a particular phenomenon that is integrally related to the final goal. For example, consider an aspect of self-esteem. People with low self-esteem often think disparaging and self-critical thoughts about themselves. A final goal relating to the problem of self-esteem could be to increase the frequency of self-approving thoughts and decrease the frequency of those that are self-critical. A client might be given or asked to purchase a simple counting mechanism (a golf scorekeeping device works well) with which to keep track of the number of self-approving and self-critical thoughts during a given time period (e.g., each day for one week). The frequency counts are then transferred to graph paper with the expectation that the change program will lead the client to increase the frequency of self-approving thoughts per day. Counting is often used during the early phase of work with clients in order to collect specific information concerning a problem behavior or event and to establish a preintervention baseline that may be used to assess the effectiveness of change efforts. Counting can be applied to many different phenomena in both person and situation spheres of concern.

Subjective rating involves the client, worker, or another person making a relative judgment concerning the extent, duration, frequency, or intensity of a targeted phenomenon. Sometimes, a client may be asked to form an imaginary ten-point scale that runs from "worst" or "least" (number 1) to "best" or "most" (number 10). Then, he is is asked to rate the phenomenon on the scale. For example, suppose a client is concerned about the relationship with his partner. The worker could make a request in this fashion: "Would you please imagine a scale that runs from 1 to 10 with 1 being the lowest possible and 10 being the highest possible? Now, on the basis of your best judgment, please rate the overall quality of the relationship as it now stands." Imagine that the client gives the relationship a 4. The worker might ask the client, and perhaps his partner as well, to conduct such a subjective rating once a week, say on Sunday evening. The request might be phrased in this manner: "Each Sunday evening just before going to bed, each of you please record in a notebook your subjective rating of the overall quality of the relationship during the past week. Please do not share your ratings with your partner until we meet together again as a threesome." Subjective rating can be used in relation to virtually all human psychological and social phenomena. Of course, because it is entirely subjective, it is highly susceptible to error. However, where the use of more objective measures is inappropriate or impossible, the use of subjective rating is certainly better than using no measure at all.

Social workers may also select from the vast array of paper-and-pencil instruments widely available. For example, Walter Hudson, a distinguished social worker, produced *The Clinical Measurement Package: A Field Manual* (1982). The Clinical Measurement Package, or CMP, contains nine scales of great utility to social workers. These scales assess phenomena that often apply to the problems and goals clients identify when they meet with social workers. The CMP scales address dimensions such as self-esteem, generalized contentment, marital satisfaction, sexual satisfaction, parental attitudes, child attitudes toward mother, child attitudes toward father, family relations, and peer relations. Each of the scales may be completed and scored quickly. Two other social workers, Kevin Corcoran and Joel Fischer, have published *Measures for Clinical Practice: A Sourcebook* (1987). It contains more than 125 Rapid Assessment Instruments (RAIs) relevant to many aspects of social work practice that measure such phenomena as spouse abuse, alcoholism, marital happiness, family adaptability and cohesion, depression, self-concept, and dozens of other dimensions of human experience. It is a rich resource of easily administered and scored instruments.

■ **Exercise 9-7: Planning for Evaluation**

Review your responses to Exercises 9-3, 9-4, 9-5, and 9-6 as they relate to the cases described above. Then, in the spaces provided, write the words you would say to identify means by which you might evaluate progress in each of those case situations. Our primary purpose here is to stimulate you to think about potential means by which you might evaluate progress in your work with clients.

1. You are in the midst of an outreach interview with Mrs. O., a seventy-seven-year-old widow who lives alone. At one point in the conversation, Mrs. O. says, "I feel just fine. Sure, I have my low points, but everybody does. I still cook my own meals and care for myself. I'm proud of that—but, with these blackouts, I'm afraid that I won't be independent much longer. I'm worried about that." In the space below, please describe two means by which you might measure progress in this situation.

2. You have begun the first interview with the seven-member, blended S. family. During the course of the exploration, Mr. S. says, "Since we married, we've had troubles with both my teenagers and her children. They dislike each other, they seem to hate us, and lately my wife and I have begun to fight. Finances have become a problem, and there's no time for anything. I don't think I've had a single minute to myself in six months. My wife and I haven't been out of the house on a weekend evening since our wedding." In the space below, please describe two means by which you might measure progress in this situation.

3. You are interviewing Mrs. F. At one point during the conversation, she says, "I've had troubles since I moved into this community. The school system is insensitive to the Hispanic population. My kids have begun to disrespect me and diminish their own heritage. The neighbors all are white and haven't even introduced themselves to us. The whites in this town seem to all be prejudiced against Hispanics." In the space below, please describe two means by which you might measure progress in this situation.

4. When you have completed the above exercises, please consider the means of evaluation you have identified in terms of the following questions: How subject to evaluator bias and error are the means you have selected? What are the ethical implications of these forms of evaluation? Do the means appear to be consistent with the fundamental values and the cultural preferences you might expect of these clients? Finally, are the means likely to measure accurately changes in the problems and goals specified in Exercises 9-3 and 9-4? In the space below, summarize the results of your review and specify those aspects of evaluation planning you need to develop further.

SUMMARIZING THE CONTRACT

Summarizing the contract involves the worker concisely repeating the essential elements of the understanding that the worker and client have reached concerning problems for work, goals, the change program, action steps, and the means by which progress is to be evaluated.

When written, the contract may be organized in accordance with the framework shown below and incorporated into the DAC. Alternately, it may be prepared separately as a formal contract using letterhead paper with spaces for client and worker to sign. In both forms, the contract provides for descriptions of problems, goals, and plans. It represents the basic agreement to work together toward the resolution of problems and the achievement of goals. Social workers usually find such contracts extremely applicable in their practice. Of course, the specific dimensions of this contract outline may not be relevant for work in all social work settings nor with all clients, all problems, or all situations. Workers in each program or agency necessarily formulate contract guidelines that best fit their needs and purposes.

III. Contract
   A. Problems
      1. Client-Defined Problems
         In this section, the problems that the client first identifies are summarized.
      2. Worker-Identified Problems
         In this section, the problems that the worker first identifies are summarized.
      3. Problems for Work
         In this section, the problems that both parties agree to attempt to resolve are summarized. These problems remain the focus for work unless or until they are renegotiated by the client and worker. Of course, either party may request that the problems for work be reconsidered or revised.
   B. Final Goals
      In this section, the final or outcome goals, derived from the problems for work as negotiated by the worker and client, are summarized. Ideally, they are defined in clear and specific terms so that progress toward their attainment may be measured.
   C. Plans
      1. Change-Program Plans
         In this section, the change program is summarized. Usually, there are notes concerning who will be involved, where the work will occur, how the process will unfold, and when it will take place and for how long.

2. Client's Action Steps
   In this section, the tasks or activities that the client agrees to undertake in his efforts toward goal attainment are outlined.
3. Worker's Action Steps
   In this section, the tasks or activities which the worker agrees to undertake in her efforts toward helping the client toward goal attainment are outlined.
4. Plans to Evaluate Progress
   In this section, the means and processes by which progress toward goal attainment is to be evaluated are outlined.

The following represents an example of the contract portion of a social worker's Description, Assessment, and Contract. Note that it is a continuation of the Chase case presented above (see Chapter Eight) in the description and assessment sections of the DAC.

III. Contract
   A. Problems
      1. Client-Defined Problems
         Mrs. Chase identified the following problems:
         a. Frequent arguments with her son Robert and, less often, with her husband Richard
         b. Increased irritability, criticism, and anger toward Robert and, to a lesser degree, toward Richard
         c. Unplanned weight loss (ten pounds)
         d. Sleep disturbance
         e. Resumption of cigarette smoking after five-year abstinence
         f. Fatigue
         g. Headaches
      2. Worker-Identified Problems
         Worker tentatively identified the following problems:
         a. Ambivalence about job at Fox Manufacturing
         b. Depression
         c. Ambivalence about Robert's adolescence
         d. Feelings of loss, disappointment, and grief because client probably cannot have another child
         e. Stress and tension; anxiety
         f. Thoughts and feelings of excessive responsibility and possibly of control
         g. Role strain and possibly role conflict among roles of mother, wife, homemaker, and employee
         h. Issues related to childhood experiences (i.e., growing up in a family system with a parent who abused alcohol; largely absent, workaholic father; unhappy incidents with

childhood peers; feeling overweight and unattractive; church-related issues; episodes of attempted molestation by maternal uncle)

     i. Interactional styles that may be classified as predominantly nonassertive with occasional periods of aggressive verbal expression

   3. Problems for Work

Worker and client agreed upon the following problems for work:

     a. Frequent arguments with her son Robert and, less often, with her husband Richard

     b. Increased irritability, criticism, and anger toward Robert and, to a lesser degree, toward Richard

     c. Sleep disturbance

     d. Ambivalence regarding job at Fox Manufacturing

     e. Stress and tension; anxiety

     f. Thoughts and feelings of excessive responsibility and possibly of control

B. Final Goals

Worker and client agreed upon the following goals for work:

   1. Within six weeks decrease by fifty percent the frequency of unwarranted arguments with Robert and Richard; and increase the frequency of satisfying interactions with them by fifty percent

   2. Within six weeks decrease by fifty percent the frequency and intensity of inappropriate feelings of irritability, criticism, and anger toward Robert and Richard; and increase appropriate feelings of comfort, understanding, and acceptance of them by fifty percent

   3. Within six weeks sleep eight full hours per night and awaken feeling refreshed at least four of seven nights weekly

   4. Within six weeks decrease the ambivalence about the job at Fox Manufacturing by deciding whether or not Lynn Chase really wants it

   5. Within six weeks decrease the stress, tension, and anxiety and increase feelings of personal comfort and calmness by fifty percent

   6. Within two weeks explore in greater depth the issue of excessuve responsibility and control; by the end of that time, decide whether maintaining or lessening the current level of responsibility and control is desirable

C. Plans

   1. Change-Program Plans

In order to achieve the identified goals, worker and client agreed upon the following change program:

Mrs. Lynn Chase and Ms. Susan Holder, social worker, will meet for eight one-hour sessions during the next two months. Our purpose is to work together toward achievement of the final goals as identified above. We will approach this work as a cooperative effort with each party contributing ideas and suggestions. On occasion, we may ask Mrs. Chase's husband or son to join us. Throughout the two-month period, we will monitor the rate and degree of progress. At the end of that time, we will determine whether to conclude our work, consult with or refer to someone else, or to contract with each other for further work together.

2. Client's Action Steps

Worker and client agree to the following action steps to be undertaken by the client during the first week of the change program. Other action steps will be developed and implemented later in the program.

a. As a first step toward addressing the goal of decreasing the stress, tension, and anxiety and increasing feelings of personal comfort and calmness, Mrs. Chase will spend fifteen minutes each day during the next week planning for or working in her garden.

b. As a first step toward addressing the goal of decreasing by fifty percent the frequency of inappropriate feelings of irritability, criticism, and anger toward Robert and Richard; and increasing appropriate feelings of comfort, understanding, and acceptance of them by fifty percent, Mrs. Chase agrees to do two things during the course of the next week: First, she will not "stuff" her feelings. Whether by writing them down on paper, verbally expressing them in a place where no one can hear, or expressing them directly to the relevant person or persons, she will express the feelings within a few minutes of the time that she becomes aware of them. Second, she will take five minutes each and every day to engage pleasantly with Robert and Richard by inquiring about them, their thoughts, feelings, and activities.

c. As a first step toward addressing the goal of determining whether a lessening of responsibility and control in some areas might be helpful, during the next week Mrs. Chase will identify and write down as many reasons as she can regarding why she should continue to maintain her current level of responsibility and control. Following that, Mrs. Chase will identify as many reasons as she can regarding why a lessening of her responsibility and control might be beneficial to her, her husband, and her son at this time. We agree to review the two lists of reasons in our next meeting.

3. Worker's Action Steps
    a. I, Susan Holder, social worker, agree to prepare this contract or agreement in written form and provide a copy to Mrs. Chase.
    b. I will assume responsibility for planning tentative agendas for our meetings together and to provide Mrs. Chase with advice and consultation concerning the implementation of the action steps and their effects.
    c. I will provide Mrs. Chase with a special notebook and related materials for completing written tasks and monitoring progress.
4. Plans to Evaluate Progress
    Progress toward achieving the goals will be evaluated in several ways. First, Mrs. Chase will keep a daily log in her notebook where she records the time and date of all "arguments" and all "satisfying interactions." Second, Mrs. Chase will also log the time and date of all inappropriate feelings of "irritability, anger, and criticism" toward Richard or Robert as well as all feelings of "comfort, understanding, and acceptance" of them. Third, Mrs. Chase will use the log book to record the number of hours slept each night and to rate, on a subjective scale of 1–10, how refreshed she feels upon awakening. Fourth, Mrs. Chase will register completion of her daily fifteen minutes of "gardening." Evaluation of progress toward other goals will be determined by the worker asking Mrs. Chase for subjective self-reports. In regard to the issues of responsibility and her job at Fox Manufacturing, progress will be indicated when Mrs. Chase reports that she has decided whether to lessen responsibility and control and whether she wants her job. A decision in either direction will reflect progress.

■ **Exercise 9-8: Summarizing the Contract**

For this exercise, please review the information you organized into the description and assessment sections of your own DAC in Exercises 8-1 and 8-2. Based upon what you know about yourself and what you included in the description and assessment, proceed to formulate a contract in your course notebook as if you were your own social worker. In creating your contract, be aware that you too, in spite of your high level of self-awareness, are still likely to miss some of the problems or issues that a professional social worker might help you to identify. Therefore, even though it concerns you—and you indeed know yourself better than anyone else does—the contract you develop should be viewed as somewhat tentative. Prepare the contract in accordance with the format provided above in Section III, Contract, of the Description, Assessment, and Contract.

SUMMARY

During the contracting phase of social work practice, the worker, on the basis of the assessment and in conjunction with the client, attempts to define clearly the problems and goals for work and to develop plans likely to resolve the identified problems and achieve the established goals. The skills especially applicable to this phase of practice include: (1) reflecting the problem, (2) sharing worker's view of the problem, (3) specifying problems for work, (4) establishing goals, (5) developing a program for change, (6) identifying action steps, (7) planning for evaluation, and (8) summarizing the contract.

■ **Exercise 9-9: Summary**

Building upon the earlier two interviews that you had with your social work student colleague, conduct a third interview for the purpose of developing the contract for work. Ensure that the interview setting is private and again tape record the meeting. Using the exploring, contracting, and other relevant social work skills, interview her with a view toward negotiating a contract. At the conclusion of the meeting, arrange for another meeting in about one week.

1. Following the interview, ask your partner for feedback concerning her thoughts and feelings about the experience. Ask her for a totally honest reaction to the following questions: (a) Did she feel comfortable and safe with you? Did she trust you? (b) Did she feel that you were sincerely interested in her and in what she had to say? (c) Did she feel that you understood what she was trying to communicate? If not, explore with her what led her to believe that you did not understand. (d) Did she enjoy the experience? (e) What are her suggestions concerning how the interview could have been better or more satisfying for her? Summarize her feedback in the space below.

2. Review your own reaction to the conversation. How did you feel about the interview? What did you like and what did you dislike about it? Do you believe that you used relevant skills during the interaction? What information did you gain that will be helpful in developing a contract? What additional information would be useful? What would you do differently if you were to redo the interview? Summarize the results of your review in the space below.

3. In your course notebook, prepare a record according to the format provided in the contract section of the Description, Assessment, and Contract.

4. After you have completed the contract, play the audiotape or videotape. Identify the specific social work skills that you used. Make notes of significant exchanges that affect the way in which you drafted the contract and revise the contract accordingly.

5. At some point during the week, share the contract section of the case record with your social work student colleague. Ask her to share her thoughts and feelings as she reads it. Request that she comment on its accuracy and correct any errors in fact or differences in interpretation concerning the contract. Ask her to respond specifically to the goals and action steps reflected in the contract section. Summarize her feedback and your own reactions to it in the space below.

6. Now that you have completed these exercises, use the rating scales below (where 0 = no proficiency and 10 = complete proficiency) to conduct a summary evaluation of your proficiency in the contracting skills.

Reflecting the Problem

0   1   2   3   4   5   6   7   8   9   10

Sharing Worker's View of the Problem

0   1   2   3   4   5   6   7   8   9   10

Specifying Problems for Work

0   1   2   3   4   5   6   7   8   9   10

Establishing Goals

0   1   2   3   4   5   6   7   8   9   10

Developing a Program for Change

0   1   2   3   4   5   6   7   8   9   10

Identifying Action Steps

0   1   2   3   4   5   6   7   8   9   10

Planning for Evaluation

0   1   2   3   4   5   6   7   8   9   10

Summarizing the Contract

0   1   2   3   4   5   6   7   8   9   10

7. Finally, review your ratings to identify those contracting skills in which you remain less proficient (e.g., a score of 7 or less). Then, in the space below, outline the steps you might take to improve your skill in these areas.

_____

WORKING

In this chapter, we make a transition from the social work skills used primarily for the purpose of collecting information, developing a relationship, formulating an assessment, and negotiating a contract to those used more frequently in the process of change. Although the latter, the working skills, do indeed build upon the experience and frame of reference of the client, they also introduce, in a much more direct fashion, the knowledge and expertise of the worker.

The skills covered in earlier chapters are primarily empathic and exploratory in nature. The worker uses them to learn about and understand the client's experience—he seeks information about the person, problem, and situation—from the client's perspective. He listens actively and reflects his understanding back to the client. The use of empathic and exploratory skill encourages the client toward further self-expression and self-exploration while solidifying a positive relationship with the worker. While the worker may go slightly beyond the literal statements of the client in his use of empathic and exploratory skills, his major focus is the experience of the client.

The working skills are significantly different. Here the worker proceeds from and expresses his own frame of reference—his own knowledge and experience. The working skills tend to reflect the worker's agenda: his thoughts, feelings, beliefs, opinions, hypotheses, deductions, and conclusions. During the beginning phase of practice, the worker uses such an expressive skill when he suggests a tentative purpose for meeting and outlines relevant policy factors. The worker also expresses his knowledge and experience when he shares his view of the problem during the assessing and contracting processes.

Occasionally, the worker's expressive skills bear little obvious relationship to the words or actions of the clients. However, they usually reflect the worker's attempt to expand the client's experience. The worker uses what he has learned from the client in order to process it from his own frame of reference and then express it in a fashion he believes will be useful to the client in progressing toward the final goals.

Because the working skills tend to be expressive rather than empathic or exploratory, the worker must be especially clear about his rationale for using an expressive skill at a particular point in time. His motivations must be professional, not personal: he should not share his knowledge, feelings, or opinions simply because he wants to; rather, the working skill selected must relate to the contract for work. In determining whether an expressive working skill is applicable, the worker may ask himself questions such as: Have we adequately explored the person, problem, and situation? Have I sufficiently communicated empathic understanding of the client's experience so that I may now appropriately consider using a work phase expressive skill? Do we have a clear contract for work? What is my objective in using this skill at this time? Will the use of this skill at this time help the client with our agreed-upon work toward problem resolution and goal attainment? How will the client react to my expression? What is the risk that using this skill at this time might endanger the client's individual or social well-being? How do I personally think and feel about this client at this time? Am I tempted to use a working skill now in order to express a personal view or impulse or to satisfy my own feeling?

Engaging in such analysis usually enables the worker to determine the relative applicability of a work phase expressive skill. If there is sufficient doubt, he may simply return to empathically oriented, exploratory skills.

During the work phase, the worker continues to use many of the empathic skills previously discussed. Reflective communications, probing, and seeking clarification are needed throughout the entire helping process. However, during the work phase, expressive skills such as rehearsing, reviewing, evaluating, focusing, reframing, and advising are increasingly used. In using the expressive skills, the worker maintains his focus on the assessment and the mutually established goals for work, guided by the contract throughout the work phase. The skills especially applicable to this phase include: (1) rehearsing action steps, (2) reviewing action steps, (3) evaluating, (4) focusing, (5) educating, (6) advising, (7) representing, (8) responding with immediacy, (9) reframing, (10) confronting, (11) pointing out endings, and (12) recording during the work phase.

REHEARSING ACTION STEPS

A primary element of the work phase involves motivating and preparing the client who has agreed to attempt an action step to actually do so. Unfortunately, the understanding gained and the commitment made by a client during an interview frequently does not transfer into action outside the worker-client context. This is one of the major obstacles social workers and clients must confront if social work intervention is to be more than a palliative experience. For change to occur beyond the interview setting and to be long lasting, some means must be incorporated within the working process to facilitate and encourage the transfer of learning from the interview into the real world of the client. Several things may be done within the context of the interview itself. Procedures such as *role-play*, *guided practice*, and *visualization* help to bridge the gap between the often special circumstances characterizing social work interviews and the more common environment of everyday life. Rehearsal activities incorporate aspects of doing with those of thinking and feeling. Involving more than talk alone, these activities constitute practice of the action step itself. Engaging several dimensions of experience (e.g., thinking, feeling, doing) in the rehearsal activity, the client moves closer to what will be necessary in the real-world context where the change must take place.

Rehearsing the action step decreases the anxiety associated with the *idea* of taking the action, increases the probability that the activity will be undertaken, and enhances the likelihood that the action step will be successful. In using this skill, the worker reviews the action step with the client and then talks through probable scenarios. Of course, many clients are quite capable of generating alternate courses of action under various circumstances. But some are not. When that is the case, the worker may assume a more active role in identifying options. The worker might propose a few different ways to complete the step or present examples of how other people might undertake it. Often, as part of the rehearsal process, the worker *models* the action step for the client by saying or doing what might be needed. The worker may also assume the role of a person with whom the action step will be undertaken and participate with the client in a *role-play* of the action step. During or following the practice, the worker provides guidance, feedback, and encouragement to the client. Another form of rehearsal involves the client *visualizing* (Lazarus, 1984) herself undertaking the action step. In using visualization, the worker first determines whether the client has the capacity to create mental pictures. The worker might phrase the question in a form such as, "If I were to ask you to imagine in your mind's eye the kitchen in the place where you live, could you do so?" If the client can form such a picture, the worker might then say, "Good, some people aren't able to imagine as well as you do. That capacity will help in this work." He would then request that the client assume a relaxed position, take a few slow, deep breaths, and, if it feels comfortable to do so, close her eyes. Closing the eyes is not essential—many people feel safer with their eyes open and can still visualize well. The worker then requests the client to imagine herself in the situation where the action step is to occur and, as if she were viewing it on a video screen, to see and experience herself undertaking the action step. He asks her to study the video in great detail, noticing all aspects. Visualization can be used for the purpose of identifying client fears and anticipating potential obstacles to successful action as well as for the purpose of rehearsal. When the worker and client understand what needs to be done, the worker may request the client to imagine herself successfully completing the action step. Following that, the worker may also ask the client to identify the positive thoughts and feelings that accompany imaginary completion of the action step.

Returning to the Chase case, the following is an excerpt from an interview in which the worker helps the client rehearse an action step through role-play:

WORKER (Ms. Holder; introducing the action step; seeking feedback): One of the steps we have identified is to express verbally your affection for both Robert and Richard at least once each day. If I understand the usual patterns correctly, this would represent a change from the way you have recently related. Is that right?

CLIENT (Mrs. Chase): Yes, it would be a big change.

WORKER: Right. It's been my experience that accomplishing changes such as this takes a good deal of planning and preparation. Unless the step is practiced ahead of time, there is a tendency for things to stay the same. With that in mind, I wonder if you would be willing to practice with me what it is you are going to say and do each day?

CLIENT: Okay.

WORKER: Good. Tell me, when you think of where and when you might make your first caring statement to Robert, what comes to mind?

CLIENT: Well, I think that I'd like to start off the day with something positive."

WORKER: Good idea! Where do you think you will be when you make the first affectionate statement?

CLIENT: Well, I think it will probably be in the kitchen.

WORKER: Okay. Let me assume the role of Robert. And, if you would, please let's imagine that it's tomorrow morning and we are now in the kitchen. What will you say to him tomorrow?

CLIENT: Well, I think I'll say something like, "Robert, I know that we have been on each other's nerves lately. I know that a lot of it has been my fault. I guess I've been more stressed out than I realized. Anyway, I want to say I'm sorry and I want you to know that I have never loved you more than I do now."

WORKER (as Robert): Geez. Thanks, Mom. I love you too.

WORKER (as herself): That sounds just great to me. I can really feel your love for Robert. How does it feel to you?

CLIENT: It feels really good. I feel warm inside. Loving toward him and also better about myself.

WORKER: I wonder, do you think Robert will react as I did or will he respond in some other way?

CLIENT: I'm not sure. But—I do think he'd like it and it would bring us closer.

WORKER: Good. Now, how do you feel as you realize that Robert will probably appreciate your comments and feel very loved?

CLIENT: Really good. I can't wait until tomorrow morning!

The following excerpt illustrates how the worker helps Mrs. Chase rehearse an action step through the use of visualization:

WORKER (Ms. Holder; introducing the step; exploring probability of action; seeking feedback): One of the steps we have identified as a means to decrease stress and increase feelings of personal comfort is to spend fifteen minutes each day planning for or working in your garden. I must admit that I wonder a bit about your ability to actually do that. You are very busy. You do so many things that I wonder whether you will really take the time to do the fifteen minutes of gardening each day. What do you think?

CLIENT (Mrs. Chase): Well, to be honest, I have known for some time that I need to get back to gardening and I haven't done it. I keep on making promises to myself and I keep on breaking them.

WORKER: Thanks for being frank with me. If we're going to get anywhere with these problems we need to be honest and open with each other. If you don't think you will actually do any of the activities we identify, please tell me.

It's been my experience that accomplishing changes such as this takes a good deal of planning and preparation. Unless the step is practiced ahead of time, there is a tendency for things to stay the same. With that in mind, I wonder if you would be willing to try a little experiment that may make it a little easier to undertake the action?

CLIENT: Well, I guess so. What kind of experiment?

WORKER: I'm sure that you've heard the old saying, "Practice makes perfect." Well, for many people, practicing in one's imagination is nearly as effective as practicing for real. If you happen to be one of the people who can form mental pictures, then we can use that capacity to increase the likelihood that you will actually begin to garden for real. Is that description clear?

CLIENT: Yes, I think so. How do I do it?

WORKER: First, let's find out about your picture-making ability. Please try now to imagine your garden as it used to be when it was in full bloom. Can you picture it?

CLIENT: Yes. I can see it now.

WORKER: Can you see it in color or is it black and white?

CLIENT: It's in color.

WORKER: Now, please imagine yourself in the garden tilling the soil around the growing plants. Is that the sort of thing you might be doing?

CLIENT: Yes. I'd be down on my knees, working the soil.

WORKER: Can you visualize that in your mind's eye?

CLIENT: Yes.

WORKER: Now, please describe what you are feeling, what you are experiencing, as you work the garden.

CLIENT: Well, I feel warm and relaxed. I feel content. I feel happy. Working the soil is, well, it's pleasurable.

WORKER: Now, please picture yourself in the garden this very evening. Can you do that?

CLIENT: Yes.

WORKER: And does that feel as good as the other picture did?

CLIENT: Yes.

WORKER: Now, let's shift to a different picture. Suppose it rains. Can you imagine planning or preparing for the garden in a way that would also be relaxing or pleasurable?

CLIENT: Yes. I can work on my drawings of the garden. I kind of draft out what plants, what fruits, what vegetables go where in the garden. I also work out what is to be planted when and approximately when they are to be harvested.

WORKER: And what do you feel in this picture?

CLIENT: I feel just as relaxed and content as when I'm in the garden itself.

WORKER: Let's create a picture of you actually doing that on rainy days when you cannot go out into the garden.

CLIENT: Okay.

As a result of rehearsing, whether through role-play, guided practice, visualization, or some combination, clients are more likely to carry out the activity in their own world.

■ **Exercise 10-1: Rehearsing Action Steps**

For these exercises, assume that you are a social worker with a family and children's counseling center. Respond in the spaces provided by describing what you would do and say in using the skill of rehearsing the action steps you identified as part of Exercise 9-6 above.

1. You are in the midst of an outreach interview with Mrs. O., a seventy-seven-year-old widow who lives alone. You have agreed upon the problems and goals for work and have identified an action step. In the space below, describe what you would do and say in using the skill of rehearsing the action step with this client. In formulating your description, anticipate what the client might say or do in response to your statements and actions.

2. You are in the midst of an interview with the seven-member, blended S. family. You have agreed upon the problems and goals for work and have identified an action step. In the space below, describe what you would do and say in using the skill of rehearsing the action step with this client. In formulating your description, anticipate what the client might say or do in response to your statements and actions.

3. You are interviewing Mrs. F. You have agreed upon the problems and goals for work and have identified an action step. In the space below, describe what you would do and say in using the skill of rehearsing the action step with this client. In formulating your description, anticipate what the client might say or do in response to your statements and actions.

REVIEWING ACTION STEPS

There are three possible outcomes when a client agrees to undertake action step activities: (1) the client may complete them; (2) she may partially complete them; or (3) she may not complete any portion of them. The first two outcomes almost always represent progress. The third outcome does not. However, even the third outcome may become useful to the client if it is examined and reviewed in order to improve the chances of success in future attempts or with other action steps. In working with clients, workers should try to increase the probability that the client will attempt and complete the agreed-upon action step. It helps for the client to rehearse the action step before she attempts it. It is also useful to *review the action step* afterward. For most clients, when the worker demonstrates his interest in the process and outcome of the client's action attempts by asking about them, he increases the probability that action steps will be attempted. By reviewing what happened, the worker also gathers information that can be used in the evaluation of progress toward goal achievement and in identifying subsequent action steps.

In reviewing action steps, the worker adopts an attitude of curiosity. If the client has partly or completely undertaken the activity, the worker may express pleasure. However, if a client has not attempted the action step, a worker would not express disapproval or criticism. Rather, he conveys his interest in a fashion such as, "What got in the way of the attempt?" In such circumstances, the worker explores with the client the thinking and feeling experiences that led the client to defer taking the action step. Additionally, the worker inquires about situational factors that may have contributed to the change in plans. Often, such exploration leads to an identification of unanticipated obstacles to activity completion. Alternate plans can then be devised and the worker and client can proceed to rehearse the revised action step. When a client has completed an action step, the worker, reflecting both pleasure and curiosity, inquires about the factors contributing to the accomplishment. He may ask, "What was different this time that enabled you to take this step?" For clients who have partly completed the activity, he may first, with pleasure and interest, inquire about those differences that enabled the client to take this "step in the right direction." Later, he explores the factors that blocked a more complete attempt and then, with the client, formulates a slightly revised plan. With clients who have partially or completely undertaken the action step, the worker encourages them to identify and express the satisfying thoughts and feelings that accompany action toward goal achievement. Frequently, the worker also shares his positive impressions about the client's efforts. Following the encouragement, the worker and client proceed toward the identification and rehearsal of additional action steps.

Example: Reviewing a Completed Action Step

WORKER (Ms. Holder):   Last time we talked, you agreed to spend fifteen minutes each day in gardening activities. If you recall, we went through the process of visualizing those activities in your mind's eye. I'm curious. How did that work out?

CLIENT (Mrs. Chase):   It was great! I did it every day, sometimes more than fifteen minutes, and I enjoyed it enormously. It spread out into other parts of my life too. I felt more calm and content throughout the day.

WORKER: Wonderful! So, it was truly effective in increasing your feelings of contentment?

CLIENT: Yes. It really worked. I had only one headache all week and I felt much better.

WORKER: Terrific! Now, is there anything about the gardening activity that we should change in order to make it better?

CLIENT: No. It's working just fine. Let's not change anything about it.

WORKER: Agreed. Let's keep the gardening activity just the same. That is, each day you will spend fifteen minutes in a gardening activity. Is that right?

CLIENT: Yes.

Example: Reviewing a Partially Completed Action Step

WORKER (Ms. Holder):   Last time we talked, you agreed to spend fifteen minutes each day in gardening activities. If you recall, we went through the process of visualizing those activities in your mind's eye. I'm curious. How did that work out?

CLIENT (Mrs. Chase):   Well, I did it on two days this week but I couldn't find the time to garden any more than that. I was just too busy.

WORKER: You were able to find time to do the gardening on two of the seven days. That's a very good beginning. On the two days that you gardened, what was it like?

CLIENT: Well, I guess at the beginning of the week I was just determined to do the gardening. I did it and I liked it. It's a lot to do, to start up a garden when you haven't worked on it for a long time. But I enjoyed it a lot and I felt good on those two days. On the third day, I just couldn't find the time.

WORKER: If I'm following you accurately, it sounds like the two days that you did the gardening were very good days for you. You felt good on those days. On the third day, when you did not garden, you didn't feel as good. Would I be correct in saying then that the gardening is definitely a helpful activity?

CLIENT: Oh, yes! If only I would do it!

WORKER: Let's see if we can figure out some way to make it easier for you to do the gardening and gain the benefits from it. What was different about the days that you did garden from the days that you didn't?

CLIENT: Well, I was really motivated on the first two days. On the third day, I had a tough time at work and I was exhausted when I got home. I just slumped into the sofa and went to sleep. I guess I was tired every night after that.

WORKER: When you come home from work, if you're tired it's harder for you to do the gardening, even though it leads to relaxing and contented feelings. I wonder, when you fall asleep on the sofa after work, do you awaken feeling as rested and relaxed as you do when you garden?

CLIENT: Actually, I feel worse after dozing on the sofa. I'm kind of grouchy for the rest of the evening. And I don't sleep very well at night. It's better when I garden.

WORKER: Now that we know that, let's see what we could do to help you garden even when you're tired and exhausted from work. Please let your eyes close and imagine that you have just come home from a stressful day at work. You're exhausted. Your usual pattern has been to crash on the sofa. However, this time, you take a drink of ice water and go out into the garden. You sit in a chair and look at your garden while drinking the ice water. You don't do anything. You just sit there. After ten minutes or so, you can feel the stress and exhaustion from work beginning to lessen. You decide to do just a little bit of gardening. After fifteen minutes, you pause and notice that you feel calm and relaxed. You're no longer tired. Instead, you're ready to go on with the rest of your evening. . . . How about it, Mrs. Chase, could you imagine that pretty clearly?

CLIENT: Yes. And I can see myself really relaxing during the gardening. I don't relax as well when I sleep on the sofa.

WORKER: In that case, what do you think about trying the fifteen minutes of gardening again during this next week—only, let's go for four days instead of all seven?

CLIENT: That sounds good. I think I'll do it this week.

Example: Reviewing an Unattempted Action Step

WORKER (Ms. Holder): Last time we talked, you agreed to spend fifteen minutes each day in gardening activities. If you recall, we went through the process of visualizing those activities in your mind's eye. I'm curious. How did that work out?

CLIENT (Mrs. Chase): Well, I thought about it but I couldn't find the time to do any gardening at all. I was just too busy.

WORKER: You were unable to find time to do the gardening at all during this past week. Tell me, during this week's time, have there been any signs that things are getting better?

CLIENT: Well, no. Things are about the same. I did feel a lot better after talking with you last time but that lasted only a day or so.

WORKER: If I'm following you accurately, it sounds like there was some temporary relief from talking about the problems with me, but there hasn't been any real progress, is that right?

CLIENT: Yes, I'm afraid so.

WORKER: Let's talk some about the gardening activity itself. In our discussion last time, you were quite sure that if you began to garden again, even for a little bit, you would soon feel better. Do you think that still holds true or have you reconsidered whether gardening would actually be helpful to you?

CLIENT: Well, I know it would help me but I just can't find the time.

WORKER: If you still think the gardening would be helpful, let's see if we can identify what gets in the way of doing it. During this past week, what did you end up doing instead of the gardening?

CLIENT: Well, on the first evening I planned to garden, Robert injured his knee playing basketball and I had to take him to the emergency room. He has been in bed all this week. I've been nursing him each evening after I get home from work.

WORKER: Your son's injury got in the way. How is his knee now?

CLIENT: Well, it's much better. He should be able to get out of bed about the middle of next week. Then he'll start walking around the house. By the first part of the following week, he should be able to return to school.

WORKER: It sounds as if your son is well on the way to recovery and you will have more time when he can get around on his own. Do you think that when he does start to walk again you will be more likely to do the gardening?

CLIENT: I think so. It depends upon how much help he needs.

WORKER: It sounds like you'll be nursing him at least for another several days. What is involved when you care for him in the evening?

CLIENT: Well, first I make him supper and then I take it to his room. Then we talk for a while. Then I clean up the kitchen and do the dishes. Then I check on Robert again. We usually talk some more. By that time, it's time for bed.

WORKER: Mrs. Chase, it seems to me that we have a choice to make here. First, if you really believe that once Robert is better you will begin the gardening, we can simply delay the starting date of the gardening activities. However, if you believe that if it were not Robert's injury, it would be something else that would prevent you from gardening, then perhaps we should take this opportunity to challenge the pattern of excessive caretaking. We have explored this before. If your decision not to garden is more a matter of neglecting yourself rather than simply a matter of unusual circumstances, perhaps we might begin to change that right now while Robert is still injured. What do you think?

CLIENT: Well, honestly, I think it's some of both. Robert's injury gives me an opportunity to take care of him and a reason not to take good care of myself by gardening.

WORKER: Okay—then what is your preference, should we delay the start-up date for the gardening activities or should we start now in order to challenge the tendency to avoid caring for yourself?

CLIENT: Well, I guess I'd like to start right now. Even with Robert's injury, I should be able to find fifteen minutes at some point during the evening.

WORKER: All right. I wonder, though, because of the extra responsibilities due to Robert's injury, should we change the plan from fifteen minutes every single day to fifteen minutes three times during the next week? That might be more reasonable given the current circumstances.

CLIENT: Yes, yes. I think that would be just about right. I know I can garden three times during the next seven days.

WORKER: Okay. Good. We've changed the plan for gardening from once every day to three times during the next week. Now, let's rehearse this a little bit.

As a result of reviewing the action steps, clients are more likely to believe that the worker is genuinely interested in whether they are carried out. Reviewing increases the probability that additional action steps will be attempted and successfully completed.

■ Exercise 10-2: Reviewing Action Steps

For these exercises, assume that you are a social worker with a family and children's counseling center. In the spaces provided, create simulated dialogues between yourself and the client that reflect how you might use the skill of reviewing action steps. Follow up on the case situations for which action steps were identified in Exercise 9-6.

1. You are in the midst of reviewing action steps with Mrs. O., a seventy-seven-year-old widow who lives alone. She reports that she has fully completed the agreed-upon action step. In the space below, write the words you might say in reviewing the action step with this client.

2. You are in the midst of reviewing action steps with the seven-member, blended S. family. The family indicates that they partly carried out the agreed-upon action step. In the space below, write the words you might say in reviewing the action step with this client.

3. You are in the midst of reviewing action steps with Mrs. F. She reports that she did not attempt the agreed-upon action step. In the space below, write the words you might say in reviewing the action step with this client.

EVALUATING

Evaluating is a crucial activity during the work phase. It is often incorporated as part of the process of reviewing action steps. The skill of evaluating engages the worker and client in a review of progress toward goal attainment. Progress may be indicated by changes in such indicators as goal attainment scales, frequency counts, subjective ratings, or standardized paper-and-pencil instruments. When recorded on paper, the presence or absence of progress, as well as the rate of change, if any, can be graphically presented. Evidence of progress may enhance clients' satisfaction and motivation to undertake further action. When, over time, progress is not reflected or when evaluation reveals change in a negative direction, the worker and client need to reconsider the assessment, the contract, and the action steps that have been formulated. Obviously, when progress toward goals is not forthcoming, social workers have an obligation to reexamine the approach.

Through the skill of evaluating, the worker engages the client in examination of the data that has been collected according to the contract's plan for evaluation of progress. The worker and client consider the information and determine whether it reflects progress toward goal attainment and problem alleviation; no change; or a change in the wrong direction (i.e., things become worse). As in reviewing action steps, when there is clear evidence of progress, the worker expresses pleasure and encourages the client to identify those factors that enabled her to make the positive changes. When there is no evidence of progress, the worker encourages the client to participate in an analysis concerning what might be preventing progress. The worker and client then consider whether a major revision in the plan is needed or whether relatively minor adjustments might suffice. Frequently, the evaluation instruments provide useful information to supplement the client's experience and the observations of the worker. When problems worsen, the worker and client engage in an intensive reanalysis. They need to determine if the planned action steps, rather than helping, are actually causing the deteriorating situation. Often, initial negative effects are an expected and predicted but temporary phenomenon. Because of the systemic nature of so many problems, it is not uncommon for "things to become worse before they get better." Also, negative effects are not always the result of the approach taken by the worker and client. They may be effects of ongoing changes in the person-situation. However, sometimes they are indeed caused by the change program itself. When that is the case, a major revision in the contract is imperative.

As an example, consider one aspect of Mrs. Chase's daily sleep log, in which she records the number of hours slept each night. The worker has reviewed these daily logs and has converted the sleep data into the graph form displayed in Figure 10-1.

As reflected by the graph, Mrs. Chase slept approximately four hours nightly during the period between June 14 and June 19. According to her, four hours has been the approximate amount she has slept each night over the last few months. On the evening of June 20, following the second interview with the social worker, Mrs. Chase implemented the change plan as devised by the worker and herself. Beginning on that night and continuing throughout the next twelve days, Mrs. Chase's daily log reflects general progress toward achieving the goal of sleeping eight hours nightly. There were only two nights when she did not sleep at least seven hours.

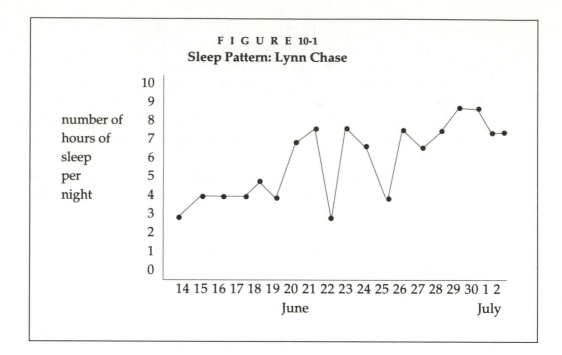

F I G U R E 10-1
Sleep Pattern: Lynn Chase

In evaluating progress, Mrs. Chase and the worker can reasonably conclude that the plan in regard to the sleeping goal is working successfully. They should also review Mrs. Chase's subjective ratings concerning how refreshed she feels upon awakening in the morning. Those ratings may also be converted into graph form for ready review.

■ **Exercise 10-3: Evaluating**

For these exercises, assume that you are a social worker with a family and children's counseling center. In the spaces provided, create simulated dialogues between yourself and the client that reflect how you might use the skill of evaluating progress toward goal attainment.

1. You are in the midst of evaluating progress toward goal attainment with Mrs. O. The measurement data clearly indicate that progress toward goal achievement has not occurred. In fact, it reveals that the problems have worsened. In the space below, create a simulated dialogue between yourself and the client as you review the data and discuss its implications.

2. You are in the midst of evaluating progress toward goal attainment with the S. family. The measurement data indicate that progress toward goal achievement has not occurred. There has been no change in either a positive or negative direction. In the space below, create a simulated dialogue between yourself and the client as you review the data and discuss its implications.

3. You are in the midst of evaluating progress toward goal attainment with Mrs. F. The measurement data clearly indicate that progress toward goal achievement has occurred. There is a definitive change in a positive direction. In the space below, create a simulated dialogue between yourself and the client as you review the data and discuss its implications.

FOCUSING

Focusing (Perlman, 1957, pp. 145–149) is a skill through which the worker helps to direct or maintain the attention of the client and worker upon the work at hand. Frequently, clients and workers wander away from the issues related to the agreed-upon purpose for work. Of course, often these digressions are very productive, leading to greater understanding and improving the chances for effective change. Sometimes, however, these departures may be clearly unproductive. Through focusing, the worker redirects energy to relevant topics. Also, something of significance may occur that goes unnoticed by the client. By quickly directing the client's attention to it, the worker may powerfully heighten the client's awareness and understanding. For example, in work with a family, the worker may observe that just as plans for an action step are about to be finalized, one family member interrupts with a complaint about some past behavior of another. Some social workers might view such behavior as resistance to change. Others might see it as an attempt to maintain family-system equilibrium. However it is regarded theoretically, the worker may use the skill of focusing to respond to the interruption. He might say to the family member who interrupts, "Would you please hold on to that thought so that we can come back to it later? I'd like to complete our plans first. Thanks." Through this form of focusing, the worker directs the family back to the work at hand. To accomplish a different purpose, that of enhancing process awareness, the worker might focus in a different way by saying something like, "I noticed that just about the time we were reaching consensus on a step to address one of the problems, Johnny brought up his concern about Sheila's past behavior. I wonder, Johnny, what do you think led you to raise the topic at this particular time?"

■ **Exercise 10-4: Focusing**

For these exercises, assume that you are a social worker with a family and children's counseling center. In the spaces provided, write the words you would say in using the skill of focusing.

1. You are reviewing action steps with Mrs. O. In the midst of this process, Mrs. O. begins to reminisce about a childhood girlfriend. It is your judgment that Mrs. O. would be better served at this time if you were to complete the process of reviewing action steps. You intend to return later in the interview to her childhood memory. In the space provided, write the words you would say in using the skill of focusing with Mrs. O. Also, anticipate Mrs. O.'s response and your reaction to it.

2. You are in the midst of exploring a new topic of importance to the S. family. Only the parents and the teenage children are present for this meeting. The subject involves the emerging sexual feelings of one of the adolescents. As the discussion begins, you observe that Mrs. S. changes the subject to a less anxiety-provoking issue. This pattern seems to occur whenever the adolescent family members begin to express sexual concerns. Based upon your professional judgment, you conclude that continuing with the topic of adolescent sexuality would be congruent with the values and cultural background of the family, helpful to the family, and represent a step toward goal achievement. You therefore decide to use the skill of focusing. In the space provided, write the words you would say in demonstrating two forms of focusing with the S. family. First, show how you would focus in order to redirect the discussion back to the topic of adolescent sexuality. Second, indicate how you might refocus in order to enhance the family's awareness of the pattern of moving to less difficult topics. Also, anticipate Mrs. S.'s response and your reaction to each of her statements.

3. You are in the midst of role-playing an action step with Mrs. F. She has assumed the role of her daughter while you play the part of mother.

After a few moments in the part of her daughter, you notice that her eyes begin to water and tears fall onto her cheeks. Mrs. F., however, shrugs it off and continues in her role. Based upon your professional judgment, you conclude that it would be consistent with your contract and that Mrs. F. would benefit from a more full expression of her feelings and an exploration of their meaning. In the space provided, write the words you would say in using the skill of focusing to call attention to the tears and the thoughts and feelings behind them. Also, anticipate Mrs. F.'s response and your reaction to it.

EDUCATING

During the work phase, it may become apparent that a client lacks certain relevant information. Frequently, there are skill deficits as well. In such circumstances, the worker may appropriately assume the role of teacher or educator. Educating involves several dimensions. Often, the worker shares knowledge and educated opinions. For example, he might inform a parent about major developmental milestones that might be expected in her six-month-old child. The worker might go on to share his ideas and opinions about how a parent could facilitate the child's development through, for instance, mutual play activities (e.g., parent moves baby's hands in patty-cake fashion while smiling and mimicking baby's sounds). Typically, the worker shares information in such a way that the client may freely consider its relevance for her particular situation and determine whether to accept it. This is particularly true when the information conveyed is opinion rather than fact. However, even when factually correct information is presented, the worker respects the right of clients to disagree.

As good teachers, social workers realize that all people do not learn in the same way. Many clients have learning styles that differ from the preferred teaching approach of the worker. Therefore, the worker attempts to individualize his educational approach in order to reach each client. For example, some clients have an affinity for abstract thinking. They enjoy theoretical concepts and principles. Once understood, they can cognitively apply, through deductive reasoning, the principles to everyday life. Other clients are stronger in concrete thinking. They may have a well-developed capacity to take a specific incident or situation and reach a clear understanding of it. Sometimes, this understanding can be applied to similar circumstances in the future, but at other times, such clients find that they must consider anew each new situation. These clients frequently benefit from examples and illustrations and from specific guidelines more than from abstract presentations. Many clients also learn better when a worker tells a story or uses a metaphor or an analogy. For example, in working with a client who feels trapped by circumstances, the worker—having thoroughly explored the situation with the client—realizes that the client is, in many ways, trapping herself. There are options, but the client has not seriously considered them. At such a time, a worker might tell a story in the following fashion:

> I remember a comic strip I once saw. In the first frame, there is this desperate-looking man, staring out between the iron bars of a jail. His eyes and head are absolutely still. He looks only through the bars and nowhere else. He appears to be highly anxious, afraid, and depressed all at the same time. In the second frame, we see the scene from a larger perspective. Again we notice the desperate man looking out between the bars. But then we notice that there are iron bars on one side of the room only. The other three sides don't have bars at all; there aren't even any walls. It's completely open. The prisoner, if he would only move his head out from between the bars and look in another direction, could easily see that he could walk away any time he wanted.

Sometimes, the worker can serve important educational functions by sharing personal feelings and experiences. It is very much like telling a story—however, it is a story about the worker himself. In self-disclosure, the worker almost always becomes a more real and genuine human being to the client. Additionally, the personal experience may carry special meaning to the client, who might attribute considerable significance to the message or moral of the worker's personal story. However, in sharing his personal feelings and experiences, the worker should be careful not to become the client's client. There should be a clear relationship between the worker's self-disclosures and the established goals for work. Also, he should not take so much time in sharing his experiences and feelings that it detracts significantly from the client's opportunity to express herself. In addition, if the worker shares too much of himself, especially personal difficulties or tragedies, the client may begin to view him as troubled or needy rather than as competent. If she does begin to consider the worker in this light, it could seriously diminish his effectiveness. The client might abruptly end the relationship with this worker and look for a "healthier" professional. Alternately, she may start to take care of the worker, assuming the role of caretaker or surrogate parent. In addition, she might begin to protect him from the full impact of her own situation. Therefore, the worker should be cautious about revealing too much of himself, too often or at too great an extent. Remember, social work services are primarily *for* the client, *not* for the worker.

■ **Exercise 10-5: Educating**

For these exercises, assume that you are a social worker with a family and children's counseling center. In the spaces provided, write the words you would say in using the skill of educating.

1. You are in the midst of discussing with Mrs. O. her eating patterns. You discover that she almost never has a hot meal and rarely eats vegetables. Her most typical meal is a bologna sandwich. You and Mrs. O. agree that more balanced meals are desirable. You then begin to educate Mrs. O. about the meals-on-wheels program available in your community. Through this program, Mrs. O. could have delivered to her apartment one or two hot, nutritionally balanced meals per day. In the space provided, outline the major elements of the information you would like to communicate to her. Then write the words you would say as you begin to educate Mrs. O. about the meals-on-wheels program.

2. You are in the midst of an individual meeting with a teenage member of the S. family. She reports to you in confidence that she is sexually active and "will continue to have sex with my boyfriend no matter what my mother says!" She reports that neither she nor her boyfriend practice birth control but that she would like to have some protection. She also mentions that she has recently begun to feel some unusual itching and discomfort "down there" (in her vaginal area). In the space provided, outline the major elements of the information you would like to communicate to her. Then write the words you would say in beginning to

educate the teenager about birth control possibilities and about medical care.

3. You are role playing an action step with Mrs. F. She plays the role of her daughter while you play the mother's part. After a few moments as her daughter, you notice that her eyes begin to water and tears fall onto her cheeks. You focus upon the tears and discover that she feels extremely

guilty about the way she has reared her children. She sobs and says, "I tried not to repeat the bad things my parents did to me, but it looks like I did them anyway." In the space provided, outline the major elements of the information you would communicate to Mrs. F. in educating her about the human tendency to repeat intergenerational family patterns even when trying not to. Then, by "telling a story" or by self-disclosing a personal experience of your own, write the words you would say in beginning to educate Mrs. F. about this human tendency.

ADVISING

Sometimes in working with a client, a worker provides advice. Making a suggestion or recommendation is a perfectly appropriate action by a social worker. However, in advising, the worker should communicate in a manner clearly conveying that the client has every opportunity to accept or reject the advice. As Maluccio (1979) has observed, clients very much value and appreciate advice. Nonetheless, almost all social workers, particularly during the early stages of their professional development, experience conflict concerning advice giving. Some may be tempted to give too much advice; others too little. Social workers are keenly aware of the values of self-determination and respect for the uniqueness of each person; in interpreting these values, some social workers conclude that they should never offer any advice, and others decide that clients are entitled to all the knowledge social workers possess and therefore provide advice whether or not it is requested. These two positions represent opposite ends of a continuum. Most social workers take a more moderate stance, giving advice in certain circumstances but not in all. Some advice giving is usually appropriate and helpful. Knowing when to, when not to, and especially how to give advice is the crux of the dilemma.

In general, the worker should resist the temptation to offer advice based upon his own personal feelings, attitudes, and preferences. This can be difficult in situations when a client asks, "What should I do?" or, "What would you do if you were in my situation?" For example, a social worker has worked for weeks with a nineteen-year-old man who is gay. As a result of their exploration together, he has become much more self-accepting and comfortable with his sexual orientation. Recently, he has raised the issue of whether to tell his tradition-bound parents the truth about his sexual preference. He asks the worker, "Should I tell them?"

Some social workers might deftly avoid answering his question by asking, "What do you think?" Others might be tempted to say, "Of course. Tell them. You have nothing to be ashamed of." Still others might experience considerable internal conflict and anxiety. Professionally, they might predict that the client would probably feel less conflicted and more personally integrated if he were to tell his parents. These workers might also anticipate that the encounter between the young man and his parents could be highly stressful; that it might even lead to the man losing his parents' approval and support, perhaps even all contact with them. Some workers might recognize that ultimately this decision is the man's alone to make. Preferring to respond directly to the question but without advising him what to do, these workers might say, "I'd be more than glad to explore this issue with you and help you make a decision. But I can't simply give you an answer to that question. The final decision is yours and yours alone."

There are also many occasions when workers should offer direct and specific advice. For example, in a situation where a client has been working on becoming more assertive with her lover, the worker and client have rehearsed assertive communication during their meetings. The client is about to take a step toward greater assertion in the relationship. The worker has learned that "soft" or caring assertions tend to solidify relationships and provide a basis for moving toward "hard" or confrontive assertions. He therefore advises the client to begin with affectionate, caring assertions and then, later, after some experience, to initiate assertive expressions that involve requests for change.

Usually, the worker provides advice in such a way that the client may freely accept or reject it. However, on some occasions he may actually have to direct the actions of others. For example, in an emergency where a child has been injured and his life is in danger, the worker might say, "We must get this child to the hospital now!"

Advising is involved in many aspects of practice. A worker might, for example, advise an adult client who grew up in a family where his father was regularly intoxicated and abusive to read books on the topics of codependence and adult children of alcoholics (ACOA). He might suggest that the client attend ACOA or Al-Anon meetings as an adjunct to their work together. The worker might guide a client through a job application or coach her about speaking to her boss about a raise. He might advise a client to seek medical care. In giving advice, the worker usually phrases it in slightly different ways to accomplish different objectives. However, unless life-threatening circumstances exist, he would nearly always express advice in a fashion conveying that it is a suggestion, perhaps even a strong recommendation, but not a command, such as an employer might give to an employee or an angry parent might deliver to a disobedient child. A typical form might be, "I have a suggestion that I'd like you to consider. I suggest/recommend/advise that you . . . "

■ **Exercise 10-6: Advising**

For these exercises, assume that you are a social worker with a family and children's counseling center. In the spaces provided, write the words you would say in using the skill of advising.

1. You are in the midst of discussing with Mrs. O. her eating patterns. You discover that she almost never has a hot meal and rarely eats vegetables. Her most typical meal is a bologna sandwich. You and Mrs. O. agree that more balanced meals would be desirable. You then begin to educate Mrs. O. about the meals-on-wheels program available in your community. Through this program, Mrs. O. could have delivered to her apartment one or two hot, nutritionally balanced meals per day. In the space provided, write the words you would say in advising Mrs. O. to participate in the meals-on-wheels program.

2. You are in the midst of an individual meeting with a teenage member of the S. family. She reports to you in confidence that she is sexually active and "will continue to have sex with my boyfriend no matter what my mother says!" She reports that neither she nor her boyfriend practice birth control but that she would like to have some protection. She also mentions that she has recently begun to feel some unusual itching and discomfort "down there" (in her vaginal area). In the space provided, write the words you would say in advising the teenager to seek medical care concerning the possible vaginal infection.

3. Following your discovery with Mrs. F. that she has perpetuated some nonfunctional parenting practices that she had experienced as a child in her own family of origin, you conclude that she might benefit from the construction of a family genogram. In the space provided, write the words you would say in advising Mrs. F. to help you complete her family genogram.

REPRESENTING

In this workbook, representing refers to the actions a worker takes on behalf of a client in pursuit of agreed-upon goals. The worker's representational activities are usually intended to facilitate the process by which a client interacts with members of various social systems. As envisioned, representing incorporates the social work interventive roles of brokering, advocating, and mediating (Compton & Galaway, 1989, pp. 505–515). Therefore, representing is a complex process indeed. It builds upon many of the skills of the preparing, beginning, and exploring phases, as well as those of assessing, contracting, and working.

However, instead of working *for* and *with* the client, the worker works *for* the client but *with* others. For example, suppose an unemployed, homeless client desperately needs immediate shelter, food, clean clothes, and financial support. Based upon their joint assessment, the worker and client concur that if the client were to apply directly to a resource agency for help, she would probably be denied. The client asks the worker to represent her in this matter. The worker consents to make the initial contact with the appropriate agency. Then, with the support of the client, he sketches out several action steps. Similar to preparation for a first meeting with a client, he carefully prepares for the contact in order to improve the chances of effectively representing the client.

During the course of the worker's career, he collects the names and phone numbers of other social workers and associates of numerous community resources. He knows people at churches, community centers, neighborhood associations, state and federal welfare organizations, and a host of other systems. He makes notes about such resource people and keeps them in a card file for easy access. Periodically, he sends contact persons friendly thank-you notes and occasionally mails commendatory letters to their supervisors and agency administrators. Such actions tend to maintain his value within the helping community.

In this particular instance, the worker may decide that a good first step would be to contact a fellow social worker at the agency in question. Once telephone contact with an appropriate agency representative is made, the worker proceeds in much the same manner as if he were beginning with a client. He introduces himself and secures an introduction in return. Depending upon the circumstances, he may make a few informal, friendly remarks to put his colleague at ease. He then outlines the purpose for the contact by saying something such as, "I have a client here with me who is in need of support right now. She is unemployed, without money. She hasn't eaten for two days and has no place to stay tonight. I'm calling in order to determine whether she might be eligible to receive some help from your agency." Following the description of purpose, the worker may seek feedback to confirm that his message has been understood. At this point in the process, he then invites his colleague to provide information about eligibility requirements or to inquire further about the client's circumstances.

Representing clients in such cases is often extremely satisfying. The exchange with the resource person may be both pleasant and productive. The client may receive what she needs and be treated decently. Workers who cultivate positive relationships with resource persons and know something about the mission and programs of contact organizations tend to be more effective in representing their clients than those workers who do not.

Representing clients, however, is not always enjoyable. Sometimes, the worker must assertively advocate on behalf of a client who is not being treated fairly. For example, consider the situation of a client who seeks help from a social worker in dealing with a landlord. In the middle of a cold winter, the heat, provided to all tenants as part of their rent, is not reaching into the client's apartment. In spite of several complaints, the landlord takes no action to rectify the situation. The client then asks the worker to contact the landlord on her behalf. The worker agrees to represent the client.

First, he uses the preparing skills in order to formulate a preliminary plan. He explores more fully with the client in order to secure detailed facts about the heating problem and to learn about her experience as a tenant in the residence. He might then consult a city official knowledgeable about housing regulations and landlord-tenant laws. He collects information to expand his knowledge base and to influence the landlord, should that become necessary. He also prepares for the initial contact with the landlord. In this instance, he decides to telephone first. He calls, gives his name, and says, "I'm a social worker with the tenants' advocacy program of the city social services agency. One of your tenants, Mrs. Wicker, has contacted us about a problem with the heating system. It seems that the family's apartment has been without heat for five days. Could you tell me what's being done to repair the problem and how much longer it will be?"

If the landlord does not acknowledge the problem and, for example, begins to denigrate the client, the worker might respond in the following manner, "Regardless of the complaints you have had about Mrs. Wicker and her family, they still need heat. As you know, it's dangerously cold and the lives of the family members are at risk if heat is not restored soon." If the landlord remains unresponsive, the worker might outline the steps he intends to take should the heating system remain unrepaired and the family continue to be at risk. In some respects, his description is similar to that of a worker beginning with a client. He states his purpose, describes his role as client advocate, and discusses the actions he intends to take should his clients continue to be in need or at risk (i.e., his policies and procedures). He also makes a specific request for action from the landlord (i.e., he outlines the landlord's role).

If the landlord acknowledges the problem, outlines a plan and a timetable for its repair, and makes a commitment to immediately protect the family from the cold, the worker would express his thanks and credit the landlord with being responsive to the worker's request. He would then apprise the client of the landlord's plan and request that he, the worker, be notified of the outcome. If the landlord follows through with the plan, the worker might again communicate appreciation for the positive action. If the landlord does not follow through, the worker would probably contact him again, report that the apartment is still dangerously cold, and begin to inform him about steps he, the worker, intends to take should the repairs remain incomplete.

Social workers frequently represent clients as a regular part of practice. They do so in order to link clients with needed community resources, to secure fair and equitable treatment, and as part of the processes of mediation and conflict resolution. In representing, workers ensure that they have the clients' informed consent to act on their behalf.

■ **Exercise 10-7: Representing**

For these exercises, assume that you are a social worker with a family and children's counseling center. In the spaces provided, outline the action steps you might take in representing the clients in the following situations. Describe how you would prepare to represent the client and then write the words you would say in beginning with the person contacted on behalf of the client.

1. With her consent, you are representing Mrs. O., an elderly person who almost never has hot or nutritionally balanced meals. You are about to contact the community meals-on-wheels program in order to seek their help in providing Mrs. O. with at least one sound meal daily. In the space provided, outline the steps you would take prior to making contact and then write the words you would say as you begin to represent Mrs. O. with the resource agency.

2. With her consent and that of her parents, you are representing Gloria, a teenage member of the S. family, in relation to some sexual issues. You have jointly decided that you will contact the office of her family physician in order to arrange for a prompt appointment to deal with a vaginal infection. (When Gloria called for an appointment, she was too embarrassed to say why she needed one right away. An appointment was scheduled for a month later.) In the space provided, outline the steps you would take prior to making contact with the physician's office and then write the words you would say in beginning to represent Gloria in this matter.

3. With the informed consent of Mrs. F., you are representing her during interactions with the principal of the school where her daughters report that they have often been harrassed by several white boys. According to the girls, the boys have spit on them and called them racist names. In

the space provided, outline the steps you would take in preparing for contact with the principal and then write the words you would say as you begin to represent Mrs. F. in this matter.

RESPONDING WITH IMMEDIACY

The skill of responding with immediacy (Carkhuff & Anthony, 1979, pp. 114–116) involves exploration of the client's experiences and feelings *as they occur*. Typically, the client's responses to the worker, the work process, or the social work relationship are the focus for immediate exploration. Such an examination may be crucial to a client's decision to continue or conclude the working relationship, to be open or closed to taking action steps, or to be an active or passive partner in the work. Immediacy makes things "real." It enhances the potency of the relationship. Responding with immediacy assists the client in exploring concerns as they emerge. Responding in an immediate manner also demonstrates (models) to the client an open communication style. It may promote greater honesty and openness on the part of the client, increase her understanding of interpersonal patterns, and reduce resistance to work on problems and goals.

One format for responding with immediacy is:

Right here and now with me you seem to be feeling/thinking/doing

_____

_____.

Usually, the worker's use of the skill applies directly to the client's immediate feelings about the worker, about their relationship, or about the nature and utility of the work. It becomes less immediate and less powerful to the degree that the worker's response moves the meaning away from the "right-here-and-right-now." For example, if the worker comments about something that happened between him and the client at some point in the past, the client may recall it differently or not at all, or she may intellectually process the information without *feeling* its full impact. Although it may still be a useful activity, exploring a past exchange rarely has as powerful an effect as does responding immediately to one occurring in the present.

In many cases, the social work relationship constitutes a sample of the client's patterns of interpersonal behavior. The client sometimes recreates in the helping context the very conditions that emerge in other relationships. When this happens, the client's reactions within the social work relationship may be illustrative of problematic interpersonal patterns with other people. Through immediate responses, the worker can help the client to recognize such patterns and develop new, more useful styles of interaction.

Responding with immediacy is not applicable in work with all clients. It depends upon the purpose for work and the contract established. Generally, workers do not respond with immediacy unless the client's reactions are clearly relevant to the problems and goals for work. Also, workers vary in the degree to which they emphasize and attend to interactions within the social work relationship. Some practice theories consider them to be highly important while others view them as less so. Nonetheless, nearly every social work practice model includes methods for using client reactions within the relationship as part of the change process. Responding with immediacy is one such skill.

For example, a social worker has begun to work with a client who identifies as problems her "lack of true friends" and a belief that her spouse does not "like" her company (the spouse confirms this). During meetings with the client, the social worker notices that she is inattentive to his statements. She seems to focus on her own thoughts and listens just enough to his words to stay somewhat involved in the conversation. In essence, the worker begins to observe, and to feel, that she "tunes him out." The worker wonders whether this interpersonal pattern contributes to her spouse's reaction to her. He concludes that responding with immediacy would be consistent with their contract. He says: "Right here and now as we talk with one another, I notice that your eyes are mostly turned away from me when I speak, and you seem uninterested in what I'm saying. Tell me, how do you feel toward me right now?"

The use of *responding with immediacy* often results in a dramatic increase in energy between the client and worker. Both parties tend to become much more oriented to the present moment and more engaged with each other. However, because it may have a powerful impact, workers should use immediate responses only after a solid relationship has been established and a contract formulated. The client should know that the worker understands her and has her interest at heart.

■ **Exercise 10-8: Responding with Immediacy**

For these exercises, assume that you are a social worker with a family and children's counseling center. In the spaces provided, write the words you would say in using the skill of responding with immediacy.

1. In the process of advising Mrs. O. to participate in a meals-on-wheels program, you observe her turning away and subtly shaking her head. You conclude that her nonverbal behavior may be saying no to your advice. In the space provided, write the words you would say in responding with immediacy to Mrs. O.'s nonverbal reaction. Also, note what you anticipate her response to your comments would be.

2. You are in the midst of an individual meeting with a teenage member of the S. family. She confides to you that although she is sexually active with her boyfriend, she often fantasizes about another person. As she says that, she looks deeply into your eyes, blushes, and then looks away in what appears to be an embarrassed reaction. You suspect that she has had sexual fantasies about you. You know that it would be quite consistent with your contract to discuss this directly. In the space provided, write the words you would say in responding with immediacy to the teenager's expression. Also, note what you anticipate her response to your comments would be.

3. Following your discovery with Mrs. F. that she has perpetuated with her own children some dysfunctional parenting practices that she had experienced as a child in her own family of origin, you observe that she sits back in her chair, crosses her arms in front of her, and appears to frown. You're not entirely certain what this reaction means but you suspect that she may be feeling ashamed and vulnerable. You think that she is afraid that you might be critical of her. In the space provided, write the words you would say in responding with immediacy to Mrs. F. Also, note what you anticipate her response to your comments would be.

REFRAMING

Reframing (Bandler & Grinder, 1982; Hartman & Laird, 1983) refers to the words a worker says and the actions he takes when introducing the client to a new way of looking at some aspect of herself, the problem, or the situation. Usually, it involves sharing a different perspective from that which the client has adopted. Clients sometimes embrace a point of view in such a determined fashion that it constitutes an obstacle to goal achievement. Fixed views are not necessarily problematic and workers should, of course, not indiscriminately attempt to challenge or reframe all of them. Reframing is used when the attitude is a fundamental part of the problem for work. It is similar to and often even a form of educating. It differs in that the overall purpose in reframing is to liberate the client from a dogmatic perspective. It usually results in changed feelings as well as cognitions.

There are several forms of reframing. One of the more common involves the worker *converting a negative into a positive*. In reframing a negative into a positive, the worker might wonder aloud in a fashion such as:

> When you talk about how stupid and indecisive you are because you have difficulty choosing from among various courses of action, I feel a bit confused because those attributes sound very desirable to me. I mean, what you refer to as indecisive appears to me to be the ability to see different points of view. It sounds like you're open-minded and willing to consider many perspectives and options. It sounds like flexibility to me. And what you suggest is stupidity sounds a great deal to me like carefulness, thoroughness, and patience. These are attributes that I find extremely appealing. Are you sure they are so bad?

Another form of reframing is *personalizing meaning* (Carkhuff & Anthony, 1979, pp. 95–131), which encourages the client to shift the attribution of responsibility away from other people, organizations, or external forces (i.e., the situation) and toward herself, so that she becomes responsible for and capable of effecting change. It helps the client to see a relationship between her own beliefs, values, attitudes, and expectations on the one hand and the feelings she experiences or the behavior she enacts on the other. This form of reframing involves the worker going beyond the communication directly expressed by the client. He alters the client's expression somewhat in order to shift an externalized or situationalized meaning toward a more internalized or personalized meaning for which the client is likely to feel greater responsibility and control. In personalizing meaning, the worker may use a format such as:

> Are you feeling/doing _____ because you think/believe/value/perceive/expect_____?

Because the skill of personalizing meaning is derived from the *worker's* rather than the *client's* frame of reference, it is an expressive rather than an empathic skill. Therefore, the worker should phrase his comments in a tentative manner. Personalizing meaning suggests that the client's thoughts, feelings, or actions are more a result of or associated with conscious individual processes than external or situational factors. It may sometimes leave clients feeling more guilty or more burdened with responsibility. However, it also conveys a sense of considerable optimism, because such feelings are a result of one's own values, beliefs, or thoughts: these are aspects of a person that are not necessarily permanent—one's beliefs and attitudes can and do change. Notice how much more positive such an explanation is than one that implies a person feels in a certain way because she is "jinxed," has a deficient superego structure, had a lousy childhood, suffers from a personality disorder, or because "that's just the way she is."

Here is an example of a social worker talking with a client who is a MSW student:

CLIENT: I'm devastated! I got a C+ in my social work field placement. I'll never make it through the program. I'm a total failure.

WORKER: Are you disappointed in yourself because you *believe* you should do better than C+ work and you *think* that getting a C+ means that you won't be able to graduate?

Situationalizing meaning is another form of reframing through which the worker changes the meaning reflected in the client's expression. Although there is certainly an empathic element, the worker again begins to alter the meaning as presented by the client. In the case of situationalizing meaning, the worker empathically reflects understanding of the client's feelings or behavior but then suggests that the reason for or the meaning associated with the feelings or behavior may also be viewed as a result of external, societal, systemic, situational, or other factors not entirely within the client's individual control or responsibility.

Frequently, situationalizing meaning results in an expansion of the client's perspective and a lessening of her sense of guilt, self-blame, or personal responsibility. For example:

CLIENT: I'm a wreck. I can't sleep or eat; I can't concentrate. I know my head is really messed up. I've always been kind of crazy.

WORKER: You feel awful; you're anxious and depressed and you have lots of problems. I wonder, though, might these feelings be a normal and understandable reaction to the recent changes in your life? Wouldn't the most well-adjusted person feel out of sorts and have some difficulty sleeping when he has recently lost his job and doesn't have any immediate prospects for another?

■ Exercise 10-9: Reframing

For these exercises, assume that you are a social worker with a family and children's counseling center. In the spaces provided, write the words you would say in using the skill of reframing.

1. You are in the midst of discussing with Mrs. O. her eating patterns. She says that she has not been eating balanced meals because, "I cannot get anyone to drive me to the grocery, it's too far to walk, and when I telephone to have it delivered they always get it wrong." In the space provided, write the words you would say in reframing Mrs. O.'s statement so that it reflects a personalized meaning. Anticipate her response. Also, experiment with another form of reframing by attempting to change her expression from a negative to a positive.

2. You are in the midst of an individual meeting with a teenage member of the S. family. She says, "My mother is always on my case. She's a wild woman. She's so controlling. I can't do anything I want to do. She thinks that I'm five years old." In the space provided, write the words you would say in reframing her statement from a negative to a positive. Anticipate her reaction. Also, experiment by reframing her statement so that it has a personalized meaning.

3. Following your discovery with Mrs. F. that she has perpetuated with her own children some dysfunctional parenting practices she had experienced as a child in her family of origin, you observe that she sits back in her chair, crosses her arms in front of her, and appears to frown. In response to your probe, Mrs. F. confirms that she is indeed feeling guilty and ashamed that she may have harmed her children. She says, "I feel so ashamed. I've done just what I've always criticized my parents

for." In the space provided, write the words you would say in reframing Mrs. F.'s statement so that it reflects a situationalized meaning. Also, note what you anticipate her response to your comments would be. Also, experiment by reframing her statement so that it has a personalized meaning.

CONFRONTING

Confronting (Carkhuff & Anthony, 1979, pp. 116–119) involves the worker directly and without disapproval pointing out to the client a discrepancy, inconsistency, or contradiction in aspects of her words and actions. In confronting, the worker challenges the client to examine different elements of herself in regard to other elements. For example, consider a situation where a client has requested help from a social worker in regard to a troubled marriage. The client says he is "willing to do whatever is necessary to save and improve the relationship." However, following a meeting with his wife and the worker during which he promised that he and his wife would go out for a "date" on the next Thursday, he worked late at his job and arrived home three hours too late. After the client missed three consecutive date nights, the worker confronted him by saying, "You said you want to improve the relationship and you agreed to several dates with your wife. However, on three consecutive occasions, you worked late on the nights you had planned to go out with your wife. What do you think this might mean?"

In confronting, the worker may use the following format (Carkhuff & Anthony, 1979, p. 117):

On the one hand you say/feel/do _____
_____ and/but/yet on the other
hand you say/feel/do _____
_____.

Confrontation can have a powerful effect upon clients. It has the potential to cause severe disequilibrium in those who are highly stressed or have fragile coping skills. Therefore, before using the skill of confronting with a particular client, the worker should be certain that the client has the psychological and social resources to endure the impact. Certainly, the relationship between worker and client should be well established prior to any confrontation. In confronting, the worker should be descriptive about the discrepancies that are observed. He should avoid judgmental or evaluative speculations and conclusions. Finally, he should usually "precede and follow confrontations with empathic" responses (Hammond, Hepworth, & Smith, 1977, p. 280).

■ Exercise 10-10: Confronting

For these exercises, assume that you are a social worker with a family and children's counseling center. In the spaces provided, write the words you would say in using the skill of confronting.

1. You are in the midst of an interview with Mrs. O. approximately two weeks after she has begun to receive daily hot meals through the meals-on-wheels program. Prior to that, she had agreed that more balanced meals would be desirable and said that she would eat the food when it was delivered. During the course of this meeting, you notice that the day's meal remains untouched. There is also evidence that Mrs. O. has not eaten the delivered meals for the past two days. In the space provided, write the words you would say in confronting Mrs. O. about the uneaten meals. Describe what Mrs. O.'s reaction to your confrontation might be.

2. You are in the midst of an individual meeting with a teenage member of the S. family, discussing sexuality. She reports that her physician had prescribed medication for the treatment of the vaginal infection. The doctor told her to abstain from sexual intercourse during the two-week period she was to take the medication. She was also told to inform her boyfriend that he should see his doctor and be treated before he resumed any sexual relations. Otherwise, they would continue to infect each other. The girl says that her boyfriend will not go to the doctor and continues to want to have sex with her. She says she'll "probably just let him have what he wants 'cause if I don't, he'll get it somewhere else." In the space provided, write the words you would say in confronting the girl about this situation. Describe what her reaction to your confrontation might be.

3. During the course of your interaction with the principal of the school where Mrs. F.'s daughters have apparently been harrassed by several white boys, the principal says, "There is no racism at this school. The F. girls will just have to learn to deal with the boys. The sisters are the only nonwhite students we have." In the space provided, write the words you would say in confronting the principal. Describe what his reaction to your confrontation might be.

POINTING OUT ENDINGS

Pointing out endings (Shulman, 1984, p. 108) involves the worker reminding "the client of the impending ending." In most cases where a contract has been established, a time frame for working toward goal achievement has been identified and agreed upon. This occurs as a significant part of developing the change program (see Chapter Nine). Periodically during the work phase, the worker makes reference to this time frame for work. Of course, the timetable may be renegotiated when the situation warrants. Ideally, however, any such revision should be considered carefully and discussed openly between the worker and client. Extending an appropriate time frame does not necessarily increase the probability of goal achievement. Sometimes, more time serves to imply to client and worker that the goals are "just too difficult" to ever accomplish. The extension may leave the impression that the relationship "need never end."

By pointing out endings, the worker motivates the client to work hard on the action steps. As Perlman has suggested (1979, pp. 48–77), the social work relationship is time limited. After all, social workers are not marrying or adopting their clients—they are their professional helpers, not members of their family. By establishing time limits and pointing out endings, the worker helps the client to prepare psychologically for the process of concluding the relationship. If the topic of the forthcoming conclusion to the relationship is avoided, the client, and the worker, can deny the immediacy of the feelings. However, denial, while affording momentary emotional respite, prevents the parties from psychologically anticipating and preparing themselves for the ending. Therefore, in spite of feelings of discomfort, the worker occasionally refers to the forthcoming conclusion to the relationship.

The skill of pointing out endings may be undertaken in several ways. Regardless of the specific form it takes, the skill leads the client to begin to consider consciously and emotionally the fact that the relationship will end. Whether it involves a transfer, referral, or termination, the worker gently reminds the client that there will soon be an ending and that there may very well be some thoughts and feelings triggered by the change.

For example, consider the case where a family and a worker have agreed to meet for eight sessions with a goal toward improving communications among the members. The work has proceeded quite well. By the fourth meeting, the family members have progressed to such an extent that they are able to express differences of opinion without feeling devalued or rejected. There has also been a noticeable decrease in tension and an increase in humor. Toward the end of the session, the worker says, "We're now finishing up our fourth session. There are four meetings left. We're halfway there."

Following such a reminder, the worker might probe for and explore thoughts and feelings associated with the idea of ending. He might say, "As we think about concluding our relationship, some thoughts or feelings may occur. I wonder, would you want to talk some about them?" Or he might ask, "How will things be different once we have concluded our work together?" Although a specific format is not universally applicable, workers should understand that the primary element in pointing out endings is the reminder. Statements such as "We have _____ meetings left" or "We will be meeting for another _____ weeks" serve the function. In the case of transfers or referrals, the worker clarifies what will happen following his ending with the client. He might say, "We have _____ meetings left before you begin to work with _____," or, "We will be meeting for another _____ weeks before you begin the program at _____."

■ **Exercise 10-11: Pointing Out Endings**

For these exercises, assume that you are a social worker with a family and children's counseling center. In the spaces provided, write the words you would say in using the skill of pointing out endings.

1. You have been working with Mrs. O. for approximately two months. Her eating patterns have improved to the point where your services are no longer needed. She is now regularly receiving and eating meals delivered by the meals-on-wheels program. Her weight has returned to normal and her energy level has improved. Three weeks earlier, you and Mrs. O. had discussed the progress and decided that you would conclude your relationship in one month. The meeting next week will be your last. In the space provided, write the words you would say in pointing out endings to Mrs. O. Describe how she might react.

2. You are in the midst of the next to last meeting with the S. family. Over the course of several months, many productive changes have occurred. Two sessions before, the family members indicated that they were well on their way to accomplishing their goals. At that time, you had agreed to meet three more times. Next week you will have the concluding session. In the space provided, write the words you would say in pointing out endings with the S. family. Describe how they might react.

3. Through a joint discussion two weeks earlier, you and Mrs. F. concluded that she could best complete work toward goal attainment by participating in a ten-week assertive training group sponsored by another community agency. The group begins in three weeks. Next week will be your last meeting together. In the space provided, write the words you would say in pointing out endings with Mrs. F. Describe how she might react.

RECORDING DURING THE WORK PHASE

Throughout all phases of practice, the professional social worker is obligated to keep records. During the work phase, the worker keeps track of any revisions to the initial assessment and contract. He incorporates within the case record progress toward goal achievement as reflected through evaluation procedures such as goal attainment scaling, subjective ratings, test scores, or graphs. He also records additional action steps and notes changes to those previously established. Particularly, he records events, issues, or themes that might relate to the process of working toward goal accomplishment. In some instances, he presents a rationale for an action he is about to take or a recommendation he intends to make. For example, when a social worker learns from an adult client that he sometimes sexually molests his infant son, the worker is required by law to report this information to governmental authorities. Usually, this means a telephone call to the child protection services division of the state or local department of welfare or human services. Because the information has been acquired during a meeting protected by the worker's ethic of confidentiality, he should meticulously record the data (i.e., the words the client said) that led him to conclude that the child may be at risk of abuse. He should also record what he said to the client in response. For example, he may have informed him that he, the worker, is required by law to report this information. He should note this. He may also have indicated that he would like to continue to serve as his social worker during this time. He should record this as well. When he makes the phone call to the relevant authorities, he should record the date and time, the person contacted, and what was said. Of course, unless the client provides informed consent to do so, the worker refrains from sharing information about the client beyond what is needed to initiate the investigation into the possibility of child abuse.

In many settings, social workers use a problem-oriented approach (Martens & Holmstrup, 1974, pp. 554–561; Burrill, 1976, pp. 67–68; and H. C. Johnson, 1978, pp. 71–77) to keeping records during the work phase. Often, the SOAP format is adopted (Kagle, 1984, p. 64). SOAP is an acronym referring to the subjective, objective, assessment, and plan sections of a case recording for each contact with a client. Under the subjective category, the workers may include new or supplementary information provided by clients or other persons with whom the workers have had contact. Under the objective category, workers describe their own observations of the person, problem, and situation. Under the assessment dimension, workers summarize their current evaluation of progress toward goal achievement and make note of their tentative impressions and hypotheses. They may also summarize results of frequency counts, subjective ratings, and standardized test results within the assessment section. Under the plan category, they record changes, if any, to the original contract and note additional action steps that they or their clients intend to take.

For example, following an interview with Mrs. Chase, the social worker might prepare a SOAP entry for the case file as follows:

July 8, 1989

S. Mrs. Chase indicated that she had accomplished the action step we had identified for this week. She reported that it was a great help. She stated that she has felt in better spirits than she has for months.

  Following our meeting, Mr. Chase telephoned to report that things are much better at home. He said, "Everybody has begun to help out at home, and we're all much happier. Thanks a lot. You've been really wonderful."

O. During today's meeting, Mrs. Chase and I talked at length about her childhood. On several occasions, she referred to her mother's drinking and the mixed feelings she experienced as a child when she dealt with her intoxicated mother. She sobbed when she talked of the embarrassment and rage she felt when a friend had visited while her mother was drunk and verbally abusive. She also revealed that she felt "somehow to blame" for her mother's drinking. She said, "I used to feel that if I were somehow better or less of a problem, then Mother wouldn't need to drink so much."

  I reminded Mrs. Chase that we had three more meetings together. She said that "she would miss me" but already "things were much better."

A. Mrs. Chase's daily logs reflect initial progress toward two of the goals: sleeping better and arguing less with Robert and Richard. The change program appears to be viable. There is no need to change it at this time.

P. We identified a new action step. In addition to those already identified last week, Mrs. Chase has agreed to read Janet Woititz's book, *Adult Children of Alcoholics*, within three weeks of today's date.

Susan Holder, BSW, MSW

■ Exercise 10-12: Recording During the Work Phase

For these exercises, assume that you are a social worker with a family and children's counseling center. In the spaces provided, prepare SOAP entries for case records concerning the following client interviews.

1. On Monday of this week, you completed an interview with Mrs. O. The meeting occurred approximately two weeks after she had begun to receive daily hot meals through the meals-on-wheels program. Prior to that, she had agreed that more balanced meals would be desirable and said that she would eat the food when it was delivered. During the course of this meeting, you noticed that the day's meal remained untouched. There was also evidence that she had not eaten the delivered meals for the previous two days. You asked her about the uneaten food and she said that she hadn't been hungry. You asked whether she would eat the meal that would be delivered tomorrow. She said, "Oh, I don't know." In the space provided, prepare a SOAP entry regarding the interview.

2. Earlier today, you completed an interview with a teenage member of the S. family. Sexuality was the topic of conversation. She reported that her physician had prescribed medication for the treatment of the vaginal infection. The doctor told her to abstain from sexual intercourse for the two-week period she was to take the medicine. She was also told to inform her boyfriend that he should see his doctor and be treated before he resumed any sexual relations. Otherwise, they would continue to infect each other. The girl said that her boyfriend will not go to the doctor and continues to want to have sex with her. She said she'll "probably just let him have what he wants 'cause if I don't, he'll get it somewhere else." You asked her what she thought would happen if she did resume sexual relations with him now. She said, "I guess I'll probably get the infection again." When asked what would happen then, she responded by saying that she would probably have to go back to the doctor. You asked whether she might then refrain from sexual contact until her boyfriend went to a doctor; she said, "Well, I guess I'll have to stop it sometime. I can't just keep on becoming infected over and over again. Maybe it would be best to stop it now." In the space provided, prepare a SOAP entry regarding the interview.

3. Earlier today, you completed an interview with Mrs. F. and the principal of the school where Mrs. F.'s daughters have apparently been harassed by several white boys. During the course of the meeting, the principal said, "There is no racism at this school. The F. girls will just have to learn to deal with the boys. The sisters are the only nonwhite students we have." When you asked what he thought might be possible in order to ensure that the girls would not be injured, he said, "If they can't handle the situation, maybe they should try another school." Mrs. F. was quiet during the meeting with the principal. Afterward, she said, "See, I told you he was as racist as could be. Maybe I should file a lawsuit." You concluded the interview with her by suggesting that "each of us" explore possible courses of action to be considered at our next meeting later in the week. In the space provided, prepare a SOAP entry regarding the interview.

SUMMARY

During the work phase of social work practice, the client and worker take action toward resolving the identified problems and achieving the established goals. In this process, the worker uses both empathic exploring skills as well as the work-related expressive skills. Several skills pertinent to the work phrase include: (1) rehearsing action steps, (2) reviewing action steps, (3) evaluating, (4) focusing, (5) educating, (6) advising, (7) representing, (8) responding with immediacy, (9) reframing, (10) confronting, (11) pointing out endings, and (12) recording during the work phase.

■ **Exercise 10-13: Summary**

Building upon the earlier interviews which you had with your student colleague, conduct another, primarily for the purpose of working toward the goals identified through the contracting process. As you did previously, ensure that the interview setting is private and once again tape record the meeting. Using empathic and especially work phase expressive skills, interview her with a view toward helping her take steps toward goal attainment. At the conclusion of the meeting, arrange for another interview in about one week and point out to her that it will be your final meeting.

1. At the conclusion of the interview, ask your partner for feedback concerning her thoughts and feelings about the experience. Ask her for a totally honest reaction to the following questions: (a) Did she feel comfortable and safe with you? Did she trust you? (b) Did she feel that you were sincerely interested in her and in what she had to say? (c) Did she feel that you understood what she was trying to communicate? If not, explore with her what led her to believe that you did not understand? (d) Did she value the experience? (e) Does she believe that she has made progress toward goal attainment? If so, what does she identify as having been most helpful to that progress? If not, what were the obstacles? Did you do or not do anything that was unhelpful? (f) What suggestions does she have for you concerning how the interview could have been better or more helpful for her? Summarize your partner's feedback in the space below.

2. In the space below, summarize your own reaction to the meeting. How did you feel about the interview? What did you like and what did you dislike about it? Do you believe that you used all the relevant empathic and expressive skills during the interaction? What would you do differently if you were to redo the interview?

3. In your course notebook, prepare a record according to the SOAP format described above.
4. After you have completed the SOAP recording, play the audiotape or videotape. Make notes of significant exchanges that affected the way in which you prepared your SOAP record. Revise the record accordingly.

   At some point during the week, share the SOAP record with your social work student colleague. Ask her to share her thoughts and feelings as she reads the record. Request that she comment on its accuracy and correct any errors or differences in interpretation. In the space below, summarize her comments and discuss what you learn from her feedback.

5. Based upon your performance in the interview, use the rating scales below (where 0 = no proficiency and 10 = complete proficiency) to assess your current level of proficiency in the following social work skills. If you did not use a particular skill, you need not simulate a rating. However, do ask yourself whether there were points during the interview when you should have used one of these skills.

Probing

```
|___|___|___|___|___|___|___|___|___|___|
0   1   2   3   4   5   6   7   8   9   10
```

Seeking Clarification

```
|___|___|___|___|___|___|___|___|___|___|
0   1   2   3   4   5   6   7   8   9   10
```

Reflecting Content

```
|___|___|___|___|___|___|___|___|___|___|
0   1   2   3   4   5   6   7   8   9   10
```

Reflecting Feeling

```
|___|___|___|___|___|___|___|___|___|___|
0   1   2   3   4   5   6   7   8   9   10
```

Reflecting Complex Communications

```
|___|___|___|___|___|___|___|___|___|___|
0   1   2   3   4   5   6   7   8   9   10
```

Partializing

```
|___|___|___|___|___|___|___|___|___|___|
0   1   2   3   4   5   6   7   8   9   10
```

Going Beyond What Is Said

```
|___|___|___|___|___|___|___|___|___|___|
0   1   2   3   4   5   6   7   8   9   10
```

6. Now that you have completed these exercises, use the rating scales below (where 0 = no proficiency and 10 = complete proficiency) to conduct a summary evaluation of your proficiency in the working skills.

Rehearsing Action Steps

| | | | | | | | | | | |
|0|1|2|3|4|5|6|7|8|9|10|

Reviewing Action Steps

| | | | | | | | | | | |
|0|1|2|3|4|5|6|7|8|9|10|

Evaluating

| | | | | | | | | | | |
|0|1|2|3|4|5|6|7|8|9|10|

Focusing

| | | | | | | | | | | |
|0|1|2|3|4|5|6|7|8|9|10|

Educating

| | | | | | | | | | | |
|0|1|2|3|4|5|6|7|8|9|10|

Advising

| | | | | | | | | | | |
|0|1|2|3|4|5|6|7|8|9|10|

Representing

| | | | | | | | | | | |
|0|1|2|3|4|5|6|7|8|9|10|

Responding with Immediacy

| | | | | | | | | | | |
|0|1|2|3|4|5|6|7|8|9|10|

Reframing

| | | | | | | | | | | |
|0|1|2|3|4|5|6|7|8|9|10|

Confronting

| | | | | | | | | | | |
|0|1|2|3|4|5|6|7|8|9|10|

Pointing Out Endings

```
|___|___|___|___|___|___|___|___|___|___|
0   1   2   3   4   5   6   7   8   9   10
```

Recording During the Work Phase

```
|___|___|___|___|___|___|___|___|___|___|
0   1   2   3   4   5   6   7   8   9   10
```

7. Finally, review your ratings to identify those working skills in which you remain less proficient (e.g., a score of 7 or less). Then, in the space below, outline the steps you might take to improve your skill in those areas.

ENDING

The four most common forms of concluding a relationship with a client are: (1) transferral, (2) referral, (3) termination, and (4) client discontinuation. The first three involve the worker and client openly discussing the ending process and jointly determining the best course of action given the circumstances. These represent the preferred modes of concluding relationships with clients. The fourth form, quite common in many agency settings, is client initiated. Often with good reason, clients sometimes decide to stop meeting with the social worker. They may do so by informing the worker during a meeting, by telephone, or by letter. They may also discontinue without notification by failing to attend a scheduled meeting—the ending message is communicated by their absence. In such cases—assuming the worker can make contact by phone or in person—it is often very useful to "seek clarification" from clients who have discontinued the relationship. However, the worker should be extremely sensitive to the client's indirect expressions during these contacts. Sometimes, in response to the worker's inquiry, a client might say he will resume the relationship "since you were so nice to call," when in fact he has truly decided to conclude his involvement. If the worker probes carefully during such contacts, she may learn something from the client about the way she presented herself or how she intervened that was a factor in his decision to discontinue. This information may be helpful with other clients in the future. Providing clients an opportunity to express themselves in regard to the service may also help them conclude the relationship in a more satisfactory manner. It may expand their view of the worker, the agency, and the experience enough to enable them to try again at some point in the future.

Clients are more likely to discontinue without notification at certain times. There is an increased probability of client discontinuation whenever changes occur. A change from a routine meeting time or a relocation from one meeting place to another may lead clients to discontinue. Transferring a client from one worker to another within the same agency involves a stressful transition that clients may resolve by discontinuing. Perhaps the most difficult of all involves referring a client to another professional in a different agency, because it involves so many changes—a new location; another agency with at least some- what disparate policies, procedures, and mission; a new meeting schedule; and, of course, a different helping professional. Although the dynamics of transfers and referrals are similar, in general, transfers are considerably easier to manage than are referrals—referrals involve more change and the psychosocial demands upon the client are greater. Nonetheless, transfers and referrals, like termination and discontinuation, involve a conclusion to the relationship be- tween the worker and client.

Ending a significant relationship is often a difficult and painful experience. It is certainly challenging for social workers. Concluding a relationship with a client can stimulate strong feelings of sadness and loss and perhaps other emotions as well. For clients, the process of ending the relationship with the worker may be even more intense. Usually, the client has viewed the worker as a kind, caring, and understanding person who listened well and had his best interests at heart. Often, he has shared personally intimate thoughts and feel- ings. This may lead him to feel simultaneously safe and vulnerable. His secrets are now entrusted to someone with whom he may never again have contact. Sometimes, the client has overcome a major problem, has turned his life toward a more adaptive direction, or has accomplished a significant goal. He may experience intense gratitude and want to make it up to the worker—perhaps with a tangible or symbolic gift. The conclusion of the relationship may stimu- late within the client a host of deep feelings. He may feel intensely sad, as if he is losing his best friend, which, in fact, he may be doing. He may feel frightened and dependent as he asks himself, How can I make it without her? He may feel guilty that he did not work as hard as he should or could have; that he did not take as much advantage of the opportunity for change and growth as he might have. He may feel rejected by the worker or angry that the relationship is ending. He may wonder, If she *really* cared about me, she wouldn't end the relation- ship—she must not care about me. The client may also deny or minimize feelings about the ending that lie beneath the surface of consciousness. There are many manifestations of the psychological and social processes associated with ending. Suffice it to say that ending nearly always provokes significant reactions from both worker and client. Ideally, these responses are explored as part of the ending process.

Although the particular form of ending may vary, there are several skills important to the process. Drawing upon the work of William Schwartz (1971) and Elizabeth Kübler-Ross (1969), Lawrence Shulman (1984) discusses the dynamics and describes several skills associated with the ending process. The skills presented here are partially derived from those he identifies. The social work ending skills include: (1) reviewing the process, (2) final evaluating, (3) sharing ending feelings and saying goodbye, and (4) recording the closing summary.

REVIEWING THE PROCESS

Reviewing the process refers to the skill of tracing what has occurred between the worker and client over the course of time they have been together. It is a mutual process. Each party shares in the retrospection. Usually, the worker begins by inviting the client to review the process from the time they first met up through the present. For example, a worker might say: "I've been thinking about our work together during these last several months. We've covered a lot of ground together and there have been some rather big changes in you and your situation. As you think back to when we first met and think about the work that we've done together, what memories come to mind?"

Following the client's expression, the worker might probe for additional thoughts and feelings from him and then might share some of her own significant recollections. This often stimulates recall of other experiences as mutual discussion of various events continues.

■ **Exercise 11-1: Reviewing the Process**

For these exercises, assume that you are a social worker with a family and children's counseling center. In the spaces provided, write the words you would say in reviewing the process with each client.

1. You have been working with Mrs. O. for approximately two months. She has accomplished the goal of improving her eating and nutritional patterns. This meeting is your last. In the space provided, write the words you would say in reviewing the process with Mrs. O.

2. You are in the midst of the final meeting with the S. family. Over the course of several months, many productive changes have occurred. In the space provided, write the words you would say in reviewing the process with the S. family.

3. This is your concluding session with Mrs. F. In two weeks she will begin a ten-week assertive training group sponsored by another community agency. In the space provided, write the words you would say in reviewing the process with Mrs. F.

FINAL EVALUATING

Building upon the mutual review of the process, the worker also engages the client in a final evaluation of progress toward problem resolution and goal attainment. For this discussion, the worker may draw upon the results of various measurement instruments such as "before-and-after" test scores and graphs. She may also share her own subjective assessment of progress and seek input from the client about his final evaluation. Especially important, the worker shares her pleasure concerning the positive changes that have occurred and credits the client for his efforts. She also, however, helps the client to identify problems that have not been completely resolved and goals that have only been partially achieved. Additional work toward such goals does not have to stop merely because the worker and client are concluding their relationship. The client himself, or with the support of friends and family members, may continue to take action steps toward desirable objectives. By the time they conclude the relationship with the social worker, many clients have become competent problem solvers in their own right. They are often quite capable of defining goals and identifying action steps on their own. This phenomenon, when it occurs, is highly satisfying for most social workers. When clients become effective problem solvers who are skilled at self-help, the worker may reasonably conclude that she has, in effect, "helped them to help themselves." The client who, as a consequence of his association with a social worker, acquires skills with which to address future problems has gained a great deal indeed.

Final evaluating is, as are most of the ending skills, a mutual process through which the worker and client share their respective evaluations of progress and jointly identify areas that may require additional work. To initiate the final evaluation, the worker may say something like: "Let's now take a final look at where we stand in regard to progress toward the goals we have established during the course of our work together. One of our major goals was _____. How far do you think we have come toward achieving it?"

Goals that have been largely or completely accomplished are discussed with appropriate pleasure and satisfaction. The worker urges the client to experience and enjoy the sense of personal competence and self-regard that accompanies goal achievement. As areas requiring additional work are clarified, the worker encourages the client to plan additional action steps that he can take after they end their relationship together. This discussion is, of course, not nearly as extensive nor as detailed as when the worker and client established action steps as part of the contracting and work processes. Rather, the worker stimulates the client to look forward to future activities that can support continued growth and development. The worker may initiate this process by asking a question such as, "What sorts of activities do you think might help you to maintain your progress toward achievement of the remaining goals?"

As part of the final evaluation, the worker may find it appropriate and extremely useful to seek feedback from the client about those things that she said or did that were helpful as well as those that were not. This kind of evaluation may be of help to the client in identifying behaviors that he can adopt for his own future use. It may also provide an opportunity for the client to share his gratitude for or express other feelings about the worker's help. However, the primary purpose for seeking feedback about helpful and unhelpful factors is to aid the social worker in her professional growth and development. In a sense, she requests that the client evaluate her performance as a social worker. Through seeking evaluative feedback, she may gain information about herself that may prove useful in her work with other current and future clients. In asking for feedback, she might say, "I would appreciate it if you would tell me about those things I did that were particularly helpful to you during our work together. . . . And now, could you identify things that I did that were not helpful."

■ Exercise 11-2: Final Evaluating

In the spaces provided, write the words you would say to engage each client in a final evaluation. Also, prepare statements to encourage each client to identify future action steps. Finally, write the words you might say in seeking evaluative feedback from each client concerning what has been helpful and what has not.

1. You have been working with Mrs. O. for approximately two months. She has accomplished the goal of improving her eating and nutritional patterns. This meeting is your last. In the space provided, write the words you would say to engage Mrs. O. in the three aspects of a final evaluation.

2. You are in the midst of the final meeting with the S. family. Over the course of several months, many productive changes have occurred. In the space provided, write the words you would say to engage the S. family in the three aspects of a final evaluation.

3. This is your concluding session with Mrs. F. In two weeks she will begin a ten-week assertive training group sponsored by another community agency. In the space provided, write the words you would say in initiating the three aspects of a final evaluation with Mrs. F.

SHARING ENDING FEELINGS AND SAYING GOODBYE

The nature and intensity of the feelings clients experience as they conclude a relationship with a social worker vary according to the clients' unique personal characteristics, the duration of service, the problem, and the function of the worker (Hess & Hess, 1989). Nonetheless, because ending is a significant event in the lives of most clients, workers should provide them an opportunity to express feelings stimulated by the ending process.

There are certain emotional responses that social workers can anticipate their clients may experience as they end their relationship with a social worker. These include anger, sadness, loss, fear, guilt, dependency, ambivalence, gratitude, and affection. A client may be hesitant to freely express his emotions. If he concludes the relationship without sharing some of these feelings, he may experience a sense of incompleteness. This "unfinished" quality may impede appropriate psychological separation from the worker and inhibit movement toward increased autonomy and independence. Therefore, the worker should encourage the client to express his ending feelings. She may say, "We've reviewed our work together and evaluated progress, but we haven't yet shared our feelings about ending the relationship with one another. As you realize that this is our final meeting together, what thoughts and feelings occur to you?"

Of course, social workers also experience feelings as they conclude relationships with clients. A client and worker may have spent several weeks or months together. During the course of their work, the client may have shared painful emotions, discussed poignant issues, or made significant progress. Despite their professional status and ethical behavior, social workers are also human. It is entirely understandable and appropriate that they experience strong feelings as they end their relationship with clients. During the ending process, a social worker may find herself feeling guilty, inadequate, proud, satisfied, sad, angry, ambivalent, relieved, or affectionate. The kind and degree of the social worker's feelings vary due to many factors. As do clients, social workers almost always experience some kind of personal reaction during the ending phase. It is often useful to share some of these feelings. However, unlike the client, the social worker, even in ending, retains her professional responsibilities. She cannot freely express whatever feelings she experiences. She must consider the potential effects upon the client. For example, consider a case where the worker feels annoyed at the client because he did not work as hard toward change as she hoped he would. The worker should not share these or any other such feelings unless to do so would help the client progress toward any remaining goals or to conclude the relationship in a beneficial manner. Even during the final meeting, the worker makes an assessment in order to determine which feelings to express and how to express them. However, the worker does not try to simply suppress feelings that are inappropriate to share with the client. Rather, she engages in the skills of self-exploration and centering (see Chapter Five) in order to address them in a personally and professionally effective fashion.

When they are relevant and appropriate, the worker can share her personal feelings about ending the relationship. For example, she might say, "When I think about the fact that we will not meet together anymore, I feel a real sense of loss. I'm really going to miss you."

Often, when the worker shares her feelings, the client responds by sharing additional feelings of his own. The worker may then reflect the client's feelings and perhaps share more of her own. Finally, however, the worker and client complete the ending process by saying goodbye.

■ Exercise 11-3: Sharing Ending Feelings and Saying Goodbye

In the spaces provided, write the words you would say to encourage each client to share feelings about ending. Also, prepare statements in which you share your own ending feelings with each client. As part of your own sharing, please specify those feelings that you think you might experience had you worked with each client. Identify those that would be appropriate to share and those that would not. Finally, note the exact words you would use in saying goodbye.

1. You have been working with Mrs. O. for approximately two months. She has accomplished the goal of improving her eating and nutritional patterns. This meeting is your last. In the space provided, write the words you would say to engage in sharing ending feelings with Mrs. O.

2. You are in the midst of the final meeting with the S. family. Over the course of several months, many productive changes have occurred. In the space provided, write the words you would say in sharing ending feelings with the S. family.

3. This is your concluding session with Mrs. F. In two weeks she will begin a ten-week assertive training group sponsored by another community agency. In the space provided, write the words you would say in sharing ending feelings with her.

RECORDING THE CLOSING SUMMARY

Following the final meeting with a client, the social worker condenses what occurred in the form of a closing summary. This final entry is usually somewhat more extensive than the typical work phase SOAP (subjective, objective, assessment, plan) recording. However, when the ending has resulted in a mutual review of the process, a summary evaluation, and a sharing of ending feelings, the worker should have most of what is needed to complete a closing summary. She should include in the final recording the following information (Wilson, 1980, pp. 119–120): (1) date of final contact; (2) names of worker and client; (3) beginning date of service; (4) the reason contact between client and worker was initiated; (5) the specified problems and goals for work; (6) the nature of the services the worker provided and the activities the client or worker undertook; (7) a summary evaluation of progress and an identification of problems and goals that remain unresolved or unaccomplished; (8) a brief assessment of the person-problem-situation as it now exists; and (9) the reason for closing the case.

For example, following the final interview with Mrs. Chase, a social worker might prepare a closing summary as follows:

Closing Summary

Process and Problems

> Today, July 29, 1989, Mrs. Lynn Chase and I, Susan Holder, MSW, met together for the eighth and final time. Mrs. Chase first contacted us on June 14, 1989. At that time, we jointly specified the following problems for work: (1) frequent arguments with and feelings of irritability and anger toward son and husband; (2) stress, tension, and anxiety; (3) sleep disturbance; (4) ambivalence about job; and (5) thoughts and feelings of excessive responsibility and possibly of control. These problems were converted into goals and an eight-week program for change was developed.

Evaluation

> In reviewing the work process and evaluating progress, Mrs. Chase reported today that the feelings of stress and anger have decreased more than seventy-five percent since the time of the first contact. She also indicated that family relations have greatly improved since they distributed housework responsibilities more evenly. She said that she assumes less of a caretaker role with them and believes that they

actually benefit when she lets them care for themselves. She stated that she now sleeps fine and has only about one headache per week. She reported that her job at Fox Manufacturing is now satisfying. And she has been engaging in more playful and pleasurable activities—particularly gardening.

Mrs. Chase indicated that the single most helpful thing was when I said to her that "doing for your husband and son may prevent them from developing some of their own potential."

Continuing Goals

Mrs. Chase indicated that she is still working on issues related to codependency and intends to do further reading. She reported that she might attend an ACOA meeting to see what it's like.

Current Assessment

Based upon the available evidence, Mrs. Chase, her son, and her husband are communicating directly, sharing household responsibilities, and experiencing considerable satisfaction in their relationships with one another. Robert, the son, seems to be negotiating the demands of adolescence in a constructive fashion, and Mrs. Chase is challenging her long-held patterns of excessive responsibility and control.

Mrs. Chase and her family have many personal strengths that I suspect will serve them well in the future. My prognosis is that Mrs. Chase will continue to grow and develop now that she has permitted herself to consider more expansive and more flexible personal roles.

Ending Process

Mrs. Chase and I concluded our work together in a positive manner. She expressed her gratitude and I shared my affection for her as well as my pleasure at the progress she has made. The case is closed in the eight-week time frame as contracted.

Susan Holder, BSW, MSW
July 29, 1989

■ **Exercise 11-4: Recording the Closing Summary**

In the spaces provided, prepare brief closing summaries for each of the following clients. You may have to simulate some information; however, by referring back to the results of earlier exercises, you should be able to find information related to problems, goals, action steps, and progress.

1. You have just completed your final meeting with Mrs. O. In the space provided, prepare a simulated closing-summary record of your work with Mrs. O.

2. You have completed the final meeting with the S. family. In the space provided, prepare a simulated closing-summary record of your work with the S. family.

3. You have now concluded the last session with Mrs. F. In the space provided, prepare a simulated closing-summary record of your work with Mrs. F.

SUMMARY

The ending process of social work practice provides the worker and client with an opportunity to look back on their relationship and the work they undertook together. They have a chance to evaluate overall progress and to identify directions for future work. But concluding the relationship can be, simultaneously, a joyful and a painful experience for both the worker and the client. Both parties may experience satisfaction concerning the progress achieved, regret about actions that might have been but were not taken, and sadness at the departure of a person who was important to them and the loss of a relationship that was significant. In optimum circumstances, these feelings are explored as part of the ending process.

Although the particular form of ending may be transferral, referral, termination, or discontinuation, there are several skills important to the process, including: (1) reviewing the process, (2) final evaluating, (3) sharing ending feelings and saying goodbye, and (4) recording the closing summary.

■ **Exercise 11-5: Summary**

Conduct a final interview with the student colleague who has served as your client during these past several weeks. As you did previously, ensure that the interview setting is private and once again tape record the meeting. Using empathic, working, and especially ending skills, interview her with a view toward concluding the relationship. This is your last meeting. Therefore, use the relevant ending skills of reviewing the work process, final evaluating, and sharing ending feelings and saying goodbye.

1. At the conclusion of the interview, ask your partner for feedback concerning her thoughts and feelings about this interview and the entire experience. Summarize your partner's feedback in the space below.

351

2. In the space below, record your own reaction to this final meeting. How did you feel about the interview? What did you like and what did you dislike about it? Do you believe that you used all the relevant empathic, expressive, and ending skills during the interaction? What would you do differently if you were to redo this interview or the entire series of interviews?

3. In your course notebook, prepare a closing summary of your work with the student-client.
4. After you have completed the closing summary, play the audiotape or videotape. Make note of significant exchanges that affected the way in which you prepared your record. Revise the record accordingly.

5. Based upon your performance in the final interview, use the rating scales below (where 0 = no proficiency and 10 = complete proficiency) to assess your current level of proficiency in the various social work skills listed. If you did not use a particular skill, you need not simulate a rating. However, do ask yourself whether there were points during the interview when you should have used that skill.

Probing

| 0 | 1 | 2 | 3 | 4 | 5 | 6 | 7 | 8 | 9 | 10 |

Seeking Clarification

| 0 | 1 | 2 | 3 | 4 | 5 | 6 | 7 | 8 | 9 | 10 |

Reflecting Content

| 0 | 1 | 2 | 3 | 4 | 5 | 6 | 7 | 8 | 9 | 10 |

Reflecting Feeling

| 0 | 1 | 2 | 3 | 4 | 5 | 6 | 7 | 8 | 9 | 10 |

Reflecting Complex Communications

| 0 | 1 | 2 | 3 | 4 | 5 | 6 | 7 | 8 | 9 | 10 |

Partializing

| 0 | 1 | 2 | 3 | 4 | 5 | 6 | 7 | 8 | 9 | 10 |

Going Beyond What Is Said

| 0 | 1 | 2 | 3 | 4 | 5 | 6 | 7 | 8 | 9 | 10 |

Reviewing Action Steps

| 0 | 1 | 2 | 3 | 4 | 5 | 6 | 7 | 8 | 9 | 10 |

Focusing

| 0 | 1 | 2 | 3 | 4 | 5 | 6 | 7 | 8 | 9 | 10 |

Educating

| | | | | | | | | | | |
|0|1|2|3|4|5|6|7|8|9|10|

Advising

| | | | | | | | | | | |
|0|1|2|3|4|5|6|7|8|9|10|

Responding with Immediacy

| | | | | | | | | | | |
|0|1|2|3|4|5|6|7|8|9|10|

Reframing

| | | | | | | | | | | |
|0|1|2|3|4|5|6|7|8|9|10|

Confronting

| | | | | | | | | | | |
|0|1|2|3|4|5|6|7|8|9|10|

Pointing Out Endings

| | | | | | | | | | | |
|0|1|2|3|4|5|6|7|8|9|10|

6. Now that you have completed these exercises, use the rating scales below (where 0 = no proficiency and 10 = complete proficiency) to conduct a summary evaluation of your proficiency in the ending skills.

Reviewing the Process

| | | | | | | | | | | |
|0|1|2|3|4|5|6|7|8|9|10|

Final Evaluating

| | | | | | | | | | | |
|0|1|2|3|4|5|6|7|8|9|10|

Sharing Ending Feelings and Saying Goodbye

| | | | | | | | | | | |
|0|1|2|3|4|5|6|7|8|9|10|

Recording the Closing Summary

| | | | | | | | | | | |
|0|1|2|3|4|5|6|7|8|9|10|

7. Review your ratings to identify those ending skills in which you remain less proficient (e.g., a score of 7 or less). Then, in the space below, outline the steps you might take to improve your skill in these areas.

SUMMARY SELF-EVALUATION: SOCIAL WORK SKILLS PROFICIENCY

You may use this instrument to conduct a summary self-evaluation of your proficiency in the social work skills. Proficiency requires the following: First, you should understand the skill and be able to describe how it might be used. Ability to recall the recommended practice format, suggested for many of the skills, reflects such an understanding. Second, you should be able to associate the skill with the phase of social work practice in which it is commonly used. Third, you should be able to demonstrate an ability to use the skill at a time and in a context that is professionally appropriate. Fourth, you should be able to demonstrate expertise in the use of the skill. Finally, you should be able to adapt the skill or combine it with others in order to meet the particular needs or demands of a unique social work situation.

Based upon your self-evaluation of the dimensions described above, rate your estimated proficiency in each of the skills identified below according to a scale where 0 = no proficiency and 10 = complete proficiency.

Self-Awareness and Self-Understanding

```
└─┴─┴─┴─┴─┴─┴─┴─┴─┴─┘
0   1   2   3   4   5   6   7   8   9   10
```

Knowledge and Understanding of Legal Duties

```
└─┴─┴─┴─┴─┴─┴─┴─┴─┴─┘
0   1   2   3   4   5   6   7   8   9   10
```

Knowledge and Understanding of Fundamental Social Work Values

```
└─┴─┴─┴─┴─┴─┴─┴─┴─┴─┘
0   1   2   3   4   5   6   7   8   9   10
```

Knowledge and Understanding of Social Work Code of Ethics

```
|   |   |   |   |   |   |   |   |   |   |
0   1   2   3   4   5   6   7   8   9   10
```

Ability to Identify Ethical Principles and Legal Duties Relevant to Specific Cases

```
|   |   |   |   |   |   |   |   |   |   |
0   1   2   3   4   5   6   7   8   9   10
```

Ability to Prioritize Applicable Ethical Principles and Legal Duties

```
|   |   |   |   |   |   |   |   |   |   |
0   1   2   3   4   5   6   7   8   9   10
```

Voice and Speech

```
|   |   |   |   |   |   |   |   |   |   |
0   1   2   3   4   5   6   7   8   9   10
```

Body Language

```
|   |   |   |   |   |   |   |   |   |   |
0   1   2   3   4   5   6   7   8   9   10
```

Hearing

```
|   |   |   |   |   |   |   |   |   |   |
0   1   2   3   4   5   6   7   8   9   10
```

Observing

```
|   |   |   |   |   |   |   |   |   |   |
0   1   2   3   4   5   6   7   8   9   10
```

Encouraging

```
|   |   |   |   |   |   |   |   |   |   |
0   1   2   3   4   5   6   7   8   9   10
```

Remembering

```
|   |   |   |   |   |   |   |   |   |   |
0   1   2   3   4   5   6   7   8   9   10
```

Active Listening

```
|   |   |   |   |   |   |   |   |   |   |
0   1   2   3   4   5   6   7   8   9   10
```

Preparatory Reviewing

```
|   |   |   |   |   |   |   |   |   |   |
0   1   2   3   4   5   6   7   8   9   10
```

357

Preparatory Exploring

| 0 | 1 | 2 | 3 | 4 | 5 | 6 | 7 | 8 | 9 | 10 |

Preparatory Consulting

| 0 | 1 | 2 | 3 | 4 | 5 | 6 | 7 | 8 | 9 | 10 |

Preparatory Arranging

| 0 | 1 | 2 | 3 | 4 | 5 | 6 | 7 | 8 | 9 | 10 |

Preparatory Empathy

| 0 | 1 | 2 | 3 | 4 | 5 | 6 | 7 | 8 | 9 | 10 |

Preliminary Planning

| 0 | 1 | 2 | 3 | 4 | 5 | 6 | 7 | 8 | 9 | 10 |

Preparatory Self-Exploration

| 0 | 1 | 2 | 3 | 4 | 5 | 6 | 7 | 8 | 9 | 10 |

Centering

| 0 | 1 | 2 | 3 | 4 | 5 | 6 | 7 | 8 | 9 | 10 |

Recording During the Preparing Phase

| 0 | 1 | 2 | 3 | 4 | 5 | 6 | 7 | 8 | 9 | 10 |

Introducing Oneself

| 0 | 1 | 2 | 3 | 4 | 5 | 6 | 7 | 8 | 9 | 10 |

Seeking Introductions

| 0 | 1 | 2 | 3 | 4 | 5 | 6 | 7 | 8 | 9 | 10 |

Describing Initial Purpose

| 0 | 1 | 2 | 3 | 4 | 5 | 6 | 7 | 8 | 9 | 10 |

Outlining the Client's Role

0   1   2   3   4   5   6   7   8   9   10

Discussing Policy and Ethical Considerations

0   1   2   3   4   5   6   7   8   9   10

Seeking Feedback

0   1   2   3   4   5   6   7   8   9   10

Probing

0   1   2   3   4   5   6   7   8   9   10

Seeking Clarification

0   1   2   3   4   5   6   7   8   9   10

Reflecting Content

0   1   2   3   4   5   6   7   8   9   10

Reflecting Feeling

0   1   2   3   4   5   6   7   8   9   10

Reflecting Complex Communications

0   1   2   3   4   5   6   7   8   9   10

Partializing

0   1   2   3   4   5   6   7   8   9   10

Going Beyond What Is Said

0   1   2   3   4   5   6   7   8   9   10

Organizing Descriptive Information

0   1   2   3   4   5   6   7   8   9   10

359

Formulating a Tentative Assessment

| 0 | 1 | 2 | 3 | 4 | 5 | 6 | 7 | 8 | 9 | 10 |

Reflecting the Problem

| 0 | 1 | 2 | 3 | 4 | 5 | 6 | 7 | 8 | 9 | 10 |

Sharing Worker's View of the Problem

| 0 | 1 | 2 | 3 | 4 | 5 | 6 | 7 | 8 | 9 | 10 |

Specifying Problems for Work

| 0 | 1 | 2 | 3 | 4 | 5 | 6 | 7 | 8 | 9 | 10 |

Establishing Goals

| 0 | 1 | 2 | 3 | 4 | 5 | 6 | 7 | 8 | 9 | 10 |

Developing a Program for Change

| 0 | 1 | 2 | 3 | 4 | 5 | 6 | 7 | 8 | 9 | 10 |

Identifying Action Steps

| 0 | 1 | 2 | 3 | 4 | 5 | 6 | 7 | 8 | 9 | 10 |

Planning for Evaluation

| 0 | 1 | 2 | 3 | 4 | 5 | 6 | 7 | 8 | 9 | 10 |

Summarizing the Contract

| 0 | 1 | 2 | 3 | 4 | 5 | 6 | 7 | 8 | 9 | 10 |

Rehearsing Action Steps

| 0 | 1 | 2 | 3 | 4 | 5 | 6 | 7 | 8 | 9 | 10 |

Reviewing Action Steps

| 0 | 1 | 2 | 3 | 4 | 5 | 6 | 7 | 8 | 9 | 10 |

Evaluating

0	1	2	3	4	5	6	7	8	9	10

Focusing

0	1	2	3	4	5	6	7	8	9	10

Educating

0	1	2	3	4	5	6	7	8	9	10

Advising

0	1	2	3	4	5	6	7	8	9	10

Representing

0	1	2	3	4	5	6	7	8	9	10

Responding with Immediacy

0	1	2	3	4	5	6	7	8	9	10

Reframing

0	1	2	3	4	5	6	7	8	9	10

Confronting

0	1	2	3	4	5	6	7	8	9	10

Pointing Out Endings

0	1	2	3	4	5	6	7	8	9	10

Recording During the Work Phase

0	1	2	3	4	5	6	7	8	9	10

Reviewing the Process

0	1	2	3	4	5	6	7	8	9	10

Final Evaluating

```
|____|____|____|____|____|____|____|____|____|____|
0    1    2    3    4    5    6    7    8    9    10
```

Sharing Ending Feelings and Saying Goodbye

```
|____|____|____|____|____|____|____|____|____|____|
0    1    2    3    4    5    6    7    8    9    10
```

Recording the Closing Summary

```
|____|____|____|____|____|____|____|____|____|____|
0    1    2    3    4    5    6    7    8    9    10
```

SOCIAL WORK SKILLS INTERVIEW RATING FORM

This rating form may be used by social workers as part of the process of evaluating their own or others' performance of the social work skills during interviews with clients. It may be used, for example, by a supervisor as she observes a social worker through a one-way window or reviews an audio or videotape recording of an interview. Please use the following rating system:

N/A During the course of the interview, the skill in question was not appropriate or necessary and was therefore not used, having no effect upon the interview.

-3 During the course of the interview, the skill in question was used at an inappropriate time or in an unsuitable context, seriously detracting from the interview.

-2 During the course of the interview, the skill in question was attempted at an appropriate time and in a suitable context but was done so in an incompetent manner, significantly detracting from the interview.

-1 During the course of the interview, the skill in question was not used at times or in contexts when it should have been, detracting from the interview.

0 During the course of the interview, the skill in question was used and demonstrated at a minimal level of competence. Its use did not detract from nor contribute to the interview.

+1 During the course of the interview, the skill in question was attempted at an appropriate time and in a suitable context and was generally demonstrated at a fair level of competence. Its use represented a small contribution to the interview.

+2 During the course of the interview, the skill in question was attempted at an appropriate time and in a suitable context and was generally demonstrated at a moderate level of competence. Its use represented a significant contribution to the interview.

363

+3 During the course of the interview, the skill in question was attempted at an appropriate time and in a suitable context and was generally demonstrated at a good level of competence. Its use represented a substantial contribution to the interview.

+4 During the course of the interview, the skill in question was attempted at an appropriate time and in a suitable context and was generally demonstrated at a superior level of performance. Its use represented a major contribution to the interview.

Talking and Listening—The Basic Interpersonal Skills

1. Voice and Speech   N/A -3 -2 -1 0 +1 +2 +3 +4
   Comments:

2. Body Language   N/A -3 -2 -1 0 +1 +2 +3 +4
   Comments:

3. Hearing   N/A -3 -2 -1 0 +1 +2 +3 +4
   Comments:

4. Observing   N/A -3 -2 -1 0 +1 +2 +3 +4
   Comments:

5. Encouraging   N/A -3 -2 -1 0 +1 +2 +3 +4
   Comments:

6. Remembering   N/A -3 -2 -1 0 +1 +2 +3 +4
   Comments:

7. Active Listening   N/A -3 -2 -1 0 +1 +2 +3 +4
   Comments:

Beginning

8. Introducing Oneself N/A -3 -2 -1 0 +1 +2 +3 +4
   Comments:

9. Seeking Introductions N/A -3 -2 -1 0 +1 +2 +3 +4
   Comments:

10. Describing Initial Purpose N/A -3 -2 -1 0 +1 +2 +3 +4
    Comments:

11. Outlining the Client's Role N/A -3 -2 -1 0 +1 +2 +3 +4
    Comments:

12. Discussing Policy and Ethical N/A -3 -2 -1 0 +1 +2 +3 +4
    Considerations
    Comments:

13. Seeking Feedback   N/A -3 -2 -1 0 +1 +2 +3 +4
      Comments:

Exploring

14. Probing   N/A -3 -2 -1 0 +1 +2 +3 +4
      Comments:

15. Seeking Clarification   N/A -3 -2 -1 0 +1 +2 +3 +4
      Comments:

16. Reflecting Content   N/A -3 -2 -1 0 +1 +2 +3 +4
      Comments:

17. Reflecting Feeling   N/A -3 -2 -1 0 +1 +2 +3 +4
      Comments:

18. Reflecting Complex   N/A -3 -2 -1 0 +1 +2 +3 +4
     Communications
      Comments:

19. Partializing   N/A -3 -2 -1 0 +1 +2 +3 +4
      Comments:

20. Going Beyond What Is Said   N/A -3 -2 -1 0 +1 +2 +3 +4
    Comments:

Contracting

21. Reflecting the Problem   N/A -3 -2 -1 0 +1 +2 +3 +4
    Comments:

22. Sharing Worker's View of   N/A -3 -2 -1 0 +1 +2 +3 +4
    the Problem
    Comments:

23. Specifying Problems for Work   N/A -3 -2 -1 0 +1 +2 +3 +4
    Comments:

24. Establishing Goals   N/A -3 -2 -1 0 +1 +2 +3 +4
    Comments:

25. Developing a Program   N/A -3 -2 -1 0 +1 +2 +3 +4
    for Change
    Comments:

26. Identifying Action Steps   N/A -3 -2 -1 0 +1 +2 +3 +4
    Comments:

27. Planning for Evaluation   N/A -3 -2 -1 0 +1 +2 +3 +4
    Comments:

28. Summarizing the Contract   N/A -3 -2 -1 0 +1 +2 +3 +4
    Comments:

Working

29. Rehearsing Action Steps   N/A -3 -2 -1 0 +1 +2 +3 +4
    Comments:

30. Reviewing Action Steps   N/A -3 -2 -1 0 +1 +2 +3 +4
    Comments:

31. Evaluating   N/A -3 -2 -1 0 +1 +2 +3 +4
    Comments:

32. Focusing   N/A -3 -2 -1 0 +1 +2 +3 +4
    Comments:

33. Educating   N/A -3 -2 -1 0 +1 +2 +3 +4
    Comments:

34. Advising   N/A   -3   -2   -1   0   +1   +2   +3   +4
     Comments:

35. Representing   N/A   -3   -2   -1   0   +1   +2   +3   +4
     Comments:

36. Responding with Immediacy   N/A   -3   -2   -1   0   +1   +2   +3   +4
     Comments:

37. Reframing   N/A   -3   -2   -1   0   +1   +2   +3   +4
     Comments:

38. Confronting   N/A   -3   -2   -1   0   +1   +2   +3   +4
     Comments:

39. Pointing Out Endings   N/A   -3   -2   -1   0   +1   +2   +3   +4
     Comments:

Ending

40. Reviewing the Process   N/A   -3   -2   -1   0   +1   +2   +3   +4
     Comments:

41. Final Evaluating   N/A -3 -2 -1 0 +1 +2 +3 +4
    Comments:

42. Sharing Ending Feelings and   N/A -3 -2 -1 0 +1 +2 +3 +4
    Saying Goodbye
    Comments:

OVERALL IMPRESSIONS:

REFERENCES
AND BIBLIOGRAPHY

Acosta, F. X., Yamamoto, J., & Evans, L. A. (1982). *Effective psychotherapy for low-income and minority patients.* New York: Plenum.

Aguilar, I. (1972). Initial contacts with Mexican-American families. *Social Work, 17,* 66–70.

Albert, R. (1986). *Law and social work practice.* New York: Springer.

Alberti, R. E., & Emmons, M. L. (1970). *Stand up, speak out, talk back.* San Luis Obispo, CA: Impact.

Altmann, H. (1973). Effects of empathy, warmth and genuineness in the initial counseling interview. *Counselor Education and Supervision, 12,* 225–229.

Anderson, J. (1988). *Foundations of social work practice.* New York: Springer.

Aronson, H., & Overall, B. (1966). Treatment expectations of patients in two social classes. *Social Work, 11,* 35–41.

Baer, B., & Federico, R. (1978). *Educating the baccalaureate social worker.* Cambridge, MA: Ballinger.

Baker, F., & Northman, J. E. (1981). *Helping: Human services for the 80's.* St. Louis, Mo.: C. V. Mosby.

Bandler, R., & Grinder, J. (1979). *Frogs into princes: Neuro-linguistic programming.* Moab, UT: Real People.

Bandler, R., & Grinder, J. (1982). *Reframing: Neuro-linguistic programing and the transformation of meaning.* Moab, UT: Real People, 5–78.

Banks, G. (1971). The effects of race on one-to-one helping interviews. *Social Service Review, 45,* 137–144.

Banville, T. G. (1978). *How to listen—how to be heard.* Chicago: Nelson/Hall.

Barker, R. L. (1987). *The social work dictionary.* Silver Spring, MD: National Association of Social Workers.

Barksdale, Lilburn S. (1973). Self-esteem index. Idyllwild, CA: The Barksdale Foundation.

Bartlett, H. (1970). *The common base of social work practice*. New York: National Association of Social Workers.

Bates, M. (1983). Using the environment to help the male skid row alcoholic. *Social Casework, 64,* 276–282.

Bernstein, B. (1977). Privileged communications to the social worker. *Social Work, 22,* 264–268.

Bernstein, B. (1978). Malpractice, an ogre on the horizon. *Social Work, 23,* 106–111.

Bernstein, S. (1960). Self-determination: King or citizen in the realm of values. *Social Work, 5* (1), 3–8.

Bertcher, H. J. (1979). *Group participation: Techniques for leaders and members.* Beverly Hills, CA: Sage Publications.

Besharov, D. J. (1985). *The vulnerable social worker: Liability for serving children and families.* Silver Spring, MD: National Association of Social Workers.

Besharov, D. J., & Besharov, S. H. (1987). Teaching about liability. *Social Work, 32* (6), 517–522.

Biagi, E. (1977). The social work stake in problem-oriented recording. *Social Work in Health Care, 3* (2), 211–222.

Biestek, F. (1957). *The casework relationship.* Chicago: Loyola University Press.

Block, C. (1979). Black Americans and the cross-cultural counseling and psychotherapy experience. In A. Marsella & P. Pederson (Eds.), *Cross-cultural counseling and psychotherapy* (pp. 177–194). New York: Pergamon.

Bloom, M. (1981). *Primary prevention: The possible science.* Englewood Cliffs, NJ: Prentice-Hall.

Bloom, M., & Fischer, J. (1982). *Evaluating practice: Guidelines for the accountable professional.* Englewood Cliffs, NJ: Prentice-Hall.

Boehm, W. (1958). The nature of social work. *Social Work, 3,* 10–19.

Bolton, R. (1979). *People skills: How to assert yourself, listen to others, and resolve conflicts.* Englewood Cliffs, NJ: Prentice-Hall.

Brill, N. I. (1985). *Working with people: The helping process* (3rd ed.). New York: Longman.

Brown, C., & Hellinger, M. (1975). Therapists' attitudes toward women. *Social Work, 20,* 266–270.

Brown, L., & Levitt, J. (1979). A methodology for problem-system identification. *Social Casework, 60,* 408–415.

Burrill, G. (1976). The problem-oriented log in social casework. *Social Work, 21* (1), 67–68.

Cameron, J., & Talavera, E. (1976). An advocacy program for Spanish-speaking people. *Social Casework, 57,* 427–431.

Campbell, David. (1974). *If you don't know where you're going you'll probably end up somewhere else.* Niles, IL: Argus Communications.

Canda, E. (1983). General implications of Shamanism for clinical social work. *International Social Work, 26,* 14–22.

Carkhuff, R. R. (1969). *Helping and human relations* (Vols. 1 & 2). New York: Holt, Rinehart and Winston.

Carkhuff, R. R. (1984). *Helping and human relations* (Vols. I & II). Amherst, MA: Human Resource Development.

Carkhuff, R. R. (1987). *The art of helping VI.* Amherst, MA: Human Resource Development.

Carkhuff, R. R., & Anthony, W. A. (1979). *The skills of helping.* Amherst, MA: Human Resource Development.

Carkhuff, R. R., & Pierce, R. (1967). Differential effects of therapist race and social class upon patient depth of self-exploration in the initial clinical interview. *Journal of Consulting Psychology, 31,* 632–634.

Carkhuff, R. R., & Truax, C. B. (1965). Training in counseling and psychotherapy. *Journal of Consulting Psychology, 29,* 333–336.

Cautela, J. R., & Kearney, A. J. (1986). *The covert conditioning handbook.* New York: Springer.

Chafetz, J. (1972). Women in social work. *Social Work, 17,* 12–18.

Compton, B., & Galaway, B. (1984). *Social work processes* (3rd ed.). Homewood, IL: Dorsey.

Compton, B., & Galaway, B. (1989). *Social work processes* (4th ed.). Belmont, CA: Wadsworth.

Cooper, S. (1978). A look at the effect of racism on clinical work. *Social Casework, 54,* 78.

Corcoran, K., & Fischer, J. (1987). *Measures for clinical practice: A sourcebook.* New York: The Free Press.

Cormier, W. H., & Cormier, L. S. (1985). *Interviewing strategies for helpers: Fundamental skills and cognitive behavioral interventions* (2nd ed.). Monterey, CA: Brooks/Cole.

Council on Social Work Education. (1976). *Teaching for competence in the delivery of direct services.* New York: Author.

Council on Social Work Education. (1982). *Curriculum policy statement.* New York: Author.

Cournoyer, B. R. (1983). Assertiveness among MSW students. *Journal of Social Work Education, 19* (1), 24–30.

Cournoyer, B. R. (1988). Personal and professional distress among social caseworkers: A developmental-interactional perspective. *Social Casework, 69* (5), 259–264.

Cournoyer, B. R. (1989). Basic communication skills for work with groups. In B. Compton & B. Galaway. *Social work processes* (4th ed.) (pp. 350–358). Belmont, CA: Wadsworth.

Cowger, C., & Atherton, C. (1974). Social control: A rationale for social welfare. *Social Work, 19,* 456–462.

Cumming, J., & Cumming, E. (1969). *Ego and milieu: Theory and practice of environmental therapy.* New York: Atherton.

Danish, S. J., & Hauer, A. L. (1973a). *Helping skills: A basic training program—leader's manual.* New York: Behavioral Publications.

Danish, S. J., & Hauer, A. L. (1973b). *Helping skills: A basic training program—trainee's workbook.* New York: Behavioral Publications.

Dauw, D. C. (1980). *Increasing your self-esteem: How to feel better about yourself.* Propect Heights, IL: Waveland.

Davenport, J., & Reims, N. (1978). Theoretical orientation and attitudes toward women. *Social Work, 23,* 306–311.

Devore, W., & Schlesinger, E. (1981). *Ethnic-sensitive social work practice.* St. Louis, MO: C. V. Mosby.

Dorfman, R. A. (Ed.). (1988). *Paradigms of clinical social work.* New York: Brunner/Mazel.

Draper, B. (1979). Black language as an adaptive response to a hostile environment. In C. Germain (Ed.), *Social work practices: People and environment* (pp. 267–281). New York: Columbia University Press.

Edleson, J. L., & Rose, S. D. (1981). Developing skills for the interview. In S. P. Schinke (Ed.), *Behavioral methods in social welfare* (pp. 257–268). New York: Aldine.

Egan, G. (1982a). *Exercises in helping skills: A training manual to accompany the skilled helper* (2nd ed.). Monterey, CA: Brooks/Cole.

Egan, G. (1982b). *The skilled helper: Model, skills, and methods for effective helping* (2nd ed.). Monterey, CA: Brooks/Cole.

Elson, M. (1986). *Self pyschology in clinical social work.* New York: W. W. Norton.

Eriksen, K. (1979). *Communications skills for the human services.* Reston, VA: Reston.

Evans, D. R., Hearn, M. T., Uhlemann, M. R., & Ivey, A. E. (1979). *Essential interviewing: A programmed approach to effective communication.* Monterey, CA: Brooks/Cole.

Everstine, D. S., & Everstine, L. (1983). *People in crisis: Strategic therapeutic interventions.* New York: Brunner/Mazel.

Everstine, L., Everstine, D. S., Heymann, G. M., True, D. H., Johnson, H. G., & Seiden, R. H. (1980). Privacy and confidentiality in psychotherapy. *American Psychologist, 35,* 828–840.

Fey, W. F. (1955). Acceptance by others and its relation to acceptance of self and others: A revaluation. *Journal of Abnormal and Social Psychology, 30,* 274–276.

Fischer, J. (1978). *Effective casework practice: An eclectic approach.* New York: McGraw-Hill.

Fischer, J., Dulaney, D., Fazio, R. T., Hudak, M. T., & Zivotofsky, E. (1976). Are social workers sexists? *Social Work, 21,* 428–433.

Fischler, R. (1980). Protecting American Indian children. *Social Work, 25,* 341–349.

Fortune, A. E. (Ed.). (1985). *Task-centered practice with families and groups.* New York: Springer.

Fox, E., Nelson, M., & Bolman, W. (1963). The termination process: A neglected dimension in social work. *Social Work, 14* (4), 53–63.

Fredman, N., & Sherman, N. (1987). *Handbook of measurements for marriage and family therapy.* New York: Brunner/Mazel.

Gambrill, E. (1983). *Casework: A competency-based approach.* Englewood Cliffs, NJ: Prentice-Hall.

Garvin, C. (1987). *Contemporary group work* (2nd ed.). Englewood Cliffs, NJ: Prentice-Hall.

Garvin, C., & Seabury, B. (1984). *Interpersonal practice in social work: Processes and procedures.* Englewood Cliffs, NJ: Prentice-Hall.

Gaylin, W. (1976). *Caring.* New York: Alfred A. Knopf.

Gaylin, W. (1979). *Feelings: Our vital signs.* New York: Harper & Row.

Germain, C. B. (Ed.). (1979). *Social work practice: People and environments—an ecological perspective.* New York: Columbia University Press.

Ghali, S. (1982). Understanding Puerto Rican traditions. *Social Work, 27,* 98–102.

Gilgun, J. F. (1989). An ecosystemic approach to assessment. In B. Compton & B. Galaway, *Social work processes* (4th ed.) (pp. 455–470). Belmont, CA: Wadsworth.

Gillespie, D. F. (1987). Ethical issues in research. *Encyclopedia of Social Work* (pp. 503–512). Washington, DC: National Association of Social Workers.

Giordano, J. (1974). Ethnics and minorities. A review of the literature. *Clinical Social Work Journal, 2,* 207–220.

Gitterman, A., & Schaeffer, A. (1972). The white professional and the black client. *Social Casework, 53,* 280–291.

Golan, N. (1981). *Passing through transitions.* New York: The Free Press.

Goldstein, E. G. (1984). *Ego psychology and social work practice.* New York: The Free Press.

Goodman, G., & Esterly, G. (1988). *The talk book: The intimate science of communicating in close relationships.* Emmaus, PA: Rodale.

Good Tracks, J. (1973). Native American noninterference. *Social Work, 18,* 30–34.

Gottesfeld, M. L., & Pharis, M. E. (1977). *Profiles in social work.* New York: Human Sciences.

Green, J. (Ed.). (1982). *Cultural awareness in the human services.* Englewood Cliffs, NJ: Prentice-Hall.

Green, R., & Cox, G. (1978). Social work and malpractice: A converging course. *Social Work, 23,* 100–104.

Haley, J. (1978). *Problem solving therapy.* San Francisco: Jossey-Bass.

Halleck, S. (1963). The impact of professional dishonesty on behavior of disturbed adolescents. *Social Work, 8,* 48–56.

Hamilton, G. (1951). *Theory and practice of social case work* (2nd ed., rev.). New York: Columbia University Press.

Hammond, D., Hepworth, D., & Smith, V. (1977). *Improving therapeutic communication.* San Francisco: Jossey-Bass.

Harris, L., & Lucas, M. (1976). Sex-role stereotyping. *Social Work, 21,* 390–395.

Hartman, A. (1978). Diagrammatic assessment of family relationships. *Social Casework, 59,* 465–476.

Hartman, A., & Laird, J. (1983). *Family-centered social work practice.* New York: The Free Press.

Hartman, B. L., & Wickey, J. M. (1978). The person-oriented record in treatment. *Social Work, 23* (4), 296–299.

Henley, N. M. (1972). *Body politics: Power, sex, and nonverbal communication.* Englewood Cliffs, NJ: Prentice-Hall.

Henry, S. (1981). *Group skills in social work.* Itasca, IL: F. E. Peacock.

Hepworth, D., & Larsen, J. (1986). *Direct social work practice: Theory and skills* (2nd ed.). Chicago: Dorsey.

Hess, H., & Hess, P.M. (1989). Termination in context. In B. Compton & B. Galaway, *Social work processes* (4th ed.) (pp. 646–657). Belmont, CA: Wadsworth.

Ho, M. (1976). Social work with Asian Americans. *Social Casework, 57,* 195–201.

Hollis, F., & Woods, M. E. (1981). *Casework: A psychosocial therapy* (3rd ed.). New York: Random House.

Howe, E. (1980). Public professions and the private model of professionalism. *Social Work, 25,* 179–191.

Hudson, W. (1982). *The clinical measurement package: A field manual.* Homewood, IL: Dorsey.

Ivey, A. E. (1971). *Microcounseling: Innovations in interview training.* Springfield, IL: Thomas.

Ivey, A. E. (1976). The counselor as teacher. *Personnel and Guidance Journal, 54,* 431–434.

Ivey, A. E. (1988). *Intentional interviewing and counseling: Facilitating client development* (2nd ed.). Pacific Grove, CA: Brooks/Cole.

Ivey, A. E., & Authier, J. (1978). *Microcounseling: Innovations in interviewing, counseling, psychotherapy, and psychoeducation.* Springfield, IL: Thomas.

Ivey, A. E., & Simek-Downing, L. (1980). *Counseling and psychotherapy: Skills, theories, and practice.* Englewood Cliffs, NJ: Prentice-Hall.

Jakubowski, P., & Lange, A. J. (1978). *The assertive option: Your rights and responsibilities.* Champaign, IL: Research Press.

Johnson, D. W. (1981). *Reaching out: Interpersonal effectiveness and self-actualization* (2nd ed.). Englewood Cliffs, NJ: Prentice-Hall.

Johnson, H. C. (1978). Integrating the problem-oriented record with a systems approach to case assessment. *Journal of Education for Social Work, 14* (3), 71–77.

Johnson, L. C. (1986). *Social work practice: A generalist approach* (2nd ed.). Newton, MA: Allyn and Bacon.

Joseph, M. V. (1985). A model for ethical decision making in clinical practice. In C. B. Germain (Ed.), *Advances in clinical social work practice: Selected papers, 1982 NASW national conference on clinical social work* (pp. 207–217). Silver Spring, MD: National Association of Social Workers.

Kadushin, A. (1972). The racial factor in the interview. *Social Work, 17,* 88–99.

Kadushin, A. (1983). *The social work interview* (2nd ed.). New York: Columbia University Press.

Kagle, J. D. (1984). *Social work records.* Homewood, IL: Dorsey.

Kane, R. A. (1974). Look to the record. *Social Work, 19* (4), 412–419.

Keefe, T. (1976). Empathy: The critical skill. *Social Work, 21,* 10–14.

Keith-Lucas, A. (1971). Ethics in social work. In *Encyclopedia of social work* (pp. 324–329). Washington, DC: National Association of Social Workers.

Keith-Lucas, A. (1972) *The giving and taking of help.* Chapel Hill: University of North Carolina Press.

Keith-Lucas, A. (1977). Ethics in social work. In *Encyclopedia of social work* (pp. 350–355). Washington, DC: National Association of Social Workers.

Kiresuk, T., & Sherman, R. E. (1968). Goal attainment scaling: A general method for evaluating comprehensive community health programs. *Community Mental Health Journal, 4,* 443–453.

Kitano, H. (Ed.). (1971). *Asians in America.* New York: Council on Social Work Education.

Knapp, M. L. (1972). *Nonverbal communication in human interaction.* New York: Holt, Rinehart and Winston.

Knoll, F. (1971). Casework services for Mexican Americans. *Social Casework, 52,* 279–284.

Kosberg, J. (1973). The nursing home: A social work paradox. *Social Work, 18,* 104–110.

Kosberg, J., & Harris, A. (1978). Attitudes toward elderly clients. *Health and Social Work, 3,* 67–90.

Krill, D. F. (1978). *Existential social work.* New York: The Free Press.

Krill, D. F. (1986). *The beat worker: Humanizing social work & psychotherapy practice.* Lanham, MD: University Press of America.

Kubler-Ross, E. (1969). *On death and dying.* New York: Macmillan.

Lambert, M. J. (1982). Relation of helping skills to treatment outcome. In E. K. Marshall and P. D Kurtz (Eds.), *Interpersonal helping skills: A guide to training methods, programs, and resources* (pp. 26–53). San Francisco: Jossey-Bass.

Lange, A. J., & Jakubowski, P. (1976). *Responsible assertive behavior: Cognitive/behavioral procedures for trainers.* Champaign, IL: Research Press.

Lazarus, A. (1984). *In the mind's eye: The power of imagery for personal enrichment.* New York: Guilford.

Levinson, H. (1977). Termination of pyschotherapy: Some salient issues. *Social Casework, 58* (8), 480–498.

Levy, C. (1976a). Personal vs. professional values: The practitioner's dilemma. *Clinical Social Work Journal 4,* 110–120.

Levy, C. (1976b). *Social work ethics.* New York: Human Sciences.

Lewis, H. (1984). Ethical assessment. *Social Casework 65,* 203–211.

Lewis, R., & Ho, M. (1975). Social work with Native Americans. *Social Work, 20,* 379–382.

Lewinsohn, P. M., Munoz, R. F., Youngren, M. A., and Zeiss, P. M. (1978). *Control your depression.* Englewood Cliffs, NJ: Prentice-Hall, 175–177.

Lieberman, F. (Ed). (1982). *Clinical social workers as psychotherapists.* New York: Gardner.

Loewenberg, F., & Dolgoff, R. (1988). *Ethical decisions for social work practice* (3rd ed.). Itasca, IL: F. E. Peacock.

Maduro, R., & Martinez, C. (1974). Latino dream analysis: Opportunity for confrontation. *Social Casework, 55,* 461–469.

Mahaffey, M. (1976). Sexism in social work. *Social Work, 2,* 419.

Maldonado, D. (1975). The Chicano aged. *Social Work, 20,* 213–216.

Maluccio, A. (1979). *Learning from clients: Interpersonal helping as viewed by clients and social workers.* New York: The Free Press.

Maluccio, A. (Ed.). (1981). *Promoting competence in clients: A new/old approach to social work practice.* New York: The Free Press.

Maluccio, A., & Marlow, W. (1974). The case for contract. *Social Work, 19,* 28–36.

Marsh, P. (Ed.). (1988). *Eye to eye: How people interact.* Topsfield, MA: Salem House.

Marshall, E. K., Charping, J. W., & Bell, W. J. (1979). Interpersonal skills training: A review of the research. *Social Work Research and Abstracts, 15,* 10–16.

Marshall, E. K., Kurtz, P. D., & Associates. (1982). *Interpersonal helping skills: A guide to training methods, programs, and resources.* San Francisco: Jossey-Bass.

Martens, W. M., & Holmstrup, E. (1974). Problem-oriented recording. *Social Casework, 55* (9), 554–561.

Matarazzo, R. G. (1978). Research on the teaching and learning of psychotherapeutic skills. In S. L. Garfield & A. E. Bergin (Eds.), *Handbook of psychotherapy and behavior change* (2nd ed.) (pp. 941–966). New York: Wiley.

Mayadas, N. S., & O'Brien, D. E. (1976). Teaching casework skills in the laboratory: Methods and techniques. In Council on Social Work Education, *Teaching for competence in the delivery of direct services* (pp. 72–82). New York: Author.

Mayer, J., & Timms, N. (1969). Clash in perspective between worker and client. *Social Casework, 50,* 32–40.

Mayfield, W. (1972). Mental health in the black community. *Social Work, 17,* 106–110.

Mays, D. T., & Franks, C. M. (1985). *Negative outcome in psychotherapy and what to do about it.* New York: Springer.

McCann, C. W. (1979). Ethics and the alleged unethical. *Social Work, 24,* 5–8.

McGoldrick, M., & Gerson, R. (1985). *Genograms in family assessment*. New York: W. W. Norton.

McIntosh, J. (1985). Suicide among the elderly: Levels and trends. *American Journal of Orthopyschiatry, 55,* 288–293.

McKay, M., Davis, M., & Fanning, P. (1983). *Messages: The communications skills book.* Oakland, CA: New Harbinger.

Medina, C., & Neyes, M. (1976). Dilemmas of Chicano counselors. *Social Work, 21,* 515–517.

Meichenbaum, D., & Turk, D. C. (1987). *Facilitating treatment adherence.* New York: Plenum.

Meyer, C. (1970). *Social work practice: A response to the urban crisis.* New York: The Free Press.

Meyer, C. (1979). What directions for direct practice? *Social Work, 24,* 267–272.

Middleman, R., & Goldberg, G. (1974). *Social service delivery: A structural approach to social work practice.* New York: Columbia University Press.

Miller, D. (1974). The influence of the patient's sex on clinical judgment. *Smith College Studies in Social Work, 44,* 89–100.

Miller, H. (1968). Value dilemmas in social casework. *Social Casework, 13,* 27–33.

Minahan, A. (1981). Social workers and oppressed people. *Social Work, 26,* 183–184.

Montagu, A., & Matson, F. (1979). *The human connection.* New York: McGraw-Hill.

Montiel, M. (1973). The Chicano family: A review of research. *Social Work, 18,* 21–23.

Morales, A. (1971). The collective preconscious and racism. *Social Casework, 52,* 285–293.

Morales, A. (1977). Beyond traditional conceptual frameworks. *Social Work, 22,* 387–393.

Morales, A. (1978). Institutional racism in mental health and criminal justice. *Social Casework, 59,* 387–395.

Morales, A. (1981). Social work with third-world people. *Social Work, 26,* 45–51.

Morales, A. (1984). Substance abuse and Mexican American youth: An overview. *Journal of Drug Issues, 14,* 297–311.

Morales, A., & Salcido, R. (1986). Social work with Mexican Americans. In A. Morales & B. Sheafor. *Social work: A profession of many faces* (4th ed.) (pp. 475–498). Boston: Allyn and Bacon.

Morales, A., & Sheafor, B. (1986). *Social work: A profession of many faces* (4th ed.). Boston: Allyn and Bacon.

Morrison, B. J., Rehr, H., & Rosenberg, G. (1985). How well are you doing? Evaluation strategies for practice. In C. B. Germain (Ed.), *Advances in clinical social work practice: Selected papers, 1982 NASW national conference on clinical social work* (pp. 218–231). Silver Spring, MD: National Association of Social Workers.

Mosko, M. (1976). Feminist theory and casework practice. In B. Ross & S. Khinduka (Eds.), *Social work in practice* (pp. 181–190). Washington, DC: National Association of Social Workers.

Moss, S., & Moss, M. (1967). When a caseworker leaves an agency: The impact on worker and client. *Social Casework, 48* (7), 433–437.

Munson, C. E. (Ed.). (1980). *Social work with families: Theory and practice.* New York: The Free Press.

Murase, K. (1977). Minorities: Asian Americans. In *Encyclopedia of Social Work* (pp. 953–960). Washington, DC: National Association of Social Workers.

National Association of Social Workers. (1980). *Code of ethics of the National Association of Social Workers.* Silver Spring, MD: Author.

National Association of Social Workers. (1981). *NASW standards for the classification of social work practice.* Silver Spring, MD: Author.

Nelsen, J. C. (1975). Social work's fields of practice, methods, and models: The choice to act. *Social Service Review, 49,* 264–270.

Nelsen, J. C. (1980). *Communication theory and social work practice.* Chicago: University of Chicago Press.

Northen, H. (1982). *Clinical social work.* New York: Columbia University Press.

Norton, D. (1978). *The dual perspective: Inclusion of ethnic minority content in the social work curriculum.* New York: Council on Social Work Education.

Ortego, P. (1971). The Chicano renaissance. *Social Casework, 52,* 294–307.

Parad, H. J. (Ed.). (1958). *Ego psychology and dynamic casework: Papers from the Smith College School for Social Work.* New York: Family Service Association of America.

Pease, A. (1981). *Signals: How to use body language for power, success and love.* New York: Bantam Books.

Perlman, H. H. (1957). *Social casework: A problem-solving process.* Chicago: University of Chicago Press.

Perlman, H. H. (1968). *Persona: Social role and personality.* Chicago: University of Chicago Press.

Perlman, H. H. (Ed.). (1969). *Helping: Charlotte Towle on social work and social casework.* Chicago: University of Chicago Press.

Perlman, H. H. (1971). *Perspectives on social casework.* Philadelphia: Temple University Press.

Perlman, H. H. (1979). *Relationship: The heart of helping people.* Chicago: University of Chicago Press.

Pilseker, C. (1978). Values: A problem for everyone. *Social Work, 23,* 54–57.

Pincus, A., & Minahan, A. (1973). *Social work practice: Model and method.* Itasca, IL: F. E. Peacock.

Pinderhughes, E. (1979). Teaching empathy in cross-cultural social work. *Social Work, 24,* 312–316.

Pinkston, E. M., Levitt, J. L., Green, G. R., Linsk, N. L., & Rzepnicki, T. L. (1982). *Effective social work practice: Advanced techniques for behavioral intervention with individuals, families, and institutional staff.* San Francisco: Jossey-Bass.

Polansky, N. (1971). *Ego psychology and communication: Theory for the interview*. New York: Atherton.

Powell, G., Yamamoto, J., Romero, A., & Morales, A. (Eds.). (1983). *The psychosocial development of minority group children*. New York: Brunner/Mazel.

Priestley, P., & McGuire, J. (1983). *Learning to help: Basic skill exercises*. London: Tavistock.

Rauch, J. (1978). Gender as a factor in practice. *Social Work, 23*, 388–395.

Reamer, F. G. (1979). Fundamental ethical issues in social work. *Social Service Review, 53*, 229–243.

Reamer, F. G. (1980). Ethical content in social work. *Social Casework, 61*, 531–540.

Reamer, F. G. (1982). *Ethical dilemmas in social service*. New York: Columbia University Press.

Reamer, F. G. (1983). Ethical dilemmas in social work practice. *Social Work, 28*, 31–35.

Reamer, F. G. (1987). Values and ethics. In *Encyclopedia of Social Work* (pp. 801–809). Washington, DC: National Association of Social Workers.

Reid, W. (1978). *The task-centered system*. New York: Columbia University Press.

Reid, W. J., & Epstein, L. (1972). *Task-centered casework*. New York: Columbia University Press.

Reid, W. J., & Epstein, L. (1977). *Task-centered practice*. New York: Columbia University Press.

Reid, W. J., & Shyne, A. W. (1969). *Brief and extended casework*. New York: Columbia University Press.

Richmond, M. E. (1944). *Social diagnosis*. New York: The Free Press. First published in 1917.

Riley, R. (1975). Family advocacy: Case to cause and back to case. *Child Welfare, 50*, 374–383.

Ripple, L. (1955). Motivation, capacity, and opportunity as related to the use of casework service: Plan of study. *Social Service Review, 29*, 172–193.

Ripple, L., & Alexander, E. (1956). Motivation, capacity, and opportunity as related to the use of casework service: Nature of client's problem. *Social Service Review, 30*, 38–54.

Roberts, R. W., & Nee, R. H. (Eds.). (1970). *Theories of social casework*. Chicago: University of Chicago Press.

Rogers, C. R. (1957). The necessary and sufficient conditions of psychotherapeutic personality change. *Journal of Consulting Psychology, 21*, 95–103.

Rogers, C. R. (1961). *On becoming a person*. Boston: Houghton Mifflin.

Rogers, C. R. (1975). Empathic: An unappreciated way of being. *Counseling Psychologist, 5*, 2–10.

Rothman, J., Gant, L., & Hnat, S. (1985). Mexican-American family culture. *Social Service Review, 59*, 197–215.

Rubenstein, H., & Bloch, M. H. (Eds). (1982). *Things that matter: Influences on helping relationships*. New York: Macmillan.

Saari, C. (1986). *Clinical social work treatment: How does it work?* New York: Gardner.

Salcido, R. (1979a). Problems of the Mexican-American elderly in an urban setting. *Social Casework, 60,* 609–615.

Salcido, R. (1979b). Undocumented aliens: A study of Mexican families. *Social Work, 24,* 306–311.

Santa Cruz, L., & Hepworth, D. (1975). News and views: Effects of cultural orientation on casework. *Social Casework, 56,* 52–57.

Satir, V. (1972). *Peoplemaking.* Palo Alto, CA: Science and Behavior Books.

Scheflen, A. E., with Scheflen, A. (1972). *Body language and social order: Communication as behavioral control.* Englewood Cliffs, NJ: Prentice-Hall.

Schinke, S. P. (Ed.). (1981a). *Behavioral methods in social welfare.* New York: Aldine.

Schinke, S. P. (1981b). Individual case evaluation. In S. P. Schinke (Ed.), *Behavioral methods in social welfare* (pp. 303–314). New York: Aldine.

Schubert, M. (1971). *Interviewing in social work practice: An introduction.* New York: Council on Social Work Education.

Schulman, E. D. (1982). *Intervention in human services: A guide to skills and knowledge* (3rd ed.). St. Louis, MO: C. V. Mosby.

Schwartz, M. (1973). Sexism in the social work curriculum. *Journal of Education for Social Work, 9,* 65–70.

Schwartz, M. (1974). Importance of sex of worker and client. *Social Work, 19,* 177–186.

Schwartz, M. (1975). Casework implications of a worker's pregnancy. *Social Casework, 56,* 27–34.

Schwartz, W. (1971). On the use of groups in social work practice. In W. Schwartz & S. Zalba (Eds.), *The practice of group work* (pp. 3–24). New York: Columbia University Press.

Schwartz, W. (1976). Between client and system: The mediating function. In R. R. Roberts & H. Northen (Eds.), *Theories of social work with groups* (pp. 188–190). New York: Columbia University Press.

Seabury, B. (1975). Negotiating sound contracts with clients. *Public Welfare, 37,* 33–39.

Seabury, B. (1976). The contract: Uses, abuses and limitations. *Social Work, 21,* 16–21.

Shelton, J. L., & Levy, R. L. (1981). *Behavioral assignments and treatment compliance.* Champaign, IL: Research Press.

Shulman, L. (1978). A study of practice skill. *Social Work, 23,* 274–280.

Shulman, L. (1981). *Identifying, measuring, and teaching helping skills.* New York: Council on Social Work Education.

Shulman, L. (1982). *Skills of supervision and staff management.* Itasca, IL: F. E. Peacock.

Shulman, L. (1984). *The skills of helping individuals and groups* (2nd ed.). Itasca, IL: F. E. Peacock.

Siporin, M. (1975). *Introduction to social work practice.* New York: Macmillan.

Skidmore, R., & Thackeray, M. G. (1982). *Introduction to social work* (3rd ed.). Englewood Cliffs, NJ: Prentice-Hall.

Smalley, R. E. (1967). *Theory for social work practice.* New York: Columbia University Press.

Sobey, F. (Ed.). (1977). *Changing roles in social work practice.* Philadelphia: Temple University Press.

Solis, F. (1971). Socioeconomic and cultural conditions of migrant workers. *Social Casework, 52,* 308–315.

Solomon, B. (1976a). *Black empowerment: Social work in oppressed communities.* New York: Columbia University Press.

Solomon, B. (1976b). Is it sex, race or class? *Social Work, 21,* 421–426.

Solomon, B. (1986). Social work with Afro-Americans. In A. Morales & B. Sheafor, *Social work: A profession of many faces* (4th ed.) (pp. 501–521). Boston: Allyn and Bacon.

Sorrels, B. D. (1983). *The nonsexist communicator.* Englewood Cliffs, NJ: Prentice-Hall.

Souflee, F., & Schmitt, G. (1974). Education for practice in the Chicano community. *Journal of Education for Social Work, 10,* 75–84.

Spiegel, J. P., & Machotka, P. (1974). *Messages of the body.* New York: The Free Press.

Stein, T. J. (1981). *Social work practice in child welfare.* Englewood Cliffs, NJ: Prentice-Hall.

Strayhorn, J. M. (1977). *Talking it out: A guide to effective communication and problem solving.* Champaign, IL: Research Press.

Sundel, S. S., & Sundel, M. (1980). *Be assertive: A practical guide for human service workers.* Beverly Hills, CA: Sage Publications.

Sydnor, G. L., Akridge, R. L., & Parkhill, N. L. (1972). *Human relations training: A programmed manual.* Minden, LA: Human Resources Development Training Institute.

Tanner, B. A., & Parrino, J. J. (1975). *Helping others: Behavioral procedures for mental health workers.* Eugene, OR: E-B Press.

Truax, D. B., & Carkhuff, R. R. (1967). *Toward effective counseling and pyschotherapy: Training and practice.* Chicago & New York: Aldine Atherton.

Turner, F. J. (Ed.). (1983). *Differential diagnosis and treatment in social work* (3rd ed.). New York: The Free Press.

Turner, F. J. (Ed.). (1986). *Social work treatment: Interlocking theoretical approaches* (3rd ed.). New York: The Free Press.

Underwood, M., & Underwood, E. (1976). Clinical observations of a pregnant therapist. *Social Work, 21,* 512–514.

Van Hoose, W. H., & Kottler, J. A. (1985). *Ethical and legal issues in counseling and psychotherapy* (2nd ed.). San Francisco: Jossey-Bass.

Velasquez, J., McClure, M., & Benavides, E. (1984). A framework for establishing social work relationships across racial/ethnic lines. In B. Compton & B. Galaway, *Social work processes* (3rd ed.) (pp. 260–267). Homewood, IL: Dorsey.

Walz, T., Willenbring, G., & deMoll, L. (1974). Environmental design. *Social Work, 19,* 38–48.

Webbink, P. (1986). *The power of the eyes.* New York: Springer.

Wegscheider-Cruse, S. (1985). *Choice-making.* Pompano Beach, FL: Health Communications.

Weil, M., & Sanchez, E. (1983). The impact of the *Tarasoff* decision on clinical social work practice. *Social Service Review, 57,* 112–124.

Wells, C. C., with Masch, M. K. (1986). *Social work ethics day to day.* New York: Longman.

Whittaker, J. K. (1974). *Social treatment: An approach to interpersonal helping.* Chicago: Aldine.

Whittaker, J. K., & Garbarino, J. (1983). *Social support networks: Informal helping in the human services.* New York: Aldine.

Wicks, R. J. (1984). *Counseling strategies and intervention techniques for the human services* (2nd ed.). New York: Longman.

Wilson, S. J. (1978). *Confidentiality in social work.* New York: The Free Press.

Wilson, S. J. (1980). *Recording: Guidelines for social workers.* New York: The Free Press.

Wodarski, J., & Bagarozzi, D. A. (1979). *Behavioral social work.* New York: Human Sciences.

Woititz, J. G. (1983). *Adult children of alcoholics.* Pompano Beach, FL: Health Communications.

Woititz, J. G. (1985). *Struggle for intimacy.* Pompano Beach, FL: Health Communications.

Yalom, I. D. (1975). *The theory and practice of group psychotherapy* (2nd ed.). New York: Basic Books.

Yelaja, S. A. (1982). *Ethical issues in social work.* Springfield, IL: Charles C. Thomas.

Zastrow, C. (1989). *The practice of social work* (3rd ed.). Chicago: Dorsey.

Zunin, L. (1972). *Contact: The first four minutes.* Los Angeles: Nash.